TRAINING THE SPORT HORSE

Christopher Bartle

with Gillian Newsum

J. A. ALLEN

Text © Christopher Bartle and Gillian Newsum 2004
Photographs © Kit Houghton
Diagrams © Trixie Hodges
Frist published in Great Britain 2004
Reprinted 2005

ISBN 0 85131 854 1

J. A. Allen
Clerkenwell House
Clerkenwell Green
London EC1R OHT

J. A. Allen is an imprint of Robert Hale Limited

Edited by John Beaton
Design and typesetting and make up by Paul Saunders

Photographs by Kit Houghton
Line illustrations by Trixie Hodges

Colour separation by Tenon & Polert Colour Scanning Limited, Hong Kong
Printed by New Era Printing Company Ltd, Hong Kong

TRAINING
THE SPORT HORSE

Dedicated to

all the horses with whom I have had the opportunity to practise and experiment over the years as I learnt and developed my training philosophy and system. I have been lucky to have had the chance to work with so many horses.

Some have gone on to be superstars and have lived the high life travelling and competing around the world, others have just had to put up with me making mistakes. None of them had the vote but I owe them everything.

I must say 'sorry' to many of them and 'thank you' to all of them.

Illustrations

All photographs are reproduced by permission of Kit Houghton with the exception of that on page 72 which is by Christopher Bartle and page 22 which is reproduced by permission of Kawasaki.

The line drawaings are all Trixie Hodges.

Contents

Preface

THE KNOWLEDGE OF A RIDER or trainer is inevitably drawn from many sources: from personal experience, from other trainers and riders, from videos, literature and from general observation. There is always more to learn. My own experience of riding racehorses, eventers and dressage horses, and of teaching other people, has helped me to develop a strong training philosophy, which has as its base a clear understanding of the partnership between horse and rider.

It has been said that too much dressage is bad for an event horse. I do not agree. Good dressage training will make a horse more gymnastic and will always help with jumping, whether it be show jumping or cross-country. Dressage is bad when the rider starts to dominate the horse and take over its responsibilities. One of my favourite expressions is that a horse has to earn its living. A horse must learn self-carriage and self-motivation; it must learn to look after itself, to stay on line, to understand a rider's body language and to accept discipline.

In teaching a horse to accept its responsibilities, the rider has responsibilities too. The objective is to train the horse to come along as part of a partnership, but one in which the rider is the senior partner. It should be a case of co-operation rather than coercion. The rider must therefore know that what is asked of the horse is fair and reasonable. To this end, the rider should have a basic knowledge of the horse's bio-mechanics and should be able to communicate effectively with the horse through the aids. It is also important to be aware of, and sensitive to, the horse's physical and mental limits, its confidence, mental attitude and physical strength.

A questioning, analytical approach to training horses was passed on to me from my mother, Nicole, who had ridden as a child in Belgium, and always had a deep academic as well as practical interest in the training of horses. In 1963 she set up the Yorkshire Riding Centre and later translated a number of equestrian books for J.A. Allen, including *The Way to Perfect Horsemanship* by Udo Berger. She was a perfectionist, and a strong believer in the responsibility of the rider/trainer to promote the welfare of the horse through correct posture and an intelligent, reasoned training system. She was not content with accepting the traditional instruction handed down through the Pony Club manual. She needed to know the 'how' and the 'why' and was always questioning the traditional systems of training.

Although I did not start riding seriously until I was fourteen, my mother encouraged me to spend a year in France between school and university to train with Commandant de Parisot, head of the Cadre Noir, the French cavalry school in Saumur. He was a brilliant man, and I think it was his inspiration, added to my mother's enthusiasm, that finally hooked me on dressage.

Nonetheless, I took a degree in Economics at Bristol University and then spent two years steeplechasing before accepting that, at 6ft, I was not ideal material for a jockey. I then returned to work at home to pursue my interest in eventing and since then I have spent my whole life avoiding getting a 'proper job'. It was around this time that I started with a horse called Wily Trout, a partner with whom I was able to fulfil many of my ambitions and dreams. I also met the man who was to influence my riding more than anyone else. My mother had invited the Swedish trainer, Hans von Blixen-Finecke, to train us at the Yorkshire Riding Centre. Blixen-Finecke had been the commander of the Swedish Cavalry School when he won the individual gold medal for eventing at the 1952 Olympic Games. He had also trained Master Rufus, the horse ridden by Col. Henri Saint Cyr who won the gold medal for dressage at the same Olympics. Blixen-Finecke had a similar approach to training as my mother, emphasizing the understanding of the biomechanics of horse and rider. When something did not work, it was not a question of coming back and doing it again, but rather of trying to work out where precisely the problem was, whether it was with the rider or the horse. Although my perspective and analyses have evolved slightly differently as a result of my own experiences, my training philosophy is still largely based on his methods. (See *The Art of Training* by Hans von Blixen-Finecke.)

In this book I have attempted to explain the processes through which horse and rider can achieve different levels of training, whether it be for pleasure riding, local events or international competition. Although the emphasis is on understanding

The author at the Sydney Olympics 2000.

the horse and working through any problems, in return there has to be discipline and respect from the horse. There is a fine balance between gaining the horse's respect and demanding obedience. The skill of the rider is get the horse to agree to his requests by making the horse realize that it is in its own best interest to do so.

The experienced horseman will always say that one never stops learning. My training system is constantly evolving and no doubt in a few years time I shall be able to write a second edition to this book incorporating what I have learned since writing this one, during which I have come to appreciate even more the complexity of the subject. There are so many interrelated variables and it is impossible to cover every possible scenario with every horse. I have tried to include some suggestions as to how to deal with the different responses one gets from the horse but there are more left out than included. The rider will develop his own database of experiences, but it is useful to be able to relate them to a system which can gradually be personalized.

Acknowledgements

J.A. Allen was the publisher that my mother, Nicole, worked with when she translated equestrian books, so I was very pleased to be involved with them for my own book. I am grateful to Gillian Newsum for providing the link between J. A. Allen and me, and for helping me produce what, I hope, is a readable text on a complex subject.

I would also like to thank Kit Houghton for allowing us to search through his extensive photograph library to find illustrations for the book, and Trixie Hodges for her painstaking work on the line drawings.

PART ONE

■

The Basics

'I study my horse; and my horse
studies me. If I am a coward, he is
one: if I am lazy, he is lazy; if I am
impatient, he is impetuous; if I am
lost in thought how dreamily
he pursues his way!'

John Osgood, Vermont Farmer, 1864

CHAPTER ONE

Partnership and Responsibility

As we move further from the time when people grew up around horses and used them for work as well as for recreation, we have tended to place the different equestrian sports into separate compartments. Yet they are all inextricably linked. Not only are the three Olympic disciplines of dressage, show jumping and eventing related, but also such diverse sports as flat racing, steeplechasing, polo and the Western sports of cutting and reining. They are linked by one common factor, the horse.

Over the centuries horses have been bred with particular functions in mind: for transport, for farm work, for war and for sport. The requirements of each of these functions gave rise to different breeds and types with the necessary characteristics for their job.

Regardless of their particular qualities, all horses still had the same basic skeletal structure; they all ate grass (if they had access to it), and they all responded to the same laws of physics and, in differing degrees, to the same stimuli. There were only *relative* variations in their skeletal structure, musculature and temperament. For example, the conformation of the racehorse, bred for speed, did not lend itself to pulling carriages, and the heavy draught horse did not have the sharpness of reaction and athleticism required of a sport horse.

Since the second half of the twentieth century the function of the horse has been primarily for sport or leisure. The emphasis in breeding has been to develop horses suitable for particular sports, and this has evolved further as the sports themselves have developed. The horse's role as a working farm animal has almost disappeared, but many of the attributes required of the sport horse are the same as those of the work horse.

The demands of the different sports can vary considerably. Grand Prix level dressage is at the opposite end of the spectrum from flat racing. However, there are common factors between the sports, and there is much to be learnt from analyzing the requirements of each of the equestrian sports and the training methods used. The training of the steeplechaser, for example, has much in common with the advanced event horse, and there are some aspects of training reining horses that are relevant to advanced dressage.

Although the training of the dressage horse, show jumper and eventer is essentially the same, the extra demands of dressage and show jumping at the top level of the sport necessitate some specialization. Dressage at Grand Prix level requires a high degree of sustained collection leading to more expressive paces, whereas the Grand Prix show jumper requires explosive power as well as courage and athleticism over a jump. The collection required of the show jumper is momentary, in the strides before the jump prior to being released over the jump. This specialization creates a slightly different order of priorities for the type of horse required and for its training, but the basics, whether in relation to the rider or the horse, remain the same for any of the three disciplines.

The most important common factor linking all horse sports is that they all involve a *partnership* between man and horse.

Man's relationship with the horse is a partnership. The cavalry soldier during war was probably closer to his horse than to a person. Great partnerships in modern times include Lester Piggott and Nijinsky, Reiner Klimke and Ahlerich, John Whitaker and Milton, Mark Todd and Charisma. Great though those riders were (and in some cases still are) they would not have been as successful if they had not

A great partnership: Reiner Klimke with Ahlerich, winning the gold medal at the Los Angeles Olympics in 1984.

Two more great partnerships: *above* Mark Todd and Charisma during their lap of honour in Seoul, where they gained their second successive Olympic gold medal. *above right* John Whitaker with Milton, who together won over one million pounds.

found such good partners. Similarly, the horses would probably not have claimed their places in the history of sport without their respective partners.

In any partnership there is a sharing of responsibilities. One of the keys to a successful partnership in the home, in business or in sport is a clear understanding by the partners of their relative responsibilities. Trust is the key ingredient that comes from this understanding. Where partners trust each other they do not interfere with each other but lend support when required. Whilst man is the senior partner in our relationship with the horse, the horse must still be allowed and trusted with its responsibilities. It must also be motivated to take on those responsibilities. The expression 'there is no such thing as a free lunch' springs to mind. There are times when my horse has to be reminded that we both have a 'living to earn'.

Success in training the horse and then in competition depends on a clear understanding of what responsibilities belong to the horse and to the rider respectively. Many of the problems that arise originate from the rider's reluctance to hand responsibility to the horse. One sees riders who do not trust their horse's ability to jump and so appear to 'lift' the horse over every fence. Some riders drive with the seat or leg at every stride, whereas others do not trust their horse to respond to the slowing aids and so keep a constant 'pull' on the reins.

Eventually such lack of trust, or reluctance on the part of the rider/trainer to hand responsibility to the horse, becomes a self-fulfiling prophecy. The horse becomes conditioned to total reliance on the rider. The result can be that the horse either becomes gradually lazier if it is driven every step, or starts to pull or lean on the hand if the rider holds all the time. It loses its initiative to look after its own balance if supported all the time. The concept can be summarized by the expression 'self-carriage'. This expression is used in dressage but applies equally, if not more importantly for safety's sake, to jumping and cross-country riding.

It is worth examining in detail the relative responsibilities of the horse and rider (see table page 7). Throughout the book I shall endeavour to explain clearly which are the rider's responsibilities and which belong to the horse. It must be emphasized, however, that the rider has a supporting role in reminding the horse of its responsibilities during training and in competition, and it may sometimes be necessary to do so even before the horse appears to need reminding. In this respect, the rider is the senior partner, and has overall responsibility for the partnership's performance.

There are sometimes 'grey areas' in which the rider's duty to remind the horse borders on taking over responsibility. The young or green horse that lacks confidence in its ability or its surroundings, or a very tired horse, for example in a race or at the end of a cross-country, may need more support during a critical moment than would be appropriate in training. This is an important difference between training and competition. There is also a difference between competitions that fall into the category of training events and those that are very important. In a particularly important competition there is a fine line between supporting and totally trusting the horse. Getting it right on the day can make the difference between winning and losing.

The good rider will always check on his own responsibilities as much as those of his horse. The rider does, at least in theory, have control over himself, and by working on perfecting his own skills as a rider and trainer, he stands the best chance of communicating effectively with his horse. The successful performer in any sport works on his own technique, fitness and mental attitude. Many times one hears relatively advanced riders comment that the horse is not performing well because it is doing this or that. But one also hears relatively novice riders accept too readily that the horse is not performing well because they are at fault. Of course both comments can be correct, but equally they can both be wrong. The novice rider can at times take on too much responsibility, and the advanced rider can fail to be sufficiently critical of his own performance.

Body Language and Position Statement

The rider has a responsibility to communicate clearly with his horse at all times through his position statement and body language, supported by the actions of hand, leg and whip. I use the terms 'Body Language' and 'Position Statement' frequently, so it is worth explaining, at the beginning, what I mean by these terms.

Body Language

Body language is a means of communication that all animals and humans use both consciously and subconsciously. It is most obvious in terms of our relationship with a horse during any work or interaction from the ground, but it is just as important when we are riding. Body language is an extension of our mind, hence the importance of clear goals being established in one's mind before doing anything. I often tell my pupils that the more they can 'be the horse' the better. In that way their body language will be the most clear. When handling a horse from the ground, the body language is a combination of posture, eye contact and body movements. When riding, body language involves posture, balance and body movements.

When handling a horse from the ground the body language is a combination of posture, eye contact and body movements.

When riding, the body language involves posture, balance and body movement.

Responsibilities

The Rider

Goal setting – long, medium and short
Setting the order of priorities – the training system

Self
Own posture
Own balance
Correct use of position statement and body language
Timing, application and coordination of the aids

Setting and monitoring:
Energy
Rhythm
The contact
Line/direction
Length of stride
The straightness (inline and online)
The flexion and bend
The angle in lateral work

Monitor and Correct:
The regularity of the steps
The posture/outline
The self-carriage
The balance

Make judgements/decisions regarding:
Physical aptitude
Mental attitude
Confidence
The energy level (tiredness/freshness)
Discipline

Self assessment:
Review, analyze and make changes where necessary
Be flexible
Learn from experience
To have self-control – physical/mental
To always seek to learn and improve

The Horse

Should always be willing to go forwards
Recognize the rider's position statement
React and respond to the rider's signals – body language
    supported by the leg and rein aids

Accept discipline
Know the 'pecking order'
Respect another person's space

Energy
Regularity
Maintain rhythm and length of stride i.e. speed
Posture – Lateral/longitudinal submission
        – Connection over the back
        – Self-carriage
Acceptance of the contact

Own balance
The straightness – inline and online (flexion and bend)
The angle in lateral work
Impulsion and elasticity of the steps
Collection

Jump the jump
'Look after itself'
Learn from experience

Be positive (try – don't give up)

Position Statement

Position statement is a term I use in order to refer to the position that the rider or trainer must adopt in *preparation* for any exercise, transition or demand they make of their horse. If the rider is consistent with his position statement, the horse will learn to recognize it and offer to respond to it with less need for supporting actions leading to the minimizing of our aids. This applies to all aspects of riding and handling a horse. The position statement eventually produces a conditioned reflex response. Body language and position statement are closely related.

Position Statement = Preparation

Body Language = Action

Goal Setting

Effective goal setting is essential to get the most enjoyment or success out of your riding and out of your horse.

Why do you ride? What do you want to achieve?

We all ride horses for our own personal reasons. We all have goals. Some time reflecting on those goals will help you to make the correct decisions as you go along. Some people are by nature competitive and want to excel in whatever sport or endeavour they are involved. They may have as their goal the winning of competitions even up to Olympic level, as I certainly did when I was in my late teens. It took me a long time to get to the Olympics, and even then I did not achieve the result that I had dreamed about as a teenager. Perhaps because of that, my competitive urge is as strong as ever, despite recognizing that time is against me.

What suits one rider does not necessarily suit another

Some riders just want to enjoy their time with their horse without placing high expectations on themselves or the horse. Not everyone wants to be an Olympic rider. Even if you are by nature competitive you may have decided that there are other aspects of your life in which you want to channel that competitive streak, and so with your horse you just want to get away from the pressure of your 'other' life. In these cases then your goal is in fact to keep the pressure off yourself and your horse. But that does not take away from your responsibility and pleasure as a rider to care for your horse and to make his life as tolerable as possible. Part of that responsibility involves making yourself as comfortable a burden on the horse's back as possible and making your signals clear without contradiction.

Is your goal to win competitions? Or to go for a quiet hack?

You're only ever as good as your horse

Not all elements are within your control. You may set yourself a goal of winning a medal at the Olympic Games, but there are many factors crucial to your attainment of that goal that are outside your control. In which case all you can do is to take a course of action that keeps open the possibility of such an achievement. Your immediate goal might be to improve your skills as a rider to the maximum of which you are capable in the hope that eventually you will be lucky enough to have a sufficiently talented horse to help you to reach your ultimate goal. Not all horses are capable of competing successfully at the very top level of the sport, but nor for that matter are all riders.

Training goals vs competition goals

I differentiate between competition goals and training goals even though there may be times when they take the same direction to the training. I can set myself a goal of winning a competition or qualifying for a championship, or I can set a goal for the training of myself and my horse. Such a training goal could be to teach my dressage horse to do flying changes or to train my event horse to jump into water willingly and confidently. Achievement of the competition goal depends, in the end, on achieving intermediate training goals, which in turn can be broken down into other goals.

Long, medium, short, macro and micro goals

The goals that you set can be broken down into long, medium and short term goals and even further into macro and micro goals that, in effect, are modified from minute to minute or even second to second. Macro goals are those that involve many aspects. Micro goals are those that relate to only one aspect or detail at a time.

Riding a circle, a shoulder-in or jumping a fence are macro goals because there are many factors involved from the rider's point of view in riding an exercise well. A micro goal would be some aspect of the horse's performance that is related to the successful completion of the macro goal. Adjusting the length of stride, the rhythm, the bend, the angle etc would be micro goals. Applying a touch of leg, an action of hand or arm, or an adjustment of position in preparation for an exercise would be a means to achieving a micro goal. Going through a process of preparations in one's position and then applying the rhythmical actions of leg and hand in setting up and riding a movement would be a means of achieving a macro goal.

It is important that the rider, not the horse, sets the agenda at all times. If you drift around an arena without a clear plan, you will find yourself responding to what the horse does, rather than the horse responding to you. Make sure you know what your goals are, and refer to the route map to plan your progress. As you move up the ladder, your training should relate to the short, medium and long term training and competition goals that you may have set yourself and your horse.

CHAPTER TWO

The System of Training – an Overview

The system of training is based on four elements:

Education/Communication

Teaching the horse to recognize your position statement and respond to body language supported by touch, sound and visual stimuli. By taking advantage of the horse's natural reflexes you develop conditioned reflexes to these stimuli. The exercises that are used to educate and develop the horse's responses then form the basis of the gymnastic exercises.

Gymnastic Exercises

A 'tool box of exercises' used initially to educate the horse by developing and testing its response to position statement, body language, leg, and rein aids. These then lead to the development of the 'posture for performance' and through that physical development and increased athleticism i.e. range of movement.

Physical Development

Maturity combined with the work (alternating with periods of rest and recovery) leads to muscular development and increased stamina within the inherent capabilities of each horse.

Educating the horse from the ground.

Mental Development

Education (resulting in clear communication) plus gymnastic exercises will lead to physical development and so to confidence. Calmness comes through discipline and

Wily Trout, aged 6, in his first career as an eventer.

below Wily Trout, aged 17, competing at Goodwood International dressage championships. These two photographs illustrate the muscular development gained through consistent training.

trust. The technical skill of the trainer in communicating with the horse is important, but so too is the ability to 'feel' and then make decisions regarding goal setting and the order of priorities. If the trainer is too demanding, the horse will lose confidence, but if he is not strict enough the horse will lose respect and see no reason to perform.

The training starts with the simplest of demands in terms of education and gymnastics and gradually becomes more complex as more elements are added. Both for the rider and the horse, the task can be likened to learning to juggle first with two balls then with three, four, five, etc. The limiting factors in this process are the rider's ability to communicate effectively and the horse's ability and willingness to perform.

Whilst the system is not rigid and is related at all times to the goals set by the trainer, there is a route map, and those trainers who try to take too many shortcuts in the horse's training will frequently find themselves at a 'dead end'. Some horses, due to their natural aptitude, are able to progress more quickly up the training road. Some are blessed with innate responses or athletic ability, which means that certain steps in their education and training can be skipped or at least not dwelt upon. Others may require a much more progressive training due to physical or mental difficulties, or because of confusion or tension caused by previous training.

Not every horse has the physical ability or mental attributes (often related) required to attain a high level in all or any of the equestrian sports. Just how good a horse is can only be found out in training. There are many *physical* attributes that can be easily identified as severely limiting potential, but without intimate knowledge of the 'family' and the attributes of the parents, the mental attitude of the horse can only be assessed or identified through the training process. A horse with positive mental attitude can often overcome physical difficulties, whilst one with a negative attitude will frequently disappoint.

However, you have to keep in mind that apparent negative attitude can often be caused by misunderstanding, a clash of personalities or by lack of confidence arising out of unsympathetic training, unsoundness or other environmental or even feeding problems. That is why one often sees a horse make a dramatic improvement with a change of rider even when the previous rider was very successful and experienced with other horses.

Much the same applies to trainers. There are those who are naturally gifted in terms of their physical and mental attributes. Their training can often skip elements that are already natural to them. No rider though is born with the knowledge and 'feel'. These can only be acquired through education and through experience acquired in training, observation and experimentation over time. (This mirrors the three coaching methods that are commonly used in any sport – 'tell and do', 'show and copy', 'trial and error'.)

Just as one says 'you are only ever as good as your horse', so you can say on behalf of your horse that 'it will only ever be as good as its trainer'. We too are limited by our physical and mental attributes. But given that we set the goals for both ourselves and our horses, we can at least try to overcome our weaknesses by making the most of our strengths. Through study, observation and experimentation we can constantly strive to be better. Even if we only ride to enjoy being transported around the countryside, we can make the horse's task of carrying us easier.

Anyone who has spent time training and competing horses knows that it can be like a game of snakes and ladders – up one minute and down the next. One quality above all is required to be consistently successful as a trainer and competitor. That is 'mental toughness'. The determination to keep striving for knowledge, experience and success in the face of innumerable setbacks due to one's own limitations or the 'slings and arrows of outrageous fortune' may bring success in the end, but even that is not guaranteed. I have known many extremely talented riders who have failed to achieve their potential due to factors outside their control. It is only too easy to become demoralized if competitive success is one's main goal in training and riding horses.

Not everyone has to have success in competition as their main goal. For some it is enough to enjoy the process of training their horses, or re-training a problem horse (in my experience, there is no such thing as a problem-free horse). Whether those horses eventually achieve great success or indeed their fullest potential is not as important as the learning process itself. The achievement of one small step on the training path with a young horse can give great satisfaction and enjoyment. Each of these small steps is a simple micro or macro goal in itself directed towards a more complex short or medium term goal.

CHAPTER THREE

The Rider

The rider's main responsibility is to communicate effectively with his horse. His ability to do this is dependent on four inter-related elements:

- **Physical elements (posture, balance, coordination and dexterity)**
- **Knowledge – biomechanics, means of communication with the horse**
- **Mental elements**
- **Feel and experience**

Physical Elements

The rider's first priority is to achieve good *posture and balance* so that he can provide a steady platform from which all his communications with the horse can emanate in a clear and precise way. Without this he cannot coordinate the actions of leg, hand and seat independently of each other. Although posture and balance are discussed separately in this chapter, it is not possible to have good balance without control of posture and vice-versa.

The *coordination* of the actions of body, seat, leg and hand is vital to communicating effectively with the horse. The ability to coordinate these actions means that the timing of them can be more accurate, thus avoiding the conflict of contradictory aids.

Dexterity, the ability to handle the reins and the whip without sending unwanted signals to the horse, is an aspect of the rider's training that is often overlooked. The adjustment of the length of rein without changing the contact is one important example.

1. Posture

'Good posture is
the key to good
riding.'

The successful athlete, gymnast or performer adopts a posture that best suits his sport or performance. Professional sports coaches often refer to this as 'core stability' which provides a base or platform for all the actions that the athlete has to perform in a controlled, coordinated and, at times, powerful way, and yet at other times in a very delicate way. Holding the correct posture without stiffness or rigidity gradually becomes second nature, but initially requires a degree of physical effort and self discipline.

The same applies to riding posture. A good rider can hold a correct posture without apparent effort and can ride many horses in a day without getting tired. This ability does not come for free. To be successful, the rider has to work at it both on and off the horse. Although I have never used it myself, I have taught many riders who have apparently benefited from the Alexander technique.

The development of the rider's posture should be seen as the means to an end, not an end in itself. There are as many instructors who focus only on the posture of the rider as there are instructors who focus only on the horse. I have seen riders who work for ever on systems of good posture, but never apply it to improving their horse's way of going.

'A good posture
is not just for
elegance it is also
for performance.'

When I was sixteen years old I came across my father's army dress uniform in a cupboard in the house. The jacket was black and had a high collar done up right to the top with brass buttons down the front. The dark breeches had a red stripe down the side. We had a German trainer staying with us at the time, and he saw me riding my horse in the arena dressed in the uniform. I kept my posture beautifully, partly because I thought I looked good, and partly because the uniform gave me no option! I felt very pleased with myself as I rode around in sitting trot on my horse that was strung out from A to Z. I can hear his voice now bringing me down to earth with a bump. 'You zit like a king, but you do nuzzink.'

Strength and fitness, as well as coordination, in the posture muscles and those that control the knee and ankle joints are the key elements in controlling our balance more effectively. A strong posture enables us to maintain position when the horse tries to take the rein from us. It gives us the ability to block without pulling. One often sees riders who have an excessively hollow back because their back muscles are stronger than their abdominal muscles.

The same applies to the muscles that control the shoulder and elbow joints. The flexors and extensors work in opposition to each other when the rider is resisting the pulling horse and, to a certain extent, when delivering the half-halt.

The link system

The rider's posture on the horse is based on a coordinated relationship between the main parts of the body, namely the trunk and the four limbs, with each part having its own role to play. To study the individual roles, the body can be divided into six links that are joined together by five joints.

The *upper body* is the primary link. It consists of one piece from the top of the

Emile Faurie showing good posture in dressage.

Posture is also important in jumping. The Italian rider, Enrico Maria Frana, maintains good posture in the upper body when in a more forward position.

head down to the seat bones. Although the body may rotate about its axis at two points (i.e. the neck and the waist) it should not flex either laterally or longitudinally at either of those points. It is as if there was a steel bar running through the centre of the body to prevent any collapse of the structure. In advanced dressage, the upper body meets the saddle more or less at the perpendicular. In jumping the body moves in front of the vertical and, at times, behind it (e.g. in cross-country riding).

'Man made of steel'

The *hip joint* connecting the upper leg to the upper body should remain relaxed and should be able to flex both longitudinally (e.g. in the rising trot) and laterally (e.g. in the turns and during the application of the stimulating action of the leg). A common fault is the closing of the hip joint, which causes the knee to grip and ride up and the lower leg to come away from the horse's sides, or be pulled back (often with the foot turned out).

The *upper leg* (thigh) should lie on the saddle in a relaxed manner. In the same way that an athlete cannot perform in tight clothes so a horse feels constrained if the thigh is clamped on to the saddle. Fresh air should occasionally pass between the thigh and the saddle. Tightness usually comes from anxiety or from the horse 'pulling' (i.e. the contact being so strong that the rider feels that he is being pulled out of the saddle).

The *knee joint,* the joint between the upper leg and the lower, flexes longitudinally with ease (e.g. in the rising trot, jumping position etc), but has very limited lateral flexion. Some riders make the mistake of using this lateral flexion to turn the foot in or out. The foot should point in exactly the same direction as the knee. The muscles that control the longitudinal flexion of the knee must have sufficient

above A relaxed hip joint leading to a relaxed knee contact and a correctly placed lower leg

right A common fault is the closing of the hip joint causing the knee to grip and the lower leg to come away from the horse's side or be pulled back.

tension to enable the knee to act as a shock absorber, but not so much that they cause the knee joint to lock. The knee joint must work in harmony with the hip and ankle joint. The straightening and locking of the knee (often associated with the rider whose stirrups are too long), or the stiffening of the joint (associated with anxiety, pain and control issues) are common faults.

The *lower leg* should be stable with as much as possible of the lower leg in contact with the horse's side at all times – this helps to give stability to the rider's position. Just how much of the lower leg is to be in contact will depend on the relationship between the size of the horse and the length of leg of the rider. The length of leg is, to an extent, affected by the length of the stirrups.

The *ankle joint* performs the same shock absorbing role as the knee. It can flex longitudinally more than it can flex laterally. The extent to which the heel drops as the ankle flexes is dependant on the ability of the calf muscles to stretch, and also on the relaxation of the hip and knee joints. The recommendation to riders to place all their weight in the heel can cause the ankle to flex too much, making it difficult for the rider to keep the lower leg stable.

The *foot* is the base upon which the weight of the leg is supported on the stirrup when sitting in the saddle in a dressage position, and upon which the whole of the body's weight is supported when riding in a light seat or galloping position. When riding without stirrups the foot is just an extension of the leg. The more even the distribution of the contact between foot and stirrup the better. The stirrup is best placed under the widest part of the ball of the foot for dressage and show jumping, but for cross-country and race riding it is better to place the foot further into the stirrup for additional security.

The *upper arm* is an independent link, but when riding in a dressage position the closer it is to the upper body the better. If the upper arm is allowed to come too far away from the body, then coordination with the upper body is lost. In the light seat or jumping position the upper arm should hang forward from the upper body at or just in front of the vertical.

The *shoulder joint* can flex both longitudinally and laterally almost equally. The elasticity of the contact will depend to a great extent on the relaxation of the shoulder joint in a longitudinal sense. The lateral flexion should be limited in order to keep the upper arm as close to the upper body as possible. This joint can also rotate in association with the elbow joint to permit the rotation of the whole arm.

The link system.

The *elbow joint* can flex longitudinally but has less ability to flex laterally, but it can rotate in conjunction with the shoulder joint. The outward rotation of the arm from neutral is a part of the correct application of the rein aids, but generally there should be no inward rotation as this produces an action of rein that is against the movement, i.e. across the body and backwards.

The *lower arm* should be considered as one continuous link with the *hand*. They

The lower arm should be one continuous link with the hand.

should act together as if the wrist were fused, so that there is no flexion of the wrist joint either inward or outward. The back of the hand should be in direct line with the lower arm at all times. The fingers should be closed around the rein, except when allowing the horse maximum freedom over a jump or when it stumbles etc. That is not to say that the fist (i.e. the closed hand) has to be tight at all times.

As the rider becomes more experienced, so the relative softness or hardness of the fist can act with finesse to fine tune the signals that are sent to the horse through the rein. With more novice riders, there is often a tendency to ride with the hands 'open' and to use the tips of the fingers. Despite the relative weakness of the fingers, this can still produce a pulling effect on the bit, which the horse may oppose or ignore. The rider should try to ride with 'quiet' hands. It has to be borne in mind that every time the fingers are opened and then closed, the contact is changed, and so a signal is sent to the horse.

2. Balance

The basis for achieving clarity in communication is good balance. To communicate effectively with our horse we have to be able to separate the actions of our body (legs, hands and body language) from the task of keeping our balance. The moment any insecurity creeps in, the rider will tend to act with his legs and hands in a way that sends a signal to the horse that it is really supposed to ignore.

If the rider is always in balance, both laterally and longitudinally, then he does not have to use his legs or hands to hold his position. Maintaining balance requires the rider to become adept at anticipating movement. (**Tip:** Use whatever chances you may have, e.g. standing on a bus, tube or moving walkway, to keep your balance without holding the rails or passenger straps tightly.) The ability to anticipate acceleration, deceleration, or lateral movement before even applying the aids not only helps the rider to stay balanced but also conveys the correct body language to the horse. Adjusting position to keep one's balance actually becomes one of the means of communicating with the horse.

Longitudinal balance

'Balance = Centre of Gravity above the base of support.'

The base of support in advanced dressage is substantially the seat bones whereas in jumping it is substantially the stirrup. Hence the emphasis changes between the work on the flat with longer stirrups and the jumping work with shorter stirrups. Even in advanced dressage, unless riding without stirrups, there should always be some weight, if only that of the leg, in the stirrup. When riding novice horses in dressage, the rider should ride with shorter stirrups to make it easier to transfer the weight from the seat to the stirrup. Much of the work with young horses is done in a rising trot or a forward canter position because of the emphasis on riding the horses forward to the contact and encouraging them to round the back.

The starting point for achieving balance is to have the stirrup leather hanging vertically down from the stirrup bar. This rule applies whether the horse is travelling on the level or up/down hill or over a jump. It also applies to the dressage position as well as to the jumping position. The ability of the rider to momentarily place more weight in the stirrup in order to lighten the seat, for example in canter, is crucial both to good dressage training and jumping, so it is important that the stirrup is in the right place at all times.

'The stirrup leather should be at the vertical.'

The shorter you have your stirrups, the more forward you have to be with your upper body from the hips in order to keep your centre of gravity above your stirrups. How short you ride is related to the speed at which you plan to travel; it is easier to control your horse at speed with shorter stirrups. The length of stirrup also affects your ability to follow the movement when the horse jumps. In race riding, jockeys ride very short, at the other extreme advanced dressage riders have very long stirrups and ride with their upper bodies at the vertical. In between these two extremes, the top show jumpers tend to ride with longer stirrups than event riders because they are not going so fast.

When sitting upright on the horse in any pace, the longitudinal balance is easier to maintain than the lateral balance, whereas in rising trot, or in the light seat, the lateral balance is easier to maintain. In the sitting trot or canter, the upper body will react by reflex when the horse accelerates or decelerates as long as the posture is maintained with a relaxed hip and the reflexes are not blocked by the nerves, which can cause the rider to grip or to reach for something to hold onto with the hands.

The inclination of the upper body ahead of the vertical is related to the length of the stirrups.

Lateral balance

The same laws of physics apply to lateral balance as to longitudinal balance. For the balance to be stable, the centre of gravity has to be above the base of support. The base of support when riding is either the stirrup or the seat bones or a combination of both. The weight should be evenly distributed when the horse is straight and travelling on a straight line, and so it is relatively easy to keep the upper body laterally vertical.

In the preparation for, and then in the execution of all turns or lateral movements, the rider must take the seat across the saddle to the inside. He will then be better able to keep the upper body at the vertical in the dressage position and keep the weight in the inside stirrup both in the light seat or in the dressage position. The faster the pace, the more the rider must pay attention to his lateral balance and make corrections frequently as part of the routine of riding the movement.

The motorbike position.

'Sit to the inside.'
'Outside shoulder back.'
'Weight in the inside stirrup.'

The racing motor bike rider provides an extreme example of the principle when preparing for, and then cornering at speed. The inside knee opens away from the body well in advance of the turn with the weight on the outside thigh and the upper body comes up towards the vertical during the period of deceleration. During the turn and as the bike accelerates, the knee nearly touches the road, while the outside shoulder is drawn back as the upper body is rotated outwards and then inclines forward during the acceleration. This position is very much exaggerated by the motor bike rider, but the rider on a horse must adopt a similar, though less exaggerated position both in cross-country riding and sometimes in riding the young horse on tight circles.

Most horses have a tendency to roll the saddle to the outside as they turn. The faster they travel on the turn the more the saddle slips. This is best seen from behind. The saddle will sometimes slip a long way over and cause the rider to end up sitting to the outside of the horse's spine with more weight in the outside stirrup. I have seen riders fall off after a jump on a turn because their weight is all in the outside stirrup, which makes the saddle slip further. Riders will often 'hang on' to the inside rein as a means of holding themselves in the saddle when that happens.

above Sitting incorrectly to the outside of the saddle.

right Sitting correctly to the inside of the saddle.

Both longitudinal balance and lateral balance are dynamic issues that require constant or repeated corrections to position in order to achieve. The good rider is not the one who never gets out of position, but the one who recognizes when he is and has a routine for correcting it as frequently as necessary. He is able to anticipate when the balance is likely to be lost in the same way as the motorbike rider does before the turns. The 'natural' rider, who is in relaxed control of his posture and balance, is also able to develop the necessary reflexes that enable him to stay in balance when the unexpected happens. The 'experienced' rider will also anticipate situations, particularly when cross-country riding, and be ready to react quickly to stay in balance.

The experienced rider will anticipate situations, particularly when cross-country riding, and will be ready to react quickly to stay in balance.

3. Coordination

The ability to coordinate the actions of body, legs and hands without tension is something we take for granted when we are walking, running, swimming etc, but even these once had to be learnt and practised. Learning a new technique that involves a number of elements often requires the rider to focus on each element independently, until he can bring them together to perform a movement without thinking about it. Sometimes it helps to use cues, or to fix one element while working on another.

Initially, when reading the instructions in a book regarding the use of hand and leg, the number of elements becomes overwhelming, and within each element there are a number of sub-elements. I find it helps to use a 'by numbers' approach in developing the coordinated techniques of body, leg and hand actions. In that way you can acquire the coordination just as you would pick up a dance routine by numbers. This is where listening to the rhythm of the horse helps, because by doing so you can check on one element within each step. Of course, it is not easy at the start, and the more you think about what you are doing the slower your reactions become, but just as a musician can gradually learn to coordinate the actions of fingers, hands and feet without thinking about it, so can the rider with practise. Good coordination relies on good body control, which in turn originates from good posture and balance.

This also applies when performing the various gymnastic or jumping exercises with your horse. If you can develop a 'system' for riding each movement then you can better coordinate the actions of body, seat, leg and hand to achieve the desired end result. Once you have a system, then you can modify it slightly from case to case and for each situation.

Develop a 'system'

4. Dexterity

A rider can only communicate effectively with his horse if he can provide a consistent contact, and then use the change in the degree of contact as a way of sending a signal to the horse via the mouth. Some riders constantly fiddle with the reins, forever adjusting them because they let them slip, or opening and closing the fist involuntarily, so changing the contact. As will be explained later, the signals down the rein (the Rein Aids) are intended to support the body and leg actions, so the horse will better understand and accept the demands of the rider if only the intended signals are sent down the rein. Of course the contact is a partnership and is shared between the horse and the rider, and despite the rider's best efforts to maintain a quiet hand the horse may be reluctant to accept the contact. At least if you handle the reins as precisely as possible you have the best chance of improving the horse's acceptance.

Key points to master include:

- Holding the reins in one hand without changing the contact or flexion.

- This ability leads to being able to shorten the rein without changing the contact.

- It also leads to the ability to 'bridge' the reins which is so useful when riding young horses or riding on the cross-country.

- Handling and using the whip. This includes the dressage whip and the short jumping whip. The objective is to use the whip precisely and with the right timing. Many people can do this well with the whip in their preferred hand, but it takes time and practise to use it as well in the other hand.

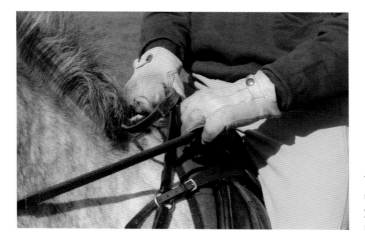

The ability to bridge the reins is useful when riding young horses or when riding across country.

Knowledge

1. Understanding the Biomechanics and Physics

Any rider wishing to influence a horse's posture, straightness and balance, should have an understanding of the elementary biomechanics of his horse. Biomechanics is the relationship between the muscles, bones and joints that are involved both in the support of the horse's body in balance and in producing the basic paces and movements. The information provided here is not intended to be very detailed or precise in scientific terms, but to give the interested horseman an understanding of the underlying logic behind the training system. The more knowledge a rider or trainer has about how the horse works, the more it will help in giving direction to the training and in problem solving.

The skeleton – bones, joints and ligaments

The bones of the horse's skeletal framework, which is held together mainly by the ligaments, act both as the supports for the body and as levers transmitting the energy into movement. These levers are operated by the muscles, which are attached to a relatively fixed point and act on the limb, either directly, or through the tendons, to produce the movement. The construction of the skeleton, and in particular the angles at which the bones meet, will influence the effectiveness of the levers to provide support and power to the movement.

When assessing a horse and its performance, the trainer has to take into account the limiting aspects of the horse's conformation. Much can be done to develop the musculature of the horse through the work and training, but the skeleton is fixed and, in the final analysis, is often the limiting factor to performance and soundness. When buying a young horse it can be easier to recognize positive and negative aspects of the horse's conformation if it is a bit lean, rather than when it is grossly fat and the producer tries to disguise the deficiencies under the fat!

The ligaments are fibrous tissues that are strong and fairly inelastic, and act like braces to keep the bones together at the joints. Two of the most important ligaments associated with the horse's posture are the nuchal ligament, which extends the length of the horse's neck, and the supraspinous ligament over the horse's back. These two ligaments, which join at the withers, connect all the vertebrae together, supporting the vertebral column rather like the ropes of a suspension bridge.

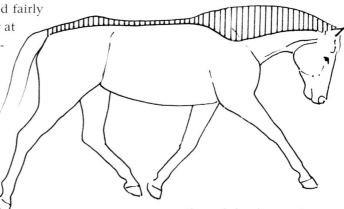

The nuchal and supraspinous ligaments.

The joints between the bones allow flexion and extension. All the lower limb joints allow longitudinal flexion and extension only. The hip joint also allows some abduction or adduction of the limb. There is no joint between the shoulder and the rib cage, instead the foreleg hangs in a sling of muscles and ligaments from the withers. It can swing forwards and backwards, and can also abduct and adduct from this cradle of muscle, as happens in the lateral work when the horse alternately takes the foreleg away from the body and across the body.

Some of the joints between the vertebrae allow a very slight flexion longitudinally and laterally, but others allow no flexion at all (see page 27, connection over the back). The cumulative effect of small degrees of lateral flexion between the vertebrae in the neck allows the horse to bend in the neck, particularly at the base, but also, to a lesser extent, right up to the poll.

The joint between the head and the first neck vertebra, the atlas or axis joint, is an important one to understand. It is only possible for this joint to flex laterally (i.e. for the horse to turn his head slightly from side to side) when the head is hanging more or less at the vertical. This is because when the nose is forward the joint locks laterally. It is therefore only possible to have *lateral flexion* at the poll when you have *longitudinal flexion*, and why obtaining the lateral flexion must mean that there is also longitudinal submission at the poll.

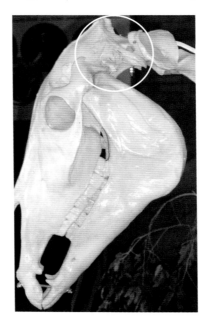

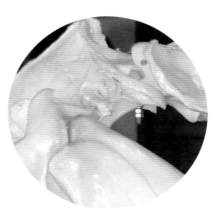

The atlas/axis joint.

The muscles

There are broadly two groups of muscles, postural muscles and locomotion muscles. *Postural muscles* act in pairs, together with the ligaments, to stabilize the frame. These muscles are short, and by opposing each other in isometric contraction they give strength to the posture and help the horse to carry the load – the same concept as 'core stability' as discussed in the section about rider's posture. How they work together is important because if one group is stronger or contracted more than the other, this will have a hollowing or rounding effect on the horse's posture. When holding the posture, these muscle groups contract and relax slowly and can maintain tension with little expenditure of energy. If the muscles are held in a permanent state of contraction, they will become stiff and the back will become rigid.

The muscles involved in *locomotion* have longer fibres and so can lengthen and shorten more rapidly. These flexors and extensors work either in pairs or singularly against gravity. A muscle can only contract, so it requires the opposing muscle (antagonist), or gravity, to lengthen it after it has contracted. Muscles of locomotion tire quickly if they have to maintain tension. If they relax and contract rhythmically, this promotes rapid excretion of the waste products, so the muscles do not tire so quickly. These muscles also have to act as shock absorbers, for example when the horse lands over a jump. When flexors and extensors oppose each other due to tension, pain or fatigue, the movement is restricted and energy is wasted. This can also be brought about by confusion caused by contradictory actions of the rider.

Although exercise develops the strength and size of the muscles, if they are in a constant state of tension they do not expel lactic acid and they become inflamed. The blood and lymph circulatory system is then impaired, and the muscles cannot absorb the nutrients and oxygen needed to develop their bulk and elasticity. There has to be a balance between work and rest both within in each phase of the movement and within each work session.

The connection over the back – posture

The key to performance in the sport horse is the back. The horse must learn to carry the rider in a way that produces a connection between the power of the hindquarters and the independent forehand. The topline of the horse can be likened to a suspension bridge. The ropes of the suspension bridge are the nuchal and supraspinous ligaments that run the length of the neck and spine. The tension is placed on the ropes by the forward pull of the muscles of the neck against the pull of the hindquarter muscles in the opposite direction as the hind leg swings forward under the body.

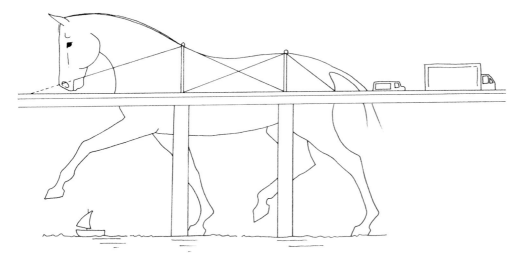

The top line of a horse can be likened to a suspension bridge.

The sacral vertebrae, in the area of the hips, are completely fused and form a 'joint' with the pelvis (*sacroiliac*). It is via this joint that the thrust of the hind leg is transmitted through the back to the forehand. The vertebrae that are connected to the ribs are also virtually fixed, so it is impossible to obtain more bend at the ribs, which some judges have been know to talk about.

The remaining thoracic and lumbar vertebrae are capable of some movement, with the most flexible part being where the last thoracic vertebrae meet the lumbar vertebrae. Normally, with a free standing horse, this area of the back is slightly bowed upwards, and this is exaggerated when the horse contracts the abdominal

'No bend in the ribs.'

muscles or when the hind legs and front legs come closer together, for example when a young horse humps its back in fright when a rider sits on it for the first time.

The main purpose of the postural back muscles is to support and stabilize the back. There are a large number of postural muscles which run along the length of the back and also laterally. All the muscles are bound together by *fasciae* (fibrous tissue), so any tension caused by discomfort or resistance in one area will extend to the whole back. Tension in the back impairs the connection between the hindquarters and the forehand.

At liberty, the horse's natural posture in walk, trot or canter, if alert, is to carry the head and neck up, with the face ahead of the vertical. This position enables it to see more easily. When the horse shows off during playtime, the neck becomes more arched, while the head tends to hang more or less vertically down from the poll in a 'proud' posture. The nervous or frightened horse may at times adopt the startle reflex, lifting his head up and hollowing the neck and back with the tail up, and setting off in a stiff-legged trot or canter.

When the horse shows off during playtime the neck becomes more arched.

The nervous or frightened horse may adopt the startled reflex.

When ridden, the just broken or weak horse will, after initially 'bowing' the back, let it sag under the weight of the rider in the same way as a plank of wood will sag if you place a heavy load on it. The muscles become slack and the bridge hangs from the pillars. The horse that lets its back sag, or that hollows and tightens it because it is tense, does not use the back elastically. The paces become tight and at times irregular. The feeling for the rider is that the back is either like a hammock or a board. In either case it is difficult to sit to the trot. The horse will also tighten its back if the rider grips too tightly with the legs, perversely, and yet understandably, because he finds the trot difficult to sit to.

The horse must initially learn to use its neck to help support the back, so that the back muscles and abdominal muscles can maintain an elastic state of tension rather than being held slack or rigid. The large group of muscles that lies between the nuchal ligament (the crest of the neck) and the neck vertebrae support the horse's head and neck. If the neck is lowered, as when a horse is grazing, the nuchal ligament and the neck muscles pull the spinous processes of the thoracic vertebrae forward, and this pull is transmitted to all the other vertebrae along the back by the supraspinous ligament and the back muscles (*semi-spinalis dorsi* and *multifidus*).

The longer the horse's neck, the easier it will be to persuade it to pull on the nuchal ligament (the ropes of the suspension bridge). Initially, the young horse will prefer to carry its head up and back just as we prefer to carry a heavy weight close to the body. The tense or frightened horse, or the horse that is reluctant to go forwards, will look back over its shoulder. The horse with a relatively long neck will soon tire of doing that, and as soon as it relaxes will drop the head and neck forward and down. The horse with a relatively short neck will be able to hold its head up and back for much longer and will be more difficult to persuade to draw the neck forward and down, especially if it is reluctant to go forwards as well.

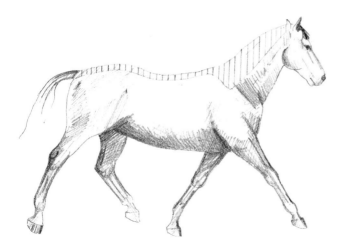

Initially the young horse will prefer to carry its head up and back into the shoulders causing the back to hollow. As it relaxes it will drop the head and neck forward and down allowing the back to become rounder.

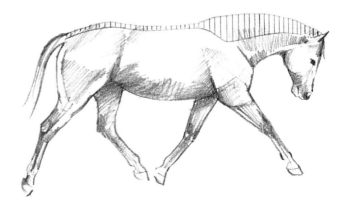

The rider can help the horse by riding in a light seat, because this will transfer the weight forward towards the withers and off the horse's back. Gravity is on our side, because the horse will eventually prefer to allow its head and neck to drop, particularly as it relaxes or becomes a bit tired.

Stretching the neck muscles is of no advantage without the activity and engagement of the hind legs. The ropes of the suspension bridge have to pull in both directions to be effective. If the pull is only in a forward direction, it will tip the balance of the structure in that direction on to the forehand. By exerting a pull in the opposite direction, by persuading the horse to step more under the body with an active hind leg, the horse will have a natural reflex to maintain its longitudinal balance by drawing the neck forwards. As it becomes stronger in the neck and can elevate the neck, so the balance will be transferred more towards the hind leg.

Once the effort of supporting the rider has been taken over by the neck and there is an equal pull in the opposite direction from the engaged hind legs, the back and abdominal muscles will develop in strength, by becoming bulkier. The horse will become able to carry the rider effectively without tightening the back. The back muscles involved in maintaining 'posture' can then provide the 'connection' that enables the muscles of locomotion, in particular the muscles of the hindquarters, to transmit their propulsive action to the forehand.

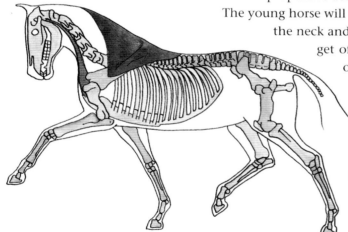

The young horse will tire quickly. When it does it will start to toss its head as the neck and back muscles become tired and sore. It is then time to get off and give it a rest. The well schooled and well developed horse has a strong, arched neck and is able to keep it still for longer, independent of the movement of the limbs. The developed muscles at the base of the neck, between the nuchal ligament and the cervical vertebrae, pull up the last cervical and first thoracic vertebrae. In this way the hollow in front of the withers will gradually disappear and the whole neck will appear longer even when elevated.

The lengthened and stronger neck, resisting the pull of gravity, and carrying itself and the head in a raised and arched appearance will support the whole forehand independent of the rider's rein contact. A horse that is 'carried' by the rider will not develop these muscles. The objective through the schooling is that the neck should become firmly stabilized by the muscles that connect it to the withers and shoulders, and in so doing reduce the oscillations up and down and from side to side.

The lengthened and stronger muscles at the base of the neck will support the whole of the forehand independently of the rider's rein contact.

The back muscles, in particular the longissimus dorsi that runs down the full length of the horse's back, have the potential to connect the propulsion generated by the hindquarters to the forehand. The actual results of that connection will differ, depending on which end the muscle is pulling from (its origin). If the hind leg is well engaged and in support (i.e with the foot fully on the floor) then the contraction of the *longissimus dorsi* lightens the forehand.

The bow of the back becomes similar to the bow on a fishing rod when a fish has been caught and is being taken out of the water. Conversely, if the fixed point is at the front, because the neck is shortened into the shoulders with a restricting contact or if the back muscles are held tight and short, rather than contracting and relaxing rhythmically, then the back is pulled downwards and the horse is said to be hollow and croup high.

The *longissimus dorsi*, which run down both sides of the horse's back, contract and relax alternately on each side in the walk and trot, as do the hindquarter muscles (*gluteals*). At the canter/gallop they contract and relax more or less simultaneously and to a greater extent, which is why cantering is often the best way to loosen a horse. Long, slow canters off the horse's back, up and down gradual inclines or hills, in a good posture with the hind leg engaged into a steady contact, will lead to the elastic development of the back muscles.

When I was in my late teens and early twenties I used to ride out racehorses for the local trainer and then spent some time as an amateur steeplechase jockey. Once the racehorses had done their initial six to eight weeks of 'legging up' on the roads, mainly in walk, they cantered one behind the other nearly every day for gradually longer periods. These horses were never intended as dressage or event horses, but one could see their 'toplines' develop and grow bigger and stronger through this work. Their abdominal muscles tightened up as well.

The contractions of the *logissimus dorsi* can be felt under your seat particularly in walk and canter, but also, if you are relaxed, in sitting trot, as they alternately bulge and then flatten. You should not rock from side to side with the movement, but rather allow the space to fill between your seat bone and the horse's back, as the muscle bulges. When the back muscles are in a permanent state of semi-contraction i.e. the back is tight, it is difficult to sit to the trot, and it is better to work the horse in rising trot until it relaxes the back.

With young horses, where the bulk of the work is initially done in rising trot for this reason, it is often difficult to go to sitting trot directly from rising trot without tightening or gripping, which then causes the horse to tighten its back muscles. You have to make a conscious effort to relax the hip and soften the contact as you go from rising to sitting, to encourage the horse to stay relaxed in the back. If that is difficult, then it is better to come back to walk and proceed into sitting trot from the walk rather than from the rising trot.

The back and hindquarter muscles must move in harmony. If the back is tight the hind leg cannot swing freely and conversely if the hind leg is inactive the back muscles cannot work properly. There is a similar relationship between the back muscles and the swing of the foreleg through the muscle (*latissimus dorsi*) that connects the *longissimus dorsi* with the withers and the foreleg (*humerus*).

The relaxed seat with a good posture absorbs the movement of the trot through relaxed buttocks, relaxed hips and the elastic relationship between back and abdominal muscles as the pelvis is inclined at or just behind the vertical. An athlete cannot perform in tight clothing, similarly the horse's back cannot function correctly if the

The bow of the horse's back becomes similar to the bow on a fishing rod when a fish has been caught.

'The more you bounce, the better they go.'

rider keeps his thigh clamped on to the saddle trying to be like a limpet. 'The more you bounce, the better they go' is what I often say to my pupils, as long as you maintain your posture without stiffness.

Flexion at the poll and relaxation of the jaw

There is a direct correlation between the tension in the jaw and tongue muscles (*mandibular* and *hyoid*) and the tightening of the muscles at the top of the neck that control the flexion at the poll. Tension in the muscles at the top of the neck will cause a tightening of the other neck muscles, and through them the back muscles. Conversely, the tightening of the back muscles has an effect on the jaw and tongue muscles, as well as on the engagement of the hind leg.

If the rider has fixed hands, or tries to force the horse into an outline by applying downward pressure on the bars of the mouth or the tongue, the horse will resist by coming against the hand and will try to come above the bit. This is usually associated with the horse opening its mouth or drawing back its tongue and locking its jaw, always more on one side than the other, and usually on the side that the horse prefers to chew. If the horse does not try to come 'above the bit' but rather drops behind the bit by bringing its nose into its chest, then the compression of the parotid glands will cause discomfort and consequent mouth problems. Draw reins or fixed hands also affect the coordination of the muscles of the topline, and lead to restricted movement of the shoulders.

It is important, therefore, that we try to obtain the outline without applying force to the mouth. We should encourage the horse to relax the muscles at the top of its neck, allowing it to hang its head towards the vertical. Whether the horse can do this will depend on its conformation and, in particular, how much space the horse has at the jowl for the parotid gland. (The jowl is the space between the vertical part of the lower jaw – the mandible – and the cervical vertebrae.) It is not necessary to have the horse's head absolutely at the vertical to be able to achieve a correct topline, particularly for the jumper or event horse. Where the space is narrow, a problem only arises with these horses at the highest level of dressage, when the neck is very elevated.

When the horse's neck is in a lengthened and strong state, and the muscles at the top of the neck allow an even flexion of the poll, so that the head hangs vertically, without tilting, the poll then provides a fixed point for the muscles that run down the side of the neck (*brachiocephallic*) and attach to the horse's foreleg (*humerus*). As the horse's head is elevated, the *brachocephallic* muscles are able to draw the limb forward and upwards in a more expressive gesture. Conversely if the neck is short and tight, the *splenius* muscle involved in elevating the neck merely hollows it and produces the 'ewe neck' effect and the downward compression of the base of the neck. The poll is consequently drawn back towards the shoulders, rather than the forelimb being drawn forward towards the poll.

As the horse's neck is elevated in a lengthened state the brachiocephalic muscles are able to draw the limb forward and upwards in a more expressive gesture.

'Lateral flexion' and 'bend'

There is an important difference between 'bend' and 'flexion'. Flexion occurs at a joint. The opposite of flexion is extension. Bend in this context occurs through a section of the body, if not the whole body, and may include several joints. Flexion at the poll refers only to the joint between the head and the neck at the poll. Whilst in the dressage test the lateral flexion should be in the direction of the turn or circle, in training it may sometimes be appropriate to flex the horse to the outside. Just as a gymnast or athlete can hold their posture absolutely straight from head to hip and yet at the same time look to the left or right as well as straight, so should the horse.

Lateral flexion at the poll.

The horse that willingly offers the lateral flexion in either direction is called 'laterally submissive'. A better word perhaps than the commonly used 'submission' is 'acceptance', because in the training we are looking for the horse to offer the flexion rather than being forced into flexing by pulling on the inside rein. When the horse offers the lateral submission/ acceptance then it must by definition offer longitudinal submission/ flexion, because the horse is physically unable to offer the lateral flexion unless his head is hanging more or less at the vertical due to the structure of the horse's skeleton, as previously explained.

The role of the hind leg – propulsion and shock absorption

Depending on the role of the horse, whether it be a racehorse or a high school dressage horse, its hind leg performs two functions – propulsion and shock absorption. The racehorse hardly uses the shock absorbing function, whereas the dressage horse requires its hind leg to be as much a shock absorber as a means of propelling the body forwards and upwards.

The *movement* of the hind leg has four phases: Forward (flexion), Impact (shock absorption), Support (store energy), Propulsion (use energy).

The hind leg acts as a shock absorber or brake by bending at the hip, stifle and hock. This requires strength in the muscles of the hind leg. To get an idea of how much strength is needed, try squatting for a long time with a 90 degree angle at the knee and without holding on to anything. It is not surprising that the horse tries to avoid this by straightening the stifle and hock before it comes to the ground, so coming croup high. During the impact and support phases of the movement, the propulsive muscles of the hind limb become the shock absorbers and the energy stores. They then reimpart that energy into the next propulsive phase of the stride.

The stifle and hock joints are connected through the stay apparatus so they have to flex together. (The stay apparatus is the mechanism that the horse has, both in the fore limb and the hind limb, which enables it to keep the leg straight and in full support of the body almost without any muscular energy. This is what allows the horse to be able to rest and almost sleep standing up. The stay apparatus of the hind leg is not quite as efficient as in the foreleg, which is why the horse is often seen resting a hind leg.)

The flexor muscles of the hindquarters are weaker than the extensors, which provide the propulsion and must act to control the flexion of the hind limb when the hind leg is loaded. The back muscles, in particular the *longissimus dorsi,* are also involved in the active roles of the hind leg, namely shock absorption and propulsion. Particularly in the canter, the flexor muscles of the loin (*ilio-psoas*) and hindquarters (*gluteus superficialis*) assisted by the abdominal muscles, cause the loin to round, and thereby allow the hind leg to come further forwards under the body. Conversely, the tight back leads to a stiff hind leg and high croup so the hind leg does not come so far forward under the horse's centre of gravity. The hamstrings towards the back of the hind leg and the quadriceps muscles at the front of the thigh also play a dual role in propulsion and then in controlling or limiting the flexion of the haunches.

The horse can resist or avoid the flexion of the hindquarters if its hindquarter muscles are weak by shortening the stride and locking the stifle and hock. It can do this by being lazy or inactive with the hind leg, by hurrying, or by putting the hind foot down to the ground early and so pushing with the hind leg. Many horses that one sees purchased for dressage with extravagant foreleg actions and impressive forehands have a pre-disposition to push with the hind leg rather than support with it. They are often more difficult to train than horses with less impressive trots but which have an inherently more engaged hind leg.

The objective in the training is:

1. To obtain the lateral submission which leads to an increased willingness to flex the hind leg. Engagement alone is not sufficient for collection; there also has to be flexion of the hind leg.

2. To increase the period of the support phase by bringing the hind leg well forward. Hence the timing of the half-halts down the outside rein as the inside hind foot comes to the floor. A longer support phase of the inside hind gives more time to the other hind leg to come forward.

3. To increase the strength of the muscles that are used to support and store the energy, or the horse will always look for a way out.

The flexor muscles of the loin and hindquarters, assisted by the abdominal muscles, cause the loin to round.

Nerves and reflexes

The nerves are the means by which the various parts of the body communicate with each other. The nervous system comprises the brain and spinal cord (central), and the nerves going from the spinal cord to the various parts of the body (peripheral). The nerves through which we communicate with the horse are situated in the skin and convey messages to the brain via the spinal cord. The brain also sends messages back to the muscles causing the contraction of the relevant muscle.

When the brain is not involved in the circuit, the nervous impulse is called a reflex, which produces a quicker reaction in the muscle. The muscles associated with posture and balance are largely, but not exclusively, stimulated into action by reflexes which control and coordinate the muscles and prevent loss of balance. In training we must distinguish between natural reflexes and conditioned reflexes. We use the natural reflexes to bring about reactions that enable us to teach the horse to respond in a certain way, which in turn become conditioned or trained reflexes.

In the early stages of training, before the conditioned reflexes have been established, there is bound to be a delay of a second or two before even the most willing of horses reacts or responds to the signal. By a process of consistent repetition, a conditioned reflex is developed. Hence it is important to use the signals, such as the touch of leg or rein, within the rhythm of the pace you are in, and not to apply more than one signal in any step, or your horse will ignore the signal overload.

Reflex reactions are involuntary. They occur without the brain being involved in making a conscious decision. However it is possible for the brain to make a conscious decision to overrule or block a reflex. Children often play games with each other to see if they can control their reflexes. Seeing how long they can avoid blinking as they stare at each other is one such game. In the same way, the horse can block these reflexes at times.

Reaction, response, effect

Given that we cannot reason or explain to a horse what we want them to do, we rely on using the natural reflexes both to bring about the basic responses that we want and to develop the more complex conditioned reflexes. Fright leading to flight is a natural reflex of the horse that we can utilize in teaching the horse to go forward on command. The horse or human has a reflex reaction to move away from a touch if he is surprised by it, and to move away from discomfort caused by irritation or pressure, or indeed to 'get rid of it', as with a fly. The horse also has a natural reflex to maintain balance and recover from a stumble. These natural reflexes are helpful in our training.

The stimulus leads to a reflex *reaction*. The degree of reaction will vary from horse to horse depending on its sensitivity. The horse can block a reflex reaction if it knows the stimulus is coming, or at least from where it is coming. The reaction in that case may not produce the desired response. Not all horses respond in exactly the same way or to the same degree to the stimulus from the trainer. Much depends on their attitude or their previous upbringing. Their respect for the trainer will play a big part in determining their response.

The *response* can be either positive i.e. the one we want, or it can be negative. For example one young unbroken horse may move or jump away from a touch of the whip or the hand on its side, while another may kick out at it. The horse that kicks out needs to be trained to have the desired response by using a sharper stimulus, to produce a natural reflex to move or run away from irritation. Gradually the horse will be trained, if necessary with the support of the whip, to respond positively to the touch of the leg as long as it is consistent. The response to the aid and the body language that goes along with it becomes a conditioned reflex because of the repeated association with the stimulus.

Riders often make the mistake of assuming that the horse has an innate knowledge of what response is required from any aid. For example, it is often assumed that the horse instinctively knows that the pressure of the leg means go forward, and therefore that a stronger pressure must necessarily mean go faster in the same way as pressing on the accelerator of the car. Each horse may respond differently to the stimulus of the aids, so the horse has to be taught to respond in the desired manner. To do this the rider must be precise and consistent in his use of the aids or signals rather than just stronger. The objective of the training is to produce conditioned reflex responses to our aids.

The '*effect of the aids*' is the result of a positive response and does not necessarily come naturally. It is brought about through the education phase of the training. For example the 'engagement of the hind leg' is the *effect* of a positive *response* to a touch of the rider's leg that causes the hind leg to step forward and under the body. That is why in dressage tests the mark for the rider includes the 'effectiveness of the aids', as well as the 'position and seat of the rider and the correct application of the aids'.

The reflex relationship between the poll, neck and action of the hind leg

Apart from the obvious fright – flight reflex, it is worth considering other reflexes that can be useful in training or, conversely, should be avoided. One reflex that should be avoided is the reflex to fight physical restraint. It is a natural reflex of the horse to pull back against the rope if they feel the pressure when tied up for the first time. Similarly it is a reflex to fight against the hand when the hand pulls the bit down and backwards against the bars of the mouth. This reaction is often seen in transitions, when riders try to hold the horse's head down during the transition.

There is also a very interesting and useful reflex relationship between the position of the head and neck and the action of the hind leg. Knowing about this will help you to understand the logic behind the training system and provide solutions to some of the problems that occur in training. The elevation of the neck causes a reflex reaction to the positioning of the hind leg, while the flexion at the poll causes a parallel reflex reaction to the flexion of the hock and stifle. As with all reflexes the horse can block this one, and will tend to do so if the back is tight, because that breaks the communication or connection between the hindquarters and the forehand.

This reflex can be divided into four positions of the head and neck and the relevant reaction on the hind limb:

1. Neck down and nose forward ➡ Hind leg out behind and relatively extended hock and stifle as in the case of the racehorse stretching out in a race.

2. Neck down and poll flexed ➡ Hind leg out behind but with hock and stifle flexing, as in the case of the horse being schooled in the 'long and low' position.

3. Neck elevated and nose forward ➡ Hind leg drawn forward under the body but with relatively extended or straight hock and stifle joints, as in the case of the Western Reining horse performing sliding stops.

4. Neck elevated and poll flexed ➡ Hind leg engaged with flexed hock and stifle as in the case of the high school dressage horse working in collection.

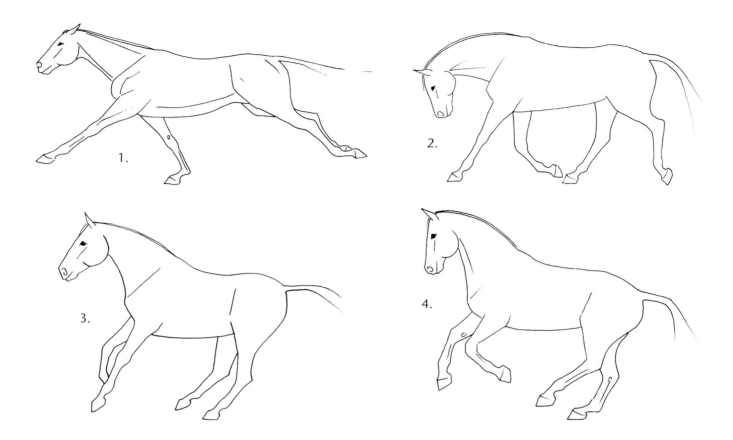

The horse's balance

The horse's centre of gravity is not situated exactly halfway between the nose and the tail. The forehand weighs more than the hind end, so its centre of gravity is situated just behind the withers. At liberty, a horse cannot change the weight of the two halves, but it can affect its balance by lengthening or shortening the neck in front of the centre of gravity or by rounding the loin and engaging the hindquarters behind it.

The horse has an innate desire to stay in balance. The horse, like a table, has four legs. It is possible for it to load the front or hind legs unevenly without falling over. So the effect of its loss of balance on the flat is usually not so serious as to cause it to fall over but when the horse jumps and lands on its forehand if it does not use its neck correctly it will lose its balance and may even fall. This is very rare when the horse is jumping at liberty. I have watched many steeplechases, and the horses that have lost their jockeys and who continue in the race almost never fall.

As with a beam on a fulcrum, it is possible to upset the balance with a very light additional weight, the more so the further away from the fulcrum it is placed. The rider represents this additional load and is able to affect the horse's balance by altering his position in the saddle, either by sitting closer to the withers or further back in the saddle. The inclination of the rider's body will also have an effect on the balance, because his centre of gravity will move forwards as he inclines forwards. In training the horse to find its own balance in self-carriage, the rider should always try

The four reflex relationships between the head, neck and the hindquarters.

1. Neck down and nose forward.

2. Neck down and poll flexed.

3. Neck elevated and nose forward.

4. Neck elevated and poll flexed.

to come back to a neutral position, even if at times he may help the horse to change or recover its balance by changing his position in the saddle.

In dressage training the rider should be aware of the effect that the light seat has, not just positively in allowing the horse to stretch the neck and come up in the back, but also negatively that it puts the horse on the forehand. So once the horse has understood the idea of lengthening and lowering the neck to round the back, you should come up into a more neutral upright position, whilst still trying to sit lightly on the back by maintaining a good posture. If at the same time you activate the hind leg to step more under the body, the frame behind the saddle will shorten and this will encourage the horse to elevate the neck.

The influence of the rider's position on the horse's balance is particularly important when jumping. In the approach to the jump, the influence of the rider can be applied in the same way as in dressage to encourage the horse to transfer its weight more towards the hindquarters. At the point of take-off, the horse engages the hind leg and lowers the croup in order to lighten the forehand, which is then drawn up by the elevating neck and propelled up and over the jump by the propulsive effect of the hindquarter muscles. If the rider gets ahead of the horse's centre of gravity at the point of take-off, the horse will find it harder to clear the front rail with its forehand.

(left) Jeanette Brakewell on The Busker showing an example of correct fold.
(above) Too much fold over the fence.

It is a common fault of event riders, particularly when show jumping, to get ahead of the centre of gravity by inclining their upper body forwards towards the horse's neck as the horse tries to lift its forehand up over the fence rather than allow the horse to come up to the rider. This is because event riders, even at advanced level, are used to jumping over relatively small jumps on the cross-country course at a higher speed, when the parabola or shape of the jump described by the horse is flatter than in pure show jumping. Particularly when jumping verticals or square oxers, you should try to stay up with the body at take-off. I often recommend to riders that they think of standing rather than folding at these jumps.

2. Understanding the System of Communication

To be able to educate a horse the rider needs to know how to communicate with it and then how to develop and refine that communication system to be able to use it when performing the gymnastic exercises that will improve the horse's way of going.

'What, how, when …'

1. We must first know *what* we want to communicate. This is related to our goals and to where the horse is on the System of Training 'ladder'.

2. We must know *how* to communicate with the horse by understanding the means of communication, namely our body language supported by touch, sound and visual signals. We also need to understand how we train our horses by using their natural reflexes.

3. We must learn *when* to communicate with the horse by coordinating our actions in such a way as to achieve the desired goal. *Timing* is very important because a horse can only respond correctly to a signal at one moment within each stride.

4. We should also ensure that we send only *complementary* and not contradictory signals to the horse to avoid confusion. The immediate goal may be to go forward, in which case at that moment the horse must not receive a contradictory message to slow down. A complementary message would be to go forward and sideways for example in leg-yielding. An advanced horse can respond correctly to more complex messages, for example the energizing action of the leg at the same time as a half-halt, but at the start of training a horse cannot distinguish between an energizing message and a 'go forward' message, so care must be taken not to confuse the horse by restraining at the same time as energizing.

The means of communication

We cannot reason with a horse no matter how clever it may be. We can only communicate naturally and directly through the senses. Horses learn by a process of trial and error based on trying to make themselves more comfortable. The best reward that a horse can receive is the absence of stimuli or signals. Gradually it may also learn to associate a pat on the neck or an appropriate use of the voice and so that becomes a reward.

'The horse was not born with an instruction manual.'

Horses react in differing degrees to sounds, touch and visual signals. (Taste and smell are also important senses, but not used so much in training.) They are very sensitive to touch in certain areas of the body and react differently to those touches. As discussed in the previous section, a horse is able to feel the touch of a small fly and react quite violently to it. We use the horse's natural reflex reactions to touch, noise and visual stimuli to train them to respond to our body language, leg and hand actions to produce the desired response.

'The hardest part of riding and training is to do nothing.'

Not all our communications are intentional. The horse has to cope with numerous signals that it is supposed to ignore, and yet learn to react and respond correctly to others, hence the importance of consistency in our communication and also reward by being 'quiet'. The hardest part of riding and training is to do nothing.

Body language supported by the leg and rein aids

The objective of the education phase of the training is to make the rider's *position statement* and *body language* the primary means of communication. The l*eg and rein actions*, supplemented by the whip, spur and bit are the secondary or supporting aids. When the partnership between horse and rider becomes so well established and they appear to be as one, then the horse is in effect just listening to the rider's thoughts through his position statement and body language. When you walk or run somewhere, when you perform an action with which you are so familiar, then you do it without thinking. It becomes your body language.

If a rider is mounted on a horse that is very responsive and willing, he only has to put himself into position for a movement and the horse will start to offer it, and then he can influence the 'way of going' through his body language. It should be possible to train a horse to respond to body language and position statement alone, so that one can ride without a bridle, but for most riders this is an unattainable goal or dream. Nevertheless it should always remain a goal at which the training is aimed. For this reason I often test myself, my horse and my pupils by riding parts of the dressage test or the jumping round with the reins in one hand.

The supporting actions of leg and hand – 'the language of touch'

The supporting actions are applied mainly through touch via the leg, whip or spur to the horse's body and through the rein to the mouth (tongue, bars and lips), sometimes to the bridge of the nose and occasionally to the poll. The rein can also communicate via touch to the side of the horse's neck. The use of noise (e.g. voice, whip cracks etc) or visual signals (e.g. waving of an arm or whip) can also be useful supporting actions.

The degree of reaction to the touches of leg and hand depends on the sensitivity of the horse and its mental state. Some horses are very sensitive and react very quickly, others are less sensitive, lazy, resistant, inattentive, so they may show little reaction. The degree of reaction to the touch may differ between the touch applied to the body, e.g. by the leg or whip, and the touch applied to the horse's mouth via the rein action. Horses are all individuals and the rider/trainer has to develop a feel and be able to recognize the clues that the horse provides as to its sensitivity and mental state, so as to apply the right amount of aggression or lightness to the touch. The same applies to the aids that appeal to the horse's sense of sight or hearing. No amount of reading can replace the need for experience in this regard.

In the case of the restraining rein actions or half-halts, I am sure that when man started to ride horses he did so without a saddle and probably with just a form of rope halter. He then found that the horse's mouth was more sensitive than the bridge of its nose and so perhaps placed the rope through the horse's mouth to gain more reaction to his half-halts, and subsequently used a metal 'bit' to further increase the reaction, particularly when the horse was distracted.

Of the aids used to motivate, the whip probably came before the refined use of the leg as a means of communicating to the horse's body, and at a later stage the spur was added to obtain a quicker reaction. The stick or whip is still used in some countries as the primary means of controlling direction on the ponies or donkeys via taps on the shoulder or neck. The leg used to communicate direction was important when the cavalry soldier had to fight as well as control his horse, hence the development of the use of the spur not just for the purpose of energizing the horse.

Different parts of the horse's body have different degrees of sensitivity. The area of the horse's sides with which the leg makes the most contact is well supplied with nerve endings, and by concentrating the actions of the leg in a relatively small area it makes the horse more sensitive to the touches in that area. The rider must avoid constantly moving the leg forward or back in an exaggerated manner. Such an exaggeration should be used only when the horse does not respond correctly or is confused. If the leg actions are always applied in the same area, the horse will gradually become more sensitive to them.

When teaching a horse to respond to the touch of the leg there may be an immediate reaction, such as the tightening of the skin, but the rider should expect a delay between the touch and response, i.e. movement. The signal (the touch of the leg) has to pass from the horse's skin to the brain and then back through the motor nerve to the appropriate muscle to produce the response. If the response is positive, the rider says 'thank you' through his position and by relaxing. Sometimes the horse will respond in the wrong way, e.g. moving towards the touch rather than away, or will under-react or over-react. If this happens, the rider repeats the original aid perhaps with the 'volume' turned up. Gradually the response should become much quicker as the horse anticipates the touch, and eventually it becomes a conditioned reflex. But one should never expect the horse, no matter how well schooled, to respond at the moment of the aid, but in the stride after the aid.

Consistent training will gradually develop conditioned reflex responses to the different signals, but at the beginning the horse learns to respond in the desired way by a process of chance discovery, or 'trial and error'. The exact place on the horse's body where the touch is applied, the manner in which it is applied by the rider, including the quickness, timing, rhythm and direction of the pressure, will all illicit a different reaction and response.

Even when the horse 'knows' the correct response, it can block both its natural reflexes and its conditioned reflexes if it 'resists'. The mental acceptance of the horse is critical to the horse's response to any leg actions and may be affected by a large

'A delayed response is normal.'

number of internal and external influences. The horse may deliberately come against the leg, may ignore the leg, may run away from the leg or may respond perfectly. In addition, different horses have different reflex responses to being touched. Some jump away from the touch, others kick out against it and others step away slowly, even a second or two later. No two horses are exactly the same, but the objective must always be to aim for a response to the most subtle of actions of leg or hand.

'The spurs are for the advanced horse, the whip for the young horse.'

The rider/trainer should not be afraid to experiment to discover the effect of the stimulus, including the whip or spur, and what natural reflexes will assist and what will hinder the training. I find that most young horses, and particularly mares, initially tighten and so brace against the touch of the spur. I sympathize with them because I can imagine what it is like to be poked in the side if one is sensitive or ticklish. The spur works well once the horse has developed the reflex response to the touch, to quicken the reaction to a lighter touch. I am more often telling my pupils to take off their spurs rather than put them on. It is better to save them for later.

'One touch is enough.'

Only ever 'touch' once in any stride whether with the leg, whip, spur, seat, or half-halt. Each touch, whether to the horse's body or mouth, is an action. The horse can only respond *after* the touch, so keeping the pressure on, or applying the touch more than once in a stride by vibrating with the leg or hand, will dull the aid and delay the response. The touch should be repeated only every other stride. To do so more often will take over the horse's responsibility for self-carriage.

'Keep your radio switched on at all times.'

Communication is like having a radio or hi-fi turned on at all times playing music that is in the appropriate rhythm and beat for the pace that you are in. The volume can be turned down almost to 0 when the horse is in self-carriage and volunteering the correct response. But if the horse does not respond or even react to your actions of leg or hand, then the volume can be turned up, if necessary quite sharply. Then when a reaction and response is forthcoming, the volume can be turned back down eventually to 0 again. But the radio should never be switched off. The rhythm to which you want your horse to relate should be in your mind at all times. This will help you to get the timing of the aids right as well.

Communicating by touch with legs, whip and spur

The *touch* of the leg, whip or spur is used for:

1. Energy To motivate the horse to be energetic both legs can be used together or separately. The 'double barrel', i.e both legs together, I save for a really sharp signal, especially if I do not have a whip or when I am using spurs with an advanced horse that understands their use. I prefer to use the energizing touch with the inside leg or the whip so that it has an effect on the inside hind. Occasionally, it is appropriate to use the outside leg or whip on the shoulder when the horse is drifting out on the turn or circle, rather than going forwards.

In training the horse to be more responsive and self-motivated, it is better to use the whip more often. The whip should be thought of as a reminder associated with the action of the leg and the body language rather than a punishment. You are saying to the horse 'come on', or 'I didn't say slow down'. If you always use your leg first and then follow it with the action of the whip, then your horse thinks of the whip as a punishment rather than a back up to the body language. As with the legs, the whip is a way of supporting your body language, and it often has the advantage that its action is quicker and sharper so you cannot hold the aid on in the same way as you can when you press with the leg, which often leads to the heel being drawn up and back. Horses have different reactions to the leg, whip and spur, and it is best to keep an open mind and use the means that works best to the lightest of touches. In the end it will lead to the horse maintaining self-carriage, rather than having to be asked or reminded every other stride.

2. Lateral response By talking specifically to one hind leg or foreleg to produce a lateral (sideways) response from that leg and so initiate a turn or a lateral movement. In this case, one leg is used at a time. This is one part of lateral submission.

The *effect* of the leg action will depend on the following three factors, which are all related: *position/direction, duration/strength and timing.*

Position of the leg
The *neutral* leg position is governed by the principle of keeping the stirrup leather hanging vertically down from the stirrup bar. Before applying the touch of the leg, the knee must be braced by lifting the toe. To *talk to the hindquarters,* the leg must be held only very slightly further back by 'opening the hip' or abducting the knee rather than by sliding the leg back. To *talk to the forehand,* the leg is used only slightly further forward by 'closing the hip' and slightly lifting the knee on that side rather than by pushing the lower leg forward which tends to take it away from the horse's side. In *canter position,* the rider sits to the inside of the saddle with the outside shoulder back and inside hip advanced. The leg hangs normally from the rider's hip, so the inside leg will then hang slightly in advance of the outside leg. Avoid pushing the inside heel forward, which takes the leg away from the horse's side.

Direction of the pressure
A horse can feel the direction of the touch against its skin. The touch of the leg action should be directed forward for energy, neutral for a purely lateral aid and only be applied backwards for the rein-back. To direct the touch *towards the forehand,* close the hip and slightly lift the knee while keeping the toe up in order to brace the knee, as for example in the pirouette. To direct the touch *towards the hindquarters,* open the hip and slightly turn the knee and foot outwards, as for example in leg-yielding. Avoid pulling the lower leg back by tightening the hamstrings and pulling up the heel.

'A horse can feel a fly.'

Duration/strength of the pressure
To increase the sensitivity of the horse to the leg actions, the lightest of pressures should be used. Always remember that there is no limit to how little you can do, but there is a limit to how much you can do. It is sometimes necessary to be sharper with the leg action to get the horse's attention, but then the duration of the pressure must be even shorter, hence the effectiveness of the whip as a supporting aid. The touch

of the spur should always be quick. It is better to repeat an action whilst gradually increasing the sharpness, than to keep the pressure on. The leg action should not last longer than one step. One often sees riders squeezing harder, keeping the pressure on the horse's side, but this only dulls the reaction.

Timing of the action
The action of the leg should always be used within the rhythm of the pace and should be applied just before the horse's leg that is being addressed leaves the ground. If the leg has already left the ground there will be no effect. Timing is most important when a sharp action of the leg, whip or spur is to be applied. The objective is to produce a reflex response to the stimulus. If applied at the wrong moment the reflex will be blocked.

For all leg, whip and spur aids, the *rider* must:

- be *clear* about what he wants the horse to do

- be *prepared* with his position statement, and *correct* it on a regular basis

- *differentiate* between the action of each leg

- be *accurate* with the timing

- *modify* the leg action according to the response, and if necessary support it with whip or spur

- *coordinate* the leg actions with the position statement and rein actions

The *horse's* responsibility is to:

- *react* – any reaction is better than no reaction with the young, uneducated horse

- *respond* correctly if it is asked correctly

- *maintain* the response until told otherwise, i.e., until there is a change to the position statement

Communicating by touch through the reins

The signals that are sent down the inside rein or outside rein (inside and outside refers to the horse's bend rather than the circle or the arena) can be divided into:

1. *Restraining* rein aids (half-halts and holding reins) ask the horse to wait and support the body language. As a general rule they should always be applied down the outside rein (see section on half-halts).

2. *Directional* rein aids (direct and indirect reins) support the leg aids and body language in turning the horse, and can be combined with a half-halt on the same rein

to produce specific reflex responses from the horse that are helpful in particular in the lateral work. The responses from these aids are called the *rein effects*.

3. *Positional* reins are related to the adjustment of the length of each rein and influence the flexion of the horse's neck at the poll (atlas/axis joint), and/or the bend at the base of the neck just in front of the withers. They have the similar effect to adjusting one side rein shorter than the other.

The rein aids only produce the desired effect when the horse has sufficient impulsion or energy (not to be confused with speed). Although they produce a reflex response from the horse, as with any reflex the horse can resist or block it.

As with the leg action, the minimum aid should be used to produce the required effect, even though it may be necessary sometimes in training to exaggerate the aid to emphasize the signal. If the aid has to be exaggerated, it is important to be clear with the position statement and the leg action. The final objective is to be able to apply the rein effect in support of the body and leg without any obviously visible movement of the arm.

For all rein aids

Always
- **Repeat** the aid in rhythm with the pace, i.e. walk, trot or canter. Don't hang-on.
- **Support** the body language and the leg actions rather than instead of.
- **Prepare position statement** before applying the rein aid. An incorrect position can cancel out the rein effect.

The allowed actions of arm and hand are: forwards, upwards and outwards.

Don't
- Pull down, backwards or across the neck with any rein aid.
- Use a rein aid on one rein that contradicts the rein aid on the other.

1. Restraining rein aids

The **half-halt** is a momentary restraining rein action that supports the body language. When riding, assuming a constant contact, the rein action produces a momentary increase in pressure on the mouth that should only last for one step/stride. It is a more or less strong signal to the horse via the mouth, which is intended to get the horse's attention and respect for the body language. When handling the horse from the ground, the rein action may be applied to the horse via the cavesson, halter or the bit.

The ideal is reached when the horse responds to the body language with little need for supporting rein actions, and yet accepts the contact with the rider's hand through the rein. When accepted, the body language combined with the half-halt produces a checking of the horse's forward motion (speed) either by slowing the rhythm or by shortening the stride.

'Slow the rhythm or
shorten the stride.'

The rider has to decide in advance whether to slow the rhythm or shorten the stride or do a combination of both. The body language will be slightly different depending on the goal. The rider asks for a *slowing of the rhythm* by setting a slower rhythm in his own mind and then riding a slower rhythm, whether in walk, trot or canter. The half-halts support his body language by asking the horse to relate to that.

The rider asks for a *shorter stride* by applying the half-halts while maintaining the same rhythm in his own mind. The following or driving action of the seat affects the length of the stride, while the leg, whip or spur energize. To shorten the stride the half-halts must be applied down the outside rein as the inside hind foot comes to the ground and at the same time the seat must stop driving.

'Reaction and
response differs
between horses.'

Horses *react* in different ways to the increased pressure on the mouth. In the case of a very sharp or strong half-halt, the reaction might vary from virtually nothing to a violent tossing of the head with or without a setting of the jaw or opening of the mouth. The *response* might vary from the horse stopping instantly to the horse running away out of fear. What the horse does and how quickly it responds will depend on its sensitivity and its understanding, and therefore to a degree on its stage of education. A young or uneducated horse cannot be expected to respond correctly to a sharp half-halt rein action. It is most likely to be frightened of it and throw its head up or 'run into the bridle'. However, an educated horse that is just inattentive or not trying can be expected to respond correctly to a sharp action because it knows what is wanted.

Not all half-halting actions of the rein should be sharp or strong. The rider must always aim to use the minimum aid. The degree of the action must be commensurate with the situation and the loudness of the rider's command to listen! The rider must have a clear idea of the goal and be assertive enough to achieve it. The key is correct goal setting combined with correct position statement and body language. It cannot be emphasized too much that the purpose of the rein action is to teach or remind the horse to respond to the body language. It will not be effective if applied on its own.

It may be necessary to repeat the action within the rhythm until the horse responds sufficiently, but by making sure that it only lasts one step we avoid 'hanging on' and giving the horse a reason for setting its jaw. The most that we should ever do is to apply a half-halt every other stride. Remember that with a young or un-educated horse it is not reasonable to expect an immediate response (see section on reflexes).

The half-halt rein

Must

- only last one step or stride
- be applied down the outside rein and be timed to coincide with the supporting phase of the stride i.e. when the inside hind foot comes to the ground
- be applied without a directly backward pull
- never be applied downwards against the bars of the mouth
- never cross the neck

If the body language is correct, then the horse is likely to respond by checking or slowing its forward momentum, even if a stride or two later. If it does not, then the rider must gradually apply sharper rein actions in the rhythm of the pace that he is in, combined with clearer body language and possibly the use of the voice.

The severity of the rein action is measured in terms of its sharpness and its strength. It may vary between a tremor to 'one in the back teeth'! The object is to get the horse's attention. What works for one horse may not necessarily work for another, and the trainer will need to experiment. The action can either whisper or shout at the horse to listen, but as with people, constant shouting will eventually cause deafness. When you hear someone whisper you instinctively try harder to listen. When a shout comes 'out of the blue', attention is obtained immediately.

Half-halts may also be supported, but not at the same moment, by other actions such as leg, the whip or spur with a view to having an 'engaging' effect on the hind leg. The expression I learnt in France as a teenager always springs to mind, 'Leg without hand, hand without leg'. The half-halt and the touch of the leg should not be applied at the same moment except with an advanced horse, where the combined action, if well timed, can produce an increase in the degree of engagement of the hind leg leading to increased collection, but it takes away from the horse's impulsion so must be used sparingly.

The *holding rein* can be used in training the green or nervous horse and should not be confused with a rider 'hanging-on'. The important difference between the 'hold' and the 'hang-on' is that the correctly applied 'hold' comes from the rider's body language and can be supported at times by placing the fist into the base of the neck; it does not come from the rider's arm alone. In the case of the untrained horse, the half-halts will not be understood and may in fact cause the horse to get excited

> 'Leg without hand, hand without leg'

 The holding rein.

and run faster. The holding rein can also be used at a later stage in the work. In the case of the racehorse or event horse, it is necessary to 'hold' the horse when galloping to keep the same pace and to help the horse to stabilize the head and neck, which improves its ability to gallop.

2. Directional rein aids

The directional rein aids are used to support the position statement both in the turns and in keeping the horse straight on the line. They are also used in supporting the leg and position statement in the lateral work. A thorough knowledge of the *rein effects* is vital in any horseman's 'tool kit', and it is important to spend time perfecting the skills of applying the rein aids correctly and recognizing the rein effects that stem from them.

The French school of riding places a higher degree of importance on the rein effects than does the German or Swedish tradition of schooling. I believe that they are very useful supporting aids, if not the primary aids. One often sees riders whose directional rein aids contradict their other aids because of ignorance of their effect.

The directional rein aids have the benefit of being natural aids in the sense that horses tend to find them easy to understand and so respond to them quickly, as long as they have the willingness, the energy and, in the case of the 'reins of opposition', the understanding of the half-halt.

The **direct (opening) rein** is applied by rotating the arm outwards and taking it slightly away from the neck as if turning the pages of a book.

The *rein effect* is to guide the horse's shoulders in the direction of the opening rein.

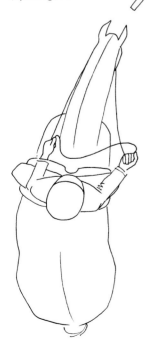

The direct (opening) rein.

- There should be no change in the weight of rein in the contact.

- The elbow should remain by the rider's side at or in front of the hip.

- It is a very basic and elementary rein effect that is used mostly with young horses. If it is used as the main turning aid it will tend to put the horse on the forehand.

- It is a very safe rein. Horses that are inclined to jib or nap on a turn are best turned using this rein aid repeatedly and very obviously.

The **indirect (neck) rein** is applied by rotating the arm outwards but at the same time bringing the rein towards and slightly up the horse's neck as if stroking the neck with the rein towards the horse's opposite ear.

The *rein effect* is to guide/nudge the shoulders in the direction away from the rein aid.

- The rein contact should remain the same.

- The rider's hand should never come across the neck.

- The indirect rein can be supported by the direct rein on the other rein especially as the horse is taught to respond to the indirect rein.

- This rein aid should be used sparingly. In my experience as a trainer it is used too often by riders instead of obtaining the response to the leg being applied to the forehand.

The **direct rein of opposition** is applied in the same manner as the simple direct rein but *with a half-halting action* on the rein as the hand is taken away from the neck.

The *rein effect* is that the horse picks up the hind foot (on the same side as the rein action) and steps across and under the body. The effect can be likened to applying the rear brake of your bicycle as you are coming around a turn.

- The half-halt should last one step. If necessary repeat the action every other stride.

- The timing of the aid is important. It should be applied just before the hind leg on the same side leaves the ground in order to encourage the hind foot to be picked up earlier in the stride.

- The aid relies on the horse having sufficient impulsion or energy in the step.

- The rein action must be supported by contact, but not resistance, on the opposite rein.

The **indirect rein of opposition** is applied in the same manner as the simple indirect (neck) rein, but with a half-halting action on the rein as the hand is brought towards the neck. The direction of the half-halt is towards the horse's hip on the opposite side.

The *rein effect* is to bring the forehand around more abruptly by stopping the forward momentum for a moment.

- The half-halt should last one step. If necessary repeat the action.

- The hand can come to the withers or neck but avoid crossing the neck because that would involve pulling rather than half-halting.

- The rein action must be supported by the contact on the opposite rein.

- The effect of the aid relies on the horse having sufficient impulsion.

- The aid should be applied as the foreleg on the same side is coming forward.

3. Positional rein aids

Adjusting the length of rein appropriately is an important part of a rider's preparation for a movement or jump. Depending on the required objective, the horse may be expected to offer lateral flexion at the poll, to increase or decrease the bend through the neck, or to change the elevation of the neck.

To obtain a correct lateral flexion at the poll to the inside, with or without bend at the base of the neck, the inside rein must be adjusted a little shorter than the outside, but the inside elbow must remain at or in front of the rider's inside hip. The

The indirect rein.

outside hand and arm should allow sufficiently to maintain the same contact on the outside rein.

If a horse willingly offers the lateral flexion, the contact will be maintained evenly in both reins. If the horse is unwilling, the contact may at times be greater on the inside rein until the horse can be persuaded to accept the lateral flexion. In the event of resistance, the inside hand and arm must avoid pulling backwards or downwards, but instead act as a side rein. It is preferable to fix the elbow against the body just in front of the hip or even fix it against some point on the horse's neck whilst working through leg and position statement, combined with relevant exercises to persuade the horse to accept the flexion. It is however better to use the gymnastic exercises explained later in the book to persuade the horse to offer the lateral flexion rather than more force being applied down the inside rein, which usually provokes more resistance.

1. To obtain the *lateral flexion* at the poll with minimum bend at the base of the neck, the inside rein should be slightly lifted and brought close to the neck, as with an indirect rein. The outside rein meanwhile should act to limit the bend at the base of the neck.

2. For an *elevated neck,* the forearm must be raised whilst keeping the elbow close to the body so that the rein aid is supporting the body language and position statement. The objective is to encourage the horse to come up through the withers and base of the neck as well as raise its poll.

3. For a *lower and round neck,* the whole arm is offered forwards towards the horse's mouth to the extent that the horse is willing to stretch the neck forward, but with the elbow kept relatively close to the body so that it can support the body if the horse tries to take too much. If a lowered and long neck is desired, the elbow is allowed to advance forward away from the body to allow the horse to stretch to the maximum, but this is only done when riding in a light seat or light rising trot.

Lateral flexion.

Elevated neck. Ferro ridden by Coby van Baalen.

Lower and round neck. Gigolo ridden by Isabel Werth.

Communicating by use of sound

The voice serves two purposes:

1. The horse reacts to noise. Sharp noises such as the click of the tongue create energy, while a prolonged soothing voice can reassure and calm the horse.

2. The use of commands when riding can also positively reinforce the rider's body language. When my young daughter was having difficulty riding her horse

through corners, I told her to shout the command to 'get into the corner!' When she shouted this with conviction she was automatically assertive enough with her body language, leg and outside rein to achieve the result she wanted, which was to stop her horse cutting the corner. It appeared to her that the horse was responding to her voice, but in fact the assertive manner in which she delivered the command produced the right response from her and perhaps attention from her horse.

3. Mental Elements (Self-Control, Confidence, Focus, Goal Setting, Self-Appraisal, Mental Toughness)

Sports psychology has long been recognized as being as much a key to successful performance as technical ability or fitness. Some riders/trainers seem to be naturals not just in respect of their physical attributes and ability to learn by copying or by experimentation but also in respect of their ability to control their emotions and make the right decisions under pressure of the competition or as professional trainers.

Goal setting and review are key factors to successful training both of the horse and rider. For the rider who is not ambitious, great pleasure and satisfaction can be gained from training and riding a horse to the highest level that both can achieve. Problems often arise where the rider/trainer sets an unattainable goal for themselves or their horses. On the one hand if you 'reach for the stars' you may 'reach the moon' but on the other hand every horse let alone rider eventually reaches its limit. It is when that limit is crossed that problems of confidence and self-control arise. The successful competition rider requires mental toughness above all else both to cope with the inevitable disappointments and to remain dedicated to the constant learning process that is 'horses'.

4. Feel and Experience (Movement, Music, Rhythm, Timing, Training Goals)

'Feel' is a vital element in a successful rider. 'Feel' in this context means two things. There is the literal meaning, in other words the ability because you are sufficiently relaxed and aware on your horse to feel the movements of the horse, to feel the contact in the reins and the changes to it, to feel the pressure applied by your legs and seat.

There is also the other meaning of 'feel' that comes through experience and imagination, the 'feel' for movement, rhythm, music and dance. Some people have the ability to be able to 'feel' or imagine what it's like to be a horse. There is no doubt that a rider who has grown up around horses and has ridden regularly since a child has an innate ability to 'feel' more on a horse than a person who has come to riding later in life and is not able to ride so often. As we move further away from the days when horses were a natural part of life and we move more into the technological age, so it becomes more difficult. The modern worker spends much of his time working over a desk or a machine with his hands, thinking then doing. Hence it is difficult to feel through the body and to communicate and feel with the body, seat and legs as well. There is a need for knowledge and understanding by the modern rider but complemented by experience which only comes from trial and error.

It is possible to be too analytical and in so doing lose the 'feeling' for the movement. In the end there is no substitute for experience but it helps to have a good imagination. In offering a system for the rider to communicate with the horse and to train it, not every permutation or nuance can be covered in a book. I hope I can help riders by providing a framework that works most of the time and from which the rider can develop their own experience and feel. In this way they will be able to react consistently with the system and yet find an individual answer to the problems with which they are faced.

CHAPTER FOUR

The Horse

THE LAST SECTION LOOKED at the way in which the rider can communicate effectively with his horse. It also explained how to educate the horse to develop the desired responses to a rider's 'body language', 'position statement', and 'language of touch'. This education process is a continuous one, which takes place throughout the horse's training with the objective of refining the communication system to the greatest possible extent. The work is never done. The dream is that you will eventually have a horse that instinctively knows what you want, and yet does not 'take charge'; that is attentive, and yet in self-carriage and able to look after itself when needed, for example when jumping.

The emphasis in this section is on using and developing that communication system to train the horse to adopt a posture, and work in a way that will make it more comfortable to ride as well as more successful as a sport horse. At any stage in its training, the horse's reaction and response to the communication system must be monitored and improved. These two aspects of the training, i.e. *education* and *gymnastics*, are inextricably linked and, together with maturity and the *physical development* that comes with work, should lead to the horse's *mental development* i.e. confidence, calmness and trust.

The route map of training

The training of the horse goes through three stages that can be likened to the stages of education of a child – nursery, primary and secondary. The route or path that the training follows is, in general terms, the same for every horse. At any stage in its training it may be necessary to take a step back, because the problems that arise as one moves along the 'route' nearly always relate back to a previous stage in the training. It is often said by experienced riders and trainers that good results come from a concentration on the basics.

The order of priorities in training

It is important to consider the order of priorities in training right from the pre-nursery stage. The horse's reaction and response to the rider or handler is always the first priority. Unless the horse has respect and does something in reaction to our communication then we cannot train it. If any element of the training is overlooked, then it will present problems later and will, at some point, have to be addressed.

At the nursery and then primary school stages, the dressage (flat work) training forms the basis of the jumping training, but in effect the jumping exercises are another form of gymnastic exercise that both develop and test the horse's basic dressage training.

1. Nursery school

The young horse must learn to:

i. Respect – accept the 'pecking order'.

ii. Respond to the handler's body language, language of touch and voice.

iii. Trust in the handler, his surroundings and the equipment.

iv. Trust and accept the rider on his back.

v. Go forward with energy and confidence.

vi. Understand and accept the basic control of the rider by staying on the line, slowing, stopping and turning.

2. Primary school

The horse must learn through gymnastic exercises to accept the lateral submission then the longitudinal submission, and so develop:

i. Regularity and rhythm within the paces.

ii. 'Connection over the back' i.e. posture.

iii. Acceptance of an even contact.

iv. 'Straightness'.

v. Confidence in basic jumping.

3. Secondary school

The work in primary school forms the basis for the work in collection, out of which comes improved control of the horse's balance leading to manoeuvrability, more expressive paces and development of the horse's jumping potential. The horse learns to improve:

i.   Longitudinal/lateral balance.

ii. Impulsion.

iii. Elasticity of the steps.

iv. Collection/extension.

v.   Jumping technique.

vi. Ability to cope with more technical demands in jumping.

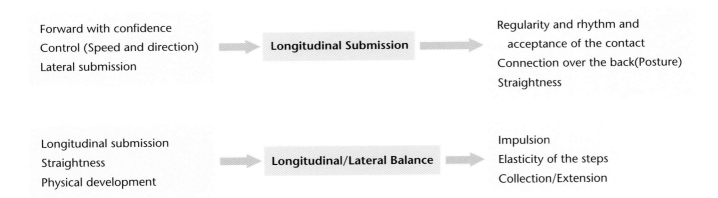

Forward with confidence
Control (Speed and direction)
Lateral submission

Longitudinal Submission

Regularity and rhythm and
   acceptance of the contact
Connection over the back(Posture)
Straightness

Longitudinal submission
Straightness
Physical development

Longitudinal/Lateral Balance

Impulsion
Elasticity of the steps
Collection/Extension

The System of Training – **Nursery School**

PHASE **1**

Handling and Backing

Taming and asserting the pecking order

Recognition of:
The forward energizing role of the touch to the horse's body.
The restraining role of the rein supported by the voice –
(initially through the cavesson and then through the bit).
The lateral effect of the touch to the horse's body
leading to:
Recognition of: The body language from the ground.

Accustoming and gaining the horse's confidence in equipment
(saddle, bridle, rugs etc).

Developing the horse's confidence and balance in carrying
a rider, accustoming it to the presence and contact
from above.

Exercises used

'Join-up' – Advance and retreat.

Leading, work in hand and simple lungeing on a cavesson
without side reins .

In the stable and then when being led and lunged.

Mounting and getting the horse used to movement on its
back. Walking and then trotting with a rider.

PHASE **2**

Energy and Control

Go The horse develops the habit of thinking forwards with
energy and confidence in response to the body language and
the energizing action of the leg and whip when being
ridden. It should enjoy the work rather finding it a chore.

Control

Stop The horse learns to respond to the body language
supported by the restraining actions of the hand applied
through the rein.
The restraining action of the hand at this stage of the training
is a holding rein rather than a half-halt and can also be
supported by the voice.

Turn The horse learns to respond to the opening or guiding
actions of the rein in support of the rider's position statement
for a turn.

Straight The horse learns to stay accurately on the line being
ridden in response to the rider's central position statement
supported by the guiding actions of the rein. At this stage
the straightness of the horse is not a priority.

Ride actively forward mainly in walk and trot but also in canter
where possible, preferably out of the arena in the countryside.
Use the horse's natural herd instinct, wherever possible, by
riding in company, sometimes following but also leading or at
least upsides.

Transitions between the paces, making sure the downward
transitions are in response to the body language and the rein
aids rather than because the horse chooses to stop going
forwards and that it continues to think forwards after the
transition. When the horse is keen, the emphasis is on
maintaining the rhythm.

The turns and circles should be as much as possible a part of
the journey rather than endless circles. The horse should be
encouraged to stay on the line by being ridden actively
forwards, preferably along a track or near a fence line rather
than out in the open at this stage unless in the company of a
more experienced horse.

The System of Training – **Primary School**

Objective

Exercises used

Dressage training (flatwork)

Turn from behind by engaging the hind leg in response to the lateral leg aid.

Control of the shoulder in response to the lateral leg aid.

Lateral submission leading to longitudinal submission.

- 'Connection over the back'.
- Rhythm and regularity of the paces.
- Acceptance of an even contact.
- Straightness – 'inline and online' – Improve lateral balance.

Recognition of position statement for turns and transition to/from canter.

Response to body language supported by leg and rein actions.

Transitions from pace to pace within a constant rhythm.

Increase the engagement of the hind leg and so improve longitudinal balance.

Develop the elasticity of the steps.

Develop the horse's ability to abduct and adduct the forelimb.

Develop the medium trot and canter.

- Recognition of the body language.
- Gradual increased length of stride within the same rhythm.

Turn about the forehand – t-a-f.

Turn about the haunches – t-a-h.

Diamond shape and zig-zag.

Combine t-a-f with circles and transitions (trot-walk-trot).

'Long and low'/'round and deep' where appropriate.

Leg-yielding – on the diagonal and on a circle in the 'corridor' exercise.

Transitions (trot-canter-trot) on the circle and out of leg-yielding.

The zone exercise (trot-walk-trot) to develop the medium trot.

Establish the halt.

The rein back.

The counter canter – starting gradually with shallow loops, then on to a circle.

Varying the stride length in canter by counting strides between markers/jumps.

Lungeing in side reins.

Working up and down a gradual incline – developing the medium trot uphill and the collection down hill.

Jumping training

Forward actively and straight but calmly over small jumps.

- Maintain the rhythm and even stride length before and after.
- Initially out of trot and then out of canter.
- Acceptance of a light even contact.

Accustom to different colours, fillers and situations.

Correct technique over the jumps – 'over the back' and 'free in the shoulder'.

Trotting poles.

Canter poles and small jumps.

Introduce fillers and take to small shows or training arenas for experience.

Introduce small simple grids including placing poles or trotting poles followed step by step by small jumps set at a comfortable distance for the stride of the horse.

Use guide poles to help with straightness when necessary.

The System of Training – **Secondary School**

Objective	Exercises used
Dressage training (flatwork)	Continued use of the exercises used in primary school especially:
Further develop the horse's posture.	• Leg-yielding.
Improve lateral suppleness.	• Corridor exercise.
Improve balance and paces.	• Zone exercise.
Transitions to and from medium trot within a constant rhythm.	• Rein back.
Improve response to the rider's body language.	• Counter canter.
Further improve straightness in the canter.	Varying the stride length within the rhythm especially in canter using the exercise of counting the strides.
Transitions to and from medium canter.	
Develop collection – improve the impulsion and expression of the paces.	Primary collecting exercises: shoulder-in, pirouette, small circles to 8 metres.
Improve the balance.	Acute transitions – trot-halt-trot, walk-canter-walk.
Improve lightness of the forehand and self-carriage.	Secondary exercises: travers, renvers and half-pass, piaffe steps. Extended paces and related transitions, Flying changes.
Jumping training	
Improve the response to the rider's body language and position.	Transitions between fences.
Related distances.	Figure of eight exercise.
Jumping off tighter turns.	Basculing exercises, including bounces and more demanding grids.
Improve technique.	
Develop experience and confidence.	Gradual increased heights and widths in training competitions.

Nursery School

This period of the horse's education covers the time from birth to starting to 'work', which is when it learns to go freely forwards under basic control, even if in its own style. It includes some essential elements that are required throughout the horse's training and career, and even with an older horse it may be necessary to go back to this stage in order to instill these elements if they have not been properly established in the past, or have been allowed to lapse. It can be difficult to do this with an older horse that is more confirmed in its way of going or its habits, but it is usually the most basic of problems that block the road ahead at the advanced stages in a horse's training and competition career.

1. Respect – Asserting the Pecking Order

A tiny foal is small enough to be carried by a person, but it soon becomes bigger and stronger than any of us, and so from the earliest stage it must accept the 'pecking order', and through that it will be easier to train.

These days many horses are bred in unnatural environments, whether on professional studs or in amateur, one-horse yards. In the wild, the horse is part of a herd that comprises a lead stallion and a group of mares with followers, ranging in age from foals upwards. Within the group below the lead stallion, there is a hierarchy. This hierarchy, or 'pecking order', is sorted out between the members of the group, and they learn to interact and respect each other's position within the herd. The hierarchy is determined by the strength of personality and courage of the individuals, as well as the natural respect for seniority that comes with age and length of time in the herd.

In our dealings with horses we have to assert the 'pecking order' between us and the horse. In recent years much has been discussed about the 'starting' or 'breaking' process. Monty Roberts has shown how we can encourage a young horse to 'volunteer' to accept a handler on the ground, rather than force it to accept us. He uses the expression 'join-up' in relation to persuading the horse to stay with the handler and accept the 'pecking order' rather than run over him or away from him.

The basis of this system is to work in a natural way. The horse learns to accept the relationship with the trainer as a partnership, in which it is the junior partner. In the wild, this relationship is established by the lead stallion in the herd, which relentlessly chases the other members of the group, particularly the mares. They soon make the choice to 'join-up' with his herd and accept his leadership, because the alternative involves expending much more effort. The important point is that the members of the group eventually make the choice to join-up. They are not forced to do so. They are not chained, tethered or in any way restrained.

Many horses are 'broken-in' and, although finally accepting the rider on their back, they have not 'joined-up'. I have found that no matter how young or old they are, the horses who do not accept the restraining aids are the ones that have not 'joined-up'. Horses can be taught to listen and respond to the restraining aids, but if they do not 'accept' them, they tend to respond less well to the body language and then the rein action has to interfere more often.

2. Response to the Handler's Body Language and the Language of Touch and Voice

Horses in a natural herd environment learn to respect the space of a more dominant or senior member of the herd in a natural way, in other words if they do not respect, they will 'receive both barrels' from the hind legs of the other horse. It is always fascinating to watch a group of horses interact in a wild or semi-wild state, or even within the paddocks of a large stud. Horses develop a reflex to get out of the way if approached by a more senior member of the herd. In a similar way the horse learns to move forward and away from the handler.

The horse that has completely 'joined-up' will walk willingly forward alongside the handler, and when the handler stops the horse will stop beside him. The less the handler has to use the restraining action of the lead rope the better. A well mannered, calm young horse that is led in-hand will respond to the handler's body language. A horse must be taught to be well mannered just as a child should be. But young horses can get excited or distracted, and so the action on the lead rope or the rein may have to re-enforce the body language. Equally the horse may have to be motivated to go forward by the use of a whip.

There is not much difference in principle between training dogs to lead and training horses to lead. It is just a question of degree. The 'half-halt' via a tug on the lead rope or the bit must be quick enough and sharp enough to produce a reaction. On its own, the action will not be sufficient; it must be supported by the body language and perhaps also the voice. The long-term effect of such training will depend on the assertiveness and consistency of the trainer.

Once the horse has learned to respond to the handler's body language, touch and voice, then it will more quickly develop a conditioned reflex response to the rider's body language, touch and voice.

Young horses learning the pecking order.

The horse that is willingly 'joined-up' will walk happily alongside the handler.

3. Trust in the Handler, Its Surroundings and in the Equipment Used

As well as respect, the horse should also develop trust in the handler. It must also trust its surroundings and the equipment used in its training and general care, including rugs, saddles, reins, stirrups etc. One of the major issues is the acceptance of the pressure of the girth (or roller) and saddle on its back. It is a natural reflex of the horse to tighten its back muscles and indeed buck or kick at the pressure, which probably arises from the natural reflex to dislodge a predator from its back.

Of course every horse is different in terms of its natural nervousness or reaction to its environment. For example, some horses never become relaxed enough to be clipped without resorting to calming drugs. It is probably the case that, if enough time was spent on accustoming a horse to the clippers, it could be done, but it might not be worth the investment of time required.

The trust that the horse acquires in being handled should never develop into a lack of respect for your space. The young horse in the herd gains confidence and trust from knowing its position in the hierarchy, and all is peaceful and relaxed until a newcomer joins the group and the process of establishing the 'pecking order' has to start again. It is not frightened of its peers, yet it remains respectful of them. So must it become with us.

4. Trust and Acceptance of the Rider on his Back

The process of gaining the horse's trust and acceptance of a rider on its back is a continuation of the work done previously to get it used to and confident with the handler and all the equipment that is used on it, particularly the roller and then the saddle. It must also get used to the presence of a person moving around it, and of being touched over areas of its body that are outside its field of vision.

There is no direct relationship between the ease of establishing this trust, the acceptance of the rider on the back and the horse's long term trainability for sport. Obviously, a naturally relaxed horse that has been well handled since birth should readily accept a rider on its back, but that does not mean that it will be any easier to train than the young horse that, at the start, has hardly been handled.

5. Go Forward with Energy and Confidence

Without energy, leading to a desire to go forwards, the horse is as trainable as a statue. Once we have some energy, then we can expect some reactions to our communication with the horse. It is not guaranteed that the young horse, let alone the experienced, well trained horse, will always channel that energy automatically in a forward direction, so the next objective of the training must be to direct that energy forwards and to control its speed and direction. Once we have the horse thinking forward under basic control, we can then work to maintain regular paces in a rhythm and develop the horse's posture, balance and straightness.

Having the right amount of *energy* or forward thought at any stage in the training is the first priority. The horse can have too much energy or too little depending on what it is being asked to do and its stage of schooling. Excess or nervous energy might come from exuberance and a feeling of well being, or it might come from fear and a desire to 'run away'. A fresh, exuberant horse may choose not to 'listen' to the rider, while a frightened or tense horse will not 'hear' the rider's signals, or even if it does then it may not attempt to understand them. On the other hand a dull or lazy horse will not bother to listen or understand.

Every horse is different. Like people, some are inherently more energetic than others, some are lazy, some are introverts, some are extroverts. I have known horses that were initially lazy and then become energetic, and I have known the reverse. With experience, the rider will become better at judging the attitude of the horse and reacting accordingly. For me, having too much energy is always better than having too little. Each rider has to find a horse whose temperament and attitude suits his own.

If your horse has too much energy you cannot make it relax. It is best to avoid an argument, so allow it to 'let off steam' in some way. Lungeing on a safe surface, or turning the horse loose for a while to have a run around and a buck as long as it is safe to do so, saves a lot of frustrating hours in the saddle. The fitter the horse is, or the more stamina it has, the longer it can take to get it to a stage where you can 'talk' to it.

'You can take a horse to water but you can't make it drink.'

Temper or fear can also affect the horse's energy level. Those young horses with an inherent nervous energy sometimes take a long time to settle. I mean by that, months if not years. They are often the stars of the future because they have natural energy, but it takes time to channel that energy in the right direction.

The young frightened horse may at first appear to have too much energy because it wants to run away from the rider and its surroundings. A calm, relaxed, patient rider will eventually persuade a frightened horse to relax and trust. You just have to keep working with the horse and wait for it to relax. The experienced rider can recognize the difference between exuberance and fear or temper from the expression on the horse's face. The eyes, ears and nostrils all tell a tale. You may not succeed in one session or even several, but if you keep working in the same patient, calm and yet disciplined way then eventually you will succeed. It never works to be in a hurry with a horse.

'Always have more time than your horse.'

The horse must learn to recognize the body language and the touch of the leg, whip or spur as a signal to *go forwards* or to have more energy. When it does not respond to our body language and touch of leg, we 'frighten' it to some degree with the whip, which causes it to be surprised and to jump forwards. This use of the whip and the leg at the same time gradually produces a reflex response to the body language as well as the touch of leg. Depending on the reactions of the horse, it is correct to combine the supporting aids at times to produce the desired response. The trainer has to develop an ability to recognize the reactions and apply the appropriate supporting aids. (See previous section 'communicating by touch'.) The horse learns gradually that the desired response is more comfortable. Going forward with energy becomes a conditioned reflex response to the body language. A horse should be trained to keep going until asked to slow down. Going forwards actively should become a habit – it is the horse's responsibility.

Motivating the horse

As you slouch in your armchair watching a film on television, your body holds no latent energy. By contrast, a performing gymnast holds energy in his posture. When you are riding, you need to recognize the effect that your posture and balance has

Learning to go forward with energy and confidence.

on a horse's energy level and desire to go forwards. You cannot expect a horse to have energy, if your own posture is slack. Equally, a tense rider will not succeed in calming an excitable horse. A rider who is consistently unbalanced and 'behind the movement' will also have trouble motivating a horse, because his body language will keep sending a contrary signal to the horse.

The rider who has no energy himself is not going to motivate his horse. There has to be a desire by the rider to have an energetic horse. Some people walk and run slowly, and they tend to ask the same of their horses. Exactly how much you want your horse to go will depend on how much you feel in control. If you are not confident of being in control, you will always convey that message to your horse through your body language. Your actions will be slightly slower or duller, and your horse will sense that you are reluctant to let it go forward.

I find that saying either aloud or to myself 'hup-two-three-four' in the trot and 'bud-a-*bum*, bud-a-*bum*' in the canter, or other such energizing expressions, has the effect of translating energetic thoughts to my body language and thereby to my horse, at the same time emphasizing the rhythm and regularity of the steps. If the horse needs more energy in its work, I usually tell my pupil to excite the horse rather than say 'use more leg'.

A number of external factors will affect the horse's attitude and energy: the type of work (dressage, jumping, galloping etc), the location (the home arena, a competition, the field etc), the company (other horses, other animals – just think what would happen if a kangaroo suddenly appeared around the corner!) Try to vary the type and place of work to keep your horse motivated. On the other hand, the horse that is too excited to concentrate on its schooling often needs to be kept in a calmer situation, at least initially, to make it possible to communicate with it.

It is important to understand the difference between length of stride and energy. Collection requires your horse to have energy within a shorter stride. Extension requires energy within a longer stride. Between jumps you sometimes want to shorten the stride without losing energy, and sometimes you want your horse to jump off a longer stride. The quick action of the leg, sometimes supported by the whip or spur, stimulates the horse to have more energy in the steps. If the horse has

'Energy starts in the rider's mind.'

'A bored person is seldom an energetic person.'

energy, it will pick the hind foot off the floor and bring it forward more actively, without necessarily lengthening the stride. The driving or pushing action of the seat lengthens the stride and sends the horse forwards, but does not necessarily energize unless accompanied by the touch of the leg or whip.

The rider's responsibility is to continuously assess the level of energy offered by the horse. The level that is sufficient will change from horse to horse, exercise to exercise, and will relate to the horse's age and stage of schooling. If the energy is insufficient, then the rider must stimulate the horse to offer more, but not take over the job for it. The same applies with the length of stride. The most you should ever do even with the laziest of horses is to remind it every second stride.

In the same way that the athletics coach, the personal fitness trainer, or the football manager motivates his players to try hard, so the rider has to think how to energize his horse, but he must do it in such a way that it does not produce paralysing tension or take over the responsibility from the horse. Horses do not all respond in the same way to the same stimulus, so the rider needs to experiment to find what works for his horse.

6. Understand and Accept Basic Control of Rider

A horse should begin learning to respond to the restraining aids when it is a foal. At that stage, and in the years before it is 'started' under saddle, it can learn to recognize and respect the body language of the handler, supported by the actions applied to the horse's head through the headcollar rope, or through the rein if walking in a bridle. If it has this respect, then it is relatively simple to teach the horse to respond to the actions applied to the mouth through the rein. The only difference is that the mouth is much more sensitive than the bridge of the horse's nose.

Once we have a horse that thinks forward, the next requirement is to be able to adjust the speed and set a rhythm by teaching the horse to respond to the restraining aids i.e. the half-halts. Ultimately, controlling the speed means being able to stop the horse even if, in the case of an excitable horse, it may not be possible to persuade it to stand still. We must always distinguish between control and calmness. It is possible to have one without the other.

Speed equals the pace (i.e. walk, trot or canter) combined with the rhythm and length of stride within that pace. To control the speed in one pace, sometimes it is desirable to slow the rhythm and at other times to adjust the length of stride, just as when driving a car one can press on the brake and/or change gear. A driver has to change gears from fourth to third to second to negotiate a tight turn, and in a similar way a rider has to ask for a shorter stride, but make sure his horse maintains the energy level, before a turn. This is what is meant by 'collection'. One of the end goals in the training is to educate the horse to recognize the body language, and be able to adjust the length of stride on command i.e. extend or collect.

In the early stages of training in nursery school, the pace is directly related to the speed. Some horses will naturally break from walk to trot sooner rather than lengthen their stride and likewise from trot to canter. I have worked with horses that have been bred and raced as trotters, and they can trot exceedingly fast before break-

'The leg is for energy the seat is for length of stride.'

'Speed = Rhythm x length of stride.'

ing to canter! The understanding of the position statement and aids for the transitions from pace to pace comes next in the horse's training.

In primary school, the horse will not be able to collect, and this limits the tightness of the turn that can be executed within the trot or canter. The size of circle demanded in a dressage test gradually becomes smaller as the horse moves from one level to the next. So too does the extent to which the horse is expected to ride deeper into the corners in the test. The same applies when jumping. The horse cannot successfully make tight turns to fences, or cope with related distances in canter, until it has learnt to control its speed by shortening its canter stride without loss of energy in the step and without breaking to trot.

The use of the bit when communicating with the horse

It can take a while before the horse settles and accepts a bit in the mouth. Each horse is different in its sensitivity, and it is not possible to force a horse to accept the bit. Any attempt to do so, such as fitting a tight noseband, tends to cause more problems than it solves because the horse fights the restriction by tightening the jaw muscles. I find that many problems, such as the reluctance of the horse to go forward to the contact, or the unsteadiness or tilting of the head, arise from the resistance to the noseband.

Much has been written and discussed about different types of bits. Horses do have different shaped mouths, which can affect how well they accept a bit, but I think that too much emphasis can be placed on the bit and not enough on the rider's responsibility in communicating through the rein. It is most important that the bit is the correct size for the horse. Too small and it will pinch, too large and it will hang too low in the horse's mouth and the 'nutcracker' action will cause discomfort. Some horses prefer a double jointed bit so that there is less nutcracker action. The long cheek eggbut snaffle suits young horses while they are being started because the bit cannot slide through the mouth. The disadvantage of them is that they seem to encourage horses to lean. The loose ring snaffle is my preferred bit, although with some horses that are 'fussy' in the mouth and are reluctant to accept the contact the eggbut snaffle works better.

When a bit is first put in a horse's mouth, it is certainly going to 'play' with it. It is unnatural for a horse to have a piece of metal in its mouth. It is important that the bit is fitted high enough in the mouth so as to be comfortably against the corners of the mouth. Too low and the horse might 'play' with the bit too much and possibly get its tongue over it. If it is too high the horse will be uncomfortable with the pressure on the corners of the mouth. Gradually the horse will accept increased pressure in the corners of the mouth to the point that the bit should be fitted to create one fold in the lip at the corners.

The parts of the horse's mouth have different degrees of sensitivity. The corner of the mouth is usually the most comfortable place for the horse to feel the pressure of the bit and therefore the actions of the rein. Pressure on the bars (jaw bone) of the mouth and the tongue is far less comfortable. Many horses resent the tongue being pinched between the bit and the lower jaw and will sometimes pull the tongue back and flip it over the bit. This leads to the rule or principle in dressage

'The straight line – elbow – hand – horse's mouth.'

that 'The hand should always be on or above the line that runs from the elbow to the horse's mouth'.

The acceptance of the bit and its effect on posture

The young horse that has just been started will naturally take a while to accept a bit in its mouth. Riders often make the mistake of trying to force the horse to lower its head by pulling downwards against the bars of the mouth. This causes the horse to contract the jaw muscles and hence the upper neck muscles (see biomechanics), and makes matters worse.

It is quite common for the horse and rider to have more contact on one particular side of the mouth (usually the left). The uneven contact occurs when the horse resists or ignores the half-halts or the turning aids causing the rider to hang on to the inside rein. This in turn causes the muscles at the top of the neck to contract unevenly, resulting in a tilting head. Some horses tilt the head away from the contact and some tilt towards. One of the outward symptoms is the bit being held to one side of the mouth. The correction must be to work on the evenness of the contact and to persuade the horse to volunteer the correct flexion in response to the body language.

Horses with a naturally longer upper neck muscle, and that are not so tight in their head/neck connection, have a tendency to carry the head behind the vertical, either if they do not want to accept the contact ('behind the bit') or if the rider allows them to lean on the contact ('overbent').

The contact is like a telephone line: it is the means through which we can send signals to the horse. The more consistent and even the contact the clearer the signals. The responsibility to maintain an even contact is a shared one. When the horse accepts the bit in its mouth and also accepts to go forward willingly and on the line that we choose, the contact can be likened to the sail on a boat in a consistent gentle breeze. Enough to keep the sail stretched and drawing the boat forward, but not so strong as to be uncomfortable in one's hands or arms. When the wind is variable and not from behind, then the sail flaps – the horse 'drops the bit'. The rider's responsibility is to maintain a constant contact by maintaining balance at all times without tension in the shoulders, arms and elbows. The relaxed elbow joint is the primary means by which the rider is able to keep an 'elastic', and therefore constant, contact.

The contact can become too strong either when the horse is too keen to go forward and the rider 'hangs-on', instead of repeating the half-halts with the appropriate severity, or when the horse looks for support in maintaining its balance or posture and leans on the bit. The rider should always avoid holding an uncomfortably strong contact in training,

The contact can be likened to the sail on a boat in a consistent, gentle breeze.

because by doing so he is taking over the horse's responsibility to carry itself and maintain the correct speed.

If the rider endeavours to maintain this elastic contact then it is ultimately the horse's responsibility to accept it. Some horses that are particularly fussy in the mouth take a while to accept the contact. They are usually reluctant to take any contact, and if they do it is a snatching one. With those horses I sometimes use elastic reins. The elastic keeps the contact with the corner of the mouth the same at all times and gradually the horse gets used to it. One can use elastic with different degrees of tension depending on the horse.

Some horses, such as ex-racehorses, have never been ridden with a view to getting them to accept a contact. These horses have all sorts of different mouth problems caused by the hands of the exercise jockeys and the horses' natural excitement. The important point to stress at all times is that we cannot *make* our horses accept the contact. We can only *wait* for them to accept it. Most horses will, eventually, if we handle the reins and apply the rein actions correctly. If your horse is willing to stand in its stable with a bit in its mouth and is not constantly fussing with it, then there is no reason why it should not eventually do so when being ridden.

Riding the young horse on a straight line

Riding the recently broken or very green horse in a straight line is relatively easy when the horse and rider both agree on where they want to go, for example back to the stables. It is not so easy when the horse is being ridden in a different direction. It will either wobble from side to side if going immediately away from the direction it wants to go, or it will hang to the left or right depending where 'home' is.

Teaching the young horse to go forward and straight.

The rider must be clear in his position and body language, he must motivate the horse to go forward and make corrections with opening reins on whichever side is appropriate to keep the horse 'on the line'. This sometimes involves riding the horse with the hands held apart to provide a 'corridor' with the rein aids and the legs. Every horse is different in its natural willingness to go forward, but following other horses, support of the lunge whip by an assistant and generally motivating the horse, is the best way to get a horse to go straight forward.

Sometimes ride the horse with the hands held apart to provide a corridor with the rein aids and with the legs.

Control of direction

The horse must also be taught in nursery and primary school to respond to the directional rein aids. As the horse progresses through the training, the directional rein aids play a smaller part in the control of direction, and the rider's position statement and body language, supported by the legs and the half-halts, become the primary means of turning the horse or keeping it on the straight line.

Before considering how to teach our horse to turn in what we conceive to be the correct way, we must first study the way it turns naturally and consider the *purpose* and *objective* of the turn. We can then teach it to turn in a way that is going to suit that purpose and objective. I deliberately differentiate between those two words.

The *purpose* can be quite obvious, such as to follow a chosen track or path, including for example a show jumping or cross-country track, but it can also be to carry out a gymnastic exercise, such as riding circles or serpentines.

The *objective* is divided into two related parts – 'during the turn' and 'after the turn'. In the case of a turn to a jump, the primary objective is what happens after the turn, even though the way the horse turns will affect his jump. When riding a circle in dressage training, the primary objective is what happens during the turn, namely the 'way of going'.

In nursery school, the purpose should only be the journey along the chosen path. It is too early to work on the horse's 'way of going' until it understands to go forward willingly along the path. The objective becomes as important as the purpose when the horse moves to primary school and starts to learn to respond to the rider's aids to turn in a particular way, rather than just turning to go in another direction.

How does the horse turn naturally?

Humans stand upright and walk and run on the hind legs only, so we can turn in one of two ways. When we turn at slow speed whether jogging on the spot or walking, we do so by rotating the inside leg outwards from the hip towards the direction we want to go, and then stepping forward and around with the other leg. When running at speed we lean into the turn.

The horse stands on four legs and so is able to turn in one of four ways. It can turn about its centre, it can turn about either the forehand or the hindquarters, and it can turn by leaning into the turn. There are three factors that affect the way it turns naturally: quickness of turn – speed of travel – tightness of turn. To turn very quickly on a tight turn, such as when spooked and 'whipping round', the horse sits momentarily on the hind leg and brings the forehand around the hindquarters. When turning in a relatively slow rhythm and virtually on the spot, as it has to do sometimes in the stable, a horse will either perform a turn about the forehand or a turn on the haunches, or a combination of both. The faster it is moving on a relatively tight turn, as in a tight bend on a racetrack, the more it leans into the turn like someone on a bike.

The objective in training depends very much on the sport the horse is aimed at. The cutting horse has to turn very quickly, and virtually on the spot, as does the polo pony, while the racehorse travels at high speed but the turns are not tight. The dressage horse has to learn to turn on the spot, for example in the canter pirouette, and should do so relatively slowly and, above all, with grace and athleticism, while the show jumper/eventer sometimes has to turn very tightly and fairly quickly, if at a slow speed, but at other times has to turn at a higher speed. The horse that achieves the fastest time in the jump-off or on the cross-country, is the one that can shorten its stride to make the tightest of turns at one moment, and then increase the speed in more gradual turns at the next, and all that without losing the quality of the canter for the jump.

Teaching the horse to turn from the opening rein

The first priority with a young or uneducated horse is to simply achieve a change in direction and for the horse to stay 'on-line' after the turn. How the horse turns is less important. Each young horse will tend to turn slightly differently to the left and right. In the same way that people are right or left handed, so are horses, and they have a preference for turning one way over the other.

Before starting the turn, the rider must prepare his position and adjust the horse's speed relative to the tightness of the turn. He then guides the horse into the turn using body language supported by an opening rein aid (see section on Rein Aids and Effects). The horse must be encouraged to maintain its energy and go forward through the turn and out of it. When the horse is reluctant to follow the direction set by the rider, it may need a more obvious opening rein combined with positive reinforcement by the body language, leg and, if necessary whip, to motivate it to go forward in the direction required. If the horse tries to turn too quickly i.e. 'falls in' on the turn, it must be controlled with the outside direct (opening) rein rather than with the inside indirect (neck) rein. Some horses will try to accelerate either to avoid turning or to turn too early by 'falling in' while others avoid turning by slowing down. The first priority, just as with a car, is to have control of the speed before insisting on the response to the rein aid.

The horse has completed its nursery education when it more or less confidently and willingly goes forward on a straight line and accepts the restraining aids and turning aids in response to simple opening rein aids. How it turns, in terms of balance and 'uniformity of bend' and posture is not important in the nursery stage nor is the straightness of the horse on the straight line. The young horse's natural crookedness will start to be corrected through the exercises and work in the next stage of its schooling – Primary school.

Primary School

'Time to move on.'

Flatwork

In the next part of the horse's training, at primary school, the objective is to develop the horse's 'way of going' to make it more pleasant to ride and to prepare it for competitions. In dressage this is sometimes referred to as 'the basics,' while in jumping it is referred to as the 'flat work'. The gymnastic exercises in primary school are used both to further educate the horse to respond to our communication and then to encourage the horse to offer the *posture, balance* and *straightness* within *regular* and *rhythmic paces* that provide the platform for the work in secondary school.

Regularity

The regularity or correctness of the steps is but one element in the quality of the pace, but is always the first priority in training. Regularity means that the walk has four even beats, that the trot is even on each diagonal, and that the canter has an even three beat with a moment of suspension when all four feet are off the ground. Not all horses have naturally correct paces, and even if you start with three good paces, the challenge is to maintain that regularity or improve it as the schooling progresses.

The regularity of the trot is the easiest to see. A horse that is not regular in trot is, in effect, lame or apparently lame. If the horse appears sound and regular in trot when lunged without a rider, even on hard ground, and yet is not regular when being ridden, this indicates a schooling problem and the horse is said to be bridle-lame. This is usually to do with the horse's posture or 'connection over the back', reflected in the unevenness of the contact and the instability of the head and neck

A lateral or pacing canter.

carriage. In my experience, bridle lameness is rare. In most cases, horses that are apparently bridle lame are in fact genuinely lame but the unsoundness may be difficult to detect.

The regularity of the walk is very important for the horse in the dressage arena, but not so for the jumper. Some breeds of horse, for example the Thoroughbred, tend to have an inherently good walk, while others do not. A good walk is recognized by most experienced trainers as indicating a good gallop. Some young horses with impressive, powerful trots often have a difficult walk with a tendency to pace in the walk. To understand a pacing walk, just watch a dog walking on a lead.

The regularity of the canter tends to be lost as the demands for collection are increased. The moment of suspension either diminishes or is lost altogether, leading to what is termed a four-beat canter. Normally, the diagonal pair, inside hind and outside foreleg, come to the floor at the same moment, but in a four-beat canter the 'lazy' inside hind comes to the ground too early and insufficiently close to the centre of gravity. The converse, namely when the outside fore leg comes to the floor earlier than the inside hind, leads to a 'lateral' or 'pacing' canter, when the horse appears to be pacing but in a canter. This happens most often with the outside lateral pair, but in severe cases with both lateral pairs. In extreme cases when you watch these horses cantering the foot of the leading leg is seen to come to the floor at the same moment as the inside hind foot, and the outside fore foot comes to the ground at the same moment as the outside hind foot. The canter appears and feels like it is 'rolling' from side to side and is very uncomfortable to sit on.

Rhythm

Once the horse has learned to go forwards in a regular pace, the priority becomes the establishment of a rhythm within the paces. Each horse has a rhythm that is appropriate to its size and type. It is to be expected that a pony will have a shorter stride and a quicker rhythm than a horse, and equally there will be a difference between a small horse and a large one. It is impossible to say exactly what is the right rhythm for each horse. As the horse develops through its schooling, the increased elasticity and energy in its steps that comes with collection will enable it to have a slightly slower rhythm by increasing the cadence in the steps. The rider must be careful, though, not to get an artificially slow rhythm. This happens when a horse avoids going forwards by using an increased cadence to push off the front legs, rather than increasing the engagement of the hind legs. This is sometimes called a hovering trot.

The *objective* is to maintain the same rhythm through the collected, working, medium and extended paces, as well as the transitions from one pace to another. Although this is very difficult to achieve it is always the ultimate goal in dressage training and gives rise to the judges' comments such as 'losing rhythm' or 'hurrying' etc.

Balance – longitudinal and lateral

The basic training gradually teaches the horse to maintain a better *longitudinal* and *lateral* balance. The balance must be an independent balance. It is the horse's responsibility to maintain its own balance on the turns and circles, no matter how small.

The advanced dressage tests require the horse to turn and perform all the movements in independent balance or 'self-carriage'. The show-jumping horse must also be able to make tight turns in balance in order to save time and maintain the quality of canter required for a good jump. Independent balance is also vitally important for an event horse on the cross-country, or a steeplechaser, even though its turns are not so tight.

The young or untrained horse's *longitudinal* balance tends to be 'on the forehand'. The basic training helps it to achieve horizontal balance, then, as the training progresses, the horse learns to carry the weight more on the hind legs in the collected paces. Collection is not just required in advanced dressage but also in advanced show jumping. The main difference is that the collection required of the dressage horse is a sustained collection, whereas that of a show jumper is a momentary collection, like the coiling of a spring. The event horse must also be collected prior to some of the more technical fences, but generally a good horizontal balance enables it to cope with the varied demands of the sport.

Lateral balance is the ability to stay 'on line' whether on straight lines or in turns. A horse is said to 'fall-in' or 'fall-out' on the turn when it loses its lateral balance. The key to achieving lateral balance is 'posture' and 'straightness', and the support of the hind leg under the centre of gravity. A horse whose conformation is fairly narrow, like some Thoroughbreds, or is 'base narrow', in other words whose feet are close together, will find it more difficult to maintain its lateral balance than a horse that has a broader base of support.

Horizontal balance.

On the forehand.

The horse's natural crookedness.

Straightness

All horses are naturally crooked. The crookedness tends to manifest itself in the same way, just as the majority of humans are right handed. The flexion at the poll is usually to the right, the bend at the base of the neck to the left and the quarters carried slightly to the right. Until they are relatively straight, horses can be like a snake to ride! It is relatively easy to drive a car in the direction you want because, in itself, it remains straight at all times, whereas a horse's head might be looking outwards, its neck bent to the inside, its shoulders drifting out while its quarters come in. Watch a dog trotting down the road and you will see that it often does so slightly sideways. A horse will naturally tend to have the same crookedness, although not always so obvious.

One of the objectives of training is to straighten the horse so that in executing turns and circles, for whatever purpose, it stays both *in-line* and *on-line*. 'On-line' means that the horse follows the track chosen by the rider, like a rally car going around the bend. As long as the car stays on the road, even if it sometimes moves sideways on a slippery surface, it is more or less 'on-line'. When it leaves the road and runs into the ditch, then it is definitely 'off-line' as is the horse that drifts outwards or falls in on the turns. In dressage tests the horse sometimes moves sideways along the line, as in lateral work, or straight down the centre line or on a circle but is still 'on-line'. The excitable jumper can sometimes be seen approaching a fence sideways, but as long as it gets to the jump, it can also be said to be 'on-line'.

'In-line' means that the horse is 'straight' through its body. The head, neck, withers, central body, hips and tail should all be 'in-line'. This can apply as much on the turn as on the straight. In a dressage test one of the requirements for a well executed circle is that the horse has a 'uniform bend'. This means that the horse is 'in-line', which includes the lateral flexion at the poll being sufficiently in the direction of the turn relative to the size of the circle. An analogy I like is that of a train with six carriages (head, neck, withers, body, hips and tail). As long as the train and carriages are not derailed, even around a bend, the train is 'in-line'. Similarly with a troop of six soldiers marching one behind the other, if any of the soldiers step out of line, the sergeant-major tells him to 'get back in line'!

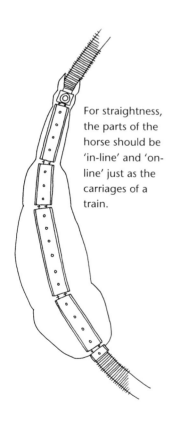

For straightness, the parts of the horse should be 'in-line' and 'on-line' just as the carriages of a train.

Posture

The word 'outline' is used when talking about a horse's posture. For riders aspiring to compete in dressage, 'outline' has a high priority. A large proportion of the marks for each movement measure the quality of the outline. Good posture provides the platform for good performance, whether in dressage or in jumping. It allows the realization of the athletic potential of the horse both in terms of the paces and expression of movement, and in the accuracy and scope of the horse's jumping. The posture required for advanced dressage differs from that required for advanced show jumping or eventing, but there are common factors.

For many riders, the word 'outline' conjures up a picture of a horse with his head hanging at the vertical. But only thinking of 'outline' in relation to the way a horse carries its head and neck is to miss out on the other important aspects of the horse's posture, namely an engaged hind leg and, most importantly, the horse's back in a state of stretched, rounded tension to support the rider and provide a strong connection between the hindquarters and the forehand. The 'straightness' of the horse is also an important part of good posture.

For the purpose of discussing outline, the horse can be divided into three parts: forehand, trunk and hindquarters. The way the horse uses the groups of muscles in each of these areas will have an effect on the muscle groups in the other two areas. Below is a summary of the conclusions that can be drawn from the study of the biomechanics in the previous section.

Correct posture requires the following:

Forehand (head and neck and shoulders):

- The acceptance of the contact leading to relaxed jaw muscles.

- Relaxed and relatively stretched upper neck muscles causing the horse's head to hang towards the vertical if its conformation allows (longitudinal submission).

- The lengthening and strengthening of the muscle at the base of the neck leading to the drawing up and forward of the neck and support of the horse's forehand. The neck is said to be 'raised and arched' in the dressage rules.

Common faults: 'Above the bit', 'against the hand', 'behind the bit', 'over bent', 'short in the neck', 'head tilting'.

Back

- The drawing forward of the raised neck combined with the active and engaged hind leg helps to pull the back up and support the rider.

- The development and interplay of the back muscles gives strength to the 'bridge' supporting the rider and links the hindquarters with the forehand. This is the basis of good posture.

Common faults: 'Hollow', 'strung out', 'crooked', 'tight in the back'.

Hindquarters

- The hind leg swinging well under the body so that the hindquarter muscles pull in the opposite direction to the neck muscles, and so act like the ropes of a suspension bridge helping to support the horse's back and thereby the rider.

- The muscles of the hindquarters being capable of bearing much of the weight of the horse when in sustained collection, and of providing the propulsive power to the show jumper and the event horse.

Common faults: 'Disengaged', 'wide behind', 'out behind', 'inactive' or 'lazy'.

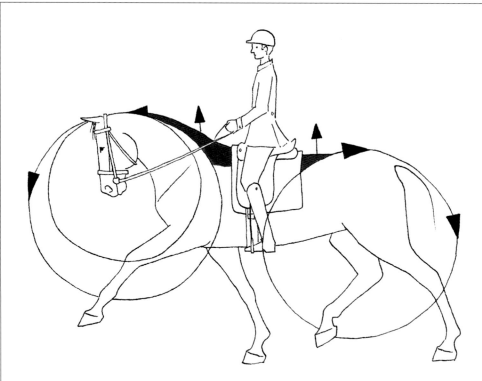

The Wheel Analogy

Imagine two bicycle wheels joined by a rope over the top. At the forehand, the reins are one of the spokes of the front wheel and at the rear, the hind legs are the spokes of the back wheel. The front wheel, rotating in a forward direction pulls on the neck muscles, while the hind wheel turning in the opposite direction pulls on the hindquarter muscles so that together both groups of muscles exert an equal and opposite pull on the elastic back muscles so helping to support the back.

The horse will overbend and go on the forehand if the front wheel is more active than the back wheel. If this happens the hind leg should be activated and the hands lowered in order to rotate the nose forward. If conversely, the horse comes above the bit with the neck shortening and the nose pushing forward, the hands should be raised to turn the front wheel in a forward direction so motivating the horse to draw forward and down into the contact, at the same time as the hind wheel is activated forward and under the body with the leg, whip or spur in order to create equal pull over the horse's back muscles.

Developing Posture, Straightness and Balance

Before you can use gymnastic exercises effectively, you have to train your horse to turn more precisely in response to your *position statement* and *body language*, supported by the touch of the legs. The rein actions become secondary to the body and leg, except in regulating the forward movement with half-halts. The 'dream' is to be able to turn the horse about either the forehand, the hindquarters, or on a very small circle, with the reins in one hand and on a light even contact. By teaching the horse to turn in this way, we set up the basis for the gymnastic exercises that are used to develop or improve the horse's posture, balance and paces.

Position statement

The *position statement* for turns and circles applies for all lateral exercises and is as follows:

1. **Sit to the inside of the saddle** with more weight in the inside stirrup (see lateral balance). The process of moving to the inside of the saddle and putting the weight in the inside stirrup lightens the rider's seat momentarily as the hind foot steps under the body, making room for the horse to come up in the back (dorsiflex). It also prevents the saddle slipping to the outside.

   When you sit to the inside of the saddle you should feel that the outside seat bone is close to the centre line of the saddle and receiving most of the rider's weight. Riders frequently make the mistake of leaning over the inside hip rather than sitting to the inside of the saddle. This is often combined with the drawing up of the inside knee and heel. If moved correctly, the inside seat bone will then be more directly above the stirrup, which enables the inside leg to reach well down. However, too much pressure into the heel will tend to push the lower leg away from the horse. The weight of the leg should be down to the ball of the foot rather than too much into the heel. A good analogy that you can practise off the horse is to sit for a while on the arm of a chair in front of a mirror whilst maintaining a good upright posture. Feel the weight distributed between the seat bone on the chair and the foot on the floor that supports your hip.

2. **Shorten the inside rein** and rotate the inside arm towards the intended direction of turn, so that when the horse offers the lateral flexion to the inside through the turn, the rider's elbow will not have to come back behind the body (see positional rein aids).

3. **Open/relax the hip joint,** particularly on the inside, and keep both the inside and outside stirrup leathers at the vertical. If you do this you can apply the inside lateral leg aid from the hip whilst keeping the contact with the outside lower leg, and without pulling up the heels. It helps to think of lifting the toe and knee on the outside to take the weight out of the outside stirrup and into the inside one.

If the rider can get into a routine of adopting the position statement, it eventually becomes automatic, and it can be repeated frequently within the movement to maintain position and to communicate with the horse.

> 'Position statement is the preparation for all turns and lateral work.'

Primary Gymnastic Exercises

The two most important exercises used to teach a horse to turn in response to the rider's position statement and body language are the turn about the forehand and the turn about the hindquarters. Once these have been understood, other primary gymnastic exercises can be introduced.

EXERCISE 1

Turn About the Forehand (T-a-F)

The objectives

- To teach the horse to turn in response to the rider's position statement and lateral leg aids, instead of the rein.

- To ask the horse to engage the inside hind leg, to 'come up' in the back (dorsiflex), stretch the neck forward and round, into an even contact, and offer the lateral flexion at the poll to the inside.

Turn about the forehand.

The exercise

The horse should turn around an imaginary post, as if it was tied to it on a very short rope. It should not pivot around the inside foreleg, instead, it should keep stepping. The inside hind should always step in front of the outside hind, and should come to the ground more or less between the footprints of the front feet. The degree to which the horse has to step across and under the body with the inside hind leg, depends on the tightness of the turn. To get an idea of what the horse has to do, push a wheelbarrow full of water around a very small circle and try not to spill a drop. You will see that you have to step across your body with your 'inside' leg. If you spill the water, it will be because you are turning like an unbalanced horse.

The hind leg should be picked up crisply, but without increasing the rhythm of the walk. The tell tale sign of a horse that is reluctant or lazy in picking up the hind foot is that it leaves 'drag' marks in the surface of the arena with its hind foot. If the hind foot is picked off the floor before it is fully extended and brought well forward as well as laterally under the body, then the horse will be encouraged to round (dorsiflex) its back and draw forward into the outside rein leading to it offering the lateral flexion at the poll to the inside. The outside rein must apply the half-halts but only as the outside front foot comes to the floor. After the inside hind steps across, then the outside rein must allow the outside foreleg to step forward and slightly across in front of the inside foreleg in order to keep walking around the imaginary post. If the outside rein blocks for too long then the horse will try to step backwards or a resistance will be provoked.

Tips for the rider

- The position statement is as for all lateral work – see above.

- To keep the horse more or less on the spot, apply half-halts down the outside rein at the moment that the horse's outside shoulder is coming back.

- The outside rein also controls the bend at the base of the neck. At the start of the T-a-F the neck should be straight and the flexion at the poll may even be to the outside. As the horse steps across with the inside hind it will offer the flexion to the inside as the outside hand allows.

- The touch of the inside leg/whip just before the inside hind foot leaves the floor talks to the inside hind to ask it to step across. Avoid a strong and prolonged pressure of the leg.

- The inside rein should maintain the contact and can support with a direct rein or even a direct rein of opposition. Most importantly, it should avoid blocking the inside foreleg by pulling backwards.

- The outside hip and knee must stay relaxed so that you can keep the contact with the lower leg on the outside at the girth, which is talking to the horse's outside foreleg and encouraging it to step forwards and round in front of the inside foreleg rather than out. A common fault is for the rider to stiffen and push the outside leg away and forwards as the pressure is applied with the inside leg so causing the horse to fall out.

- Lighten the seat as the inside hind comes off the floor to allow the horse's back to 'round'. This is also the moment to correct the seat position to the inside of the saddle if necessary.

Common problems

Horse comes against the touch of the leg or whip rather than moves away from it.

- It may be necessary to work them in hand to teach them to respect the leg. It may also be necessary to support the leg action with a direct rein of opposition on the inside rein(see rein effects).

Horse overbends the neck to the inside and walks forward or sideways and ignores the half-halt down the outside rein.

- Immediately halt before touching with the leg or whip again.

- Use the outside rein to restrict the bend in the neck.

- Avoid pulling back on the inside rein.

● Work in hand to teach the horse to move away from the touch of the whip followed by the support of the whip if appropriate when riding.

Horse abducts the outside hind in response to the leg aid to avoid engaging the inside hind.

● Could be the rider incorrectly sitting to the outside of the saddle and/or not supporting with the outside leg to encourage the horse to keep thinking forward.

● Could be the rider blocking the movement by pulling back with the outside rein.

● Could be incorrect timing of the leg action.

● Could be reluctance of the horse to engage the inside hind leg. It may be necessary to work the horse in hand and then when riding support the leg action with the whip.

The engagement of the hind leg through the T-a-F is a necessary, but not a sufficient, condition for balance and collection.

● Although the T-a-F places the hind foot under the body, it also tends to put the horse on the forehand and can lead to the horse 'escaping' through the outside shoulder. It should not be used for too long before the rider 'talks' with his outside leg to the forehand. It is when the horse can also bring the forehand around the hindquarters in the turn about the hindquarters that the longitudinal and lateral balance will be improved.

EXERCISE 2

Turn About the Hindquarters (T-a-H)

The objectives

● To teach the horse to turn in response to the rider's position statement and outside leg aid instead of the rein.

● To improve the lateral balance on the turns and the straightness by controlling the shoulder.

● To teach the horse to stretch into the outside rein contact when it is offered at the same moment as the outside foreleg steps across the body, thereby improving the lateral flexion to the inside.

The exercise

This requires the horse to alternately cross the outside foreleg in front of the inside foreleg and then abduct the inside foreleg. Meanwhile, the hind legs remain actively stepping within the rhythm more or less on the spot, or on a very small circle, but never backwards. To do this exercise well, the horse has to keep the inside hind leg under the body and it should remain active. That is why this exercise should not be taught before the horse has understood and accepted the T-a-F.

The T-a-H is the basis of the pirouette. In the true pirouette, performed by the advanced dressage horse, the degree of collection is greater (see section on Collection in Pure Dressage) and the hind feet are expected to mark time on the spot.

Turn about the hindquarters.

Tips for the rider

● The position statement is the same as for all lateral work – sit to the inside, shorten the inside rein, relax the hips.

● It helps to prepare the horse by engaging the inside hind through at least one step of T-a-F, which will lead to the horse offering the lateral flexion to the inside. When this happens, the horse is ready to start the T-a-H.

● Half-halts down the outside rein as the outside fore comes to the floor to shorten the step and control the degree the horse is allowed to move forwards, i.e. the size of the T-a-H.

● Touch of the outside leg at the girth with the foot and knee closing and slightly lifting at the moment that the outside fore comes off the floor, combined with the slight releasing of the outside rein contact to encourage the outside foreleg to step across the body in the direction of the turn.

● Touch of the inside leg of varying intensity, when necessary, to encourage the inside hind to remain active and stepping forward or on the spot rather than abducting away from the body.

● Inside rein held upwards towards the neck as an indirect rein without increasing the contact in order to encourage the horse to maintain the flexion to the inside and to avoid blocking the movement.

Common problems

The horse loses the lateral flexion and comes against the contact on the inside rein.

● Revert for at least one step to the T-a-F until the lateral flexion is re-established.

● Check on position statement, especially 'sitting to the inside' (it is normal to slip to the outside after the first few steps) and make sure that the horse has 'room' under the inside seat bone by distributing the weight between the inside stirrup and the outside seat bone.

● Make sure the outside rein is coordinated with the outside foreleg and allows the T-a-H. Riders often make the mistake of using an indirect rein of opposition to bring the forehand around, combined with the outside leg talking to the hindquarters instead of the forehand.

The horse steps backwards or does not reach across with the outside foreleg.

- Allow with the outside hand as the outside leg touches.

The horse swings the quarters out.

- Inside elbow must avoid pulling back behind the hip.

- The inside rein should not come away from the neck as a direct rein or direct rein of opposition.

- The half-halts should be applied down the outside rein towards the outside hip (as a direct rein of opposition), rather than across the body, and they should be applied within the rhythm as the horse's outside shoulder is coming back.

Useful Exercises to Reinforce the Understanding of the T-a-F and T-a-H

1. The Box Exercise to work on the T-a-F: Create a box by laying out four jump poles on the floor with a suitable centre point such as a jump stand or barrel. Ask your assistant to 'open the box' by rolling back one pole. Walk in to the box and then have it closed. Once in the box the objective is to walk around the post but without pulling on the inside rein and so causing the horse to bend excessively in the neck. If you can do it without either touching the jump stand or leaving the box and without bending the neck then you will have a correct T-a-F. A further challenge would be to perform the exercise with the reins in one hand!

2. Diamond/Square shape: T-a-F or T-a-H one or two steps only and then walk forward as soon as the horse turns.

3. Zig-zag: T-a-F or T-a-H one or two steps, forward, change position and prepare, T-a-F or T-a-H one or two steps in the other direction.

Primary Gymnastic Exercises – Continued

Once you have educated your horse through these simple yet initially complex exercises to understand the position statement, the reins (half-halts, directional and positional aids) and the leg, whip, spur (energizing and lateral aids) you are then able to make use of that basic understanding in reinforcing your body language in the turns, circles and transitions, from pace to pace and then in due course within the pace. The first step in training the horse is education and, as with any child, once they have been taught something and have had enough practice at it then, although they may have to be reminded, it can be assumed that they do understand. Whether or not the horse continues to respond to your position and action of leg and hand from day to day will depend on a number of factors – motivation, confidence,

The box exercise.

below left The diamond/square exercise.
below right The zig-zag exercise.

freedom from pain, clarity of signal and your attitude. You now get to the stage in the training where the exercises are used to further develop the horse's way of going and recognition of your position statement.

Within basic training, the primary exercises not only reinforce the understanding and acceptance of the body language, leg and rein aids, but also encourage the horse to offer the posture, straightness and balance that will improve the quality of the paces. The quality is measured in terms of regularity, rhythm and impulsion, leading to the freedom and expression of the paces. The secondary exercises (see page 148) develop the horse's ability to collect (shorten) or extend (lengthen) the stride within the rhythm.

The exercises develop the horse's range of movement and also provide targets to aim for in the training, or as proof of the training in dressage competitions. Both groups of exercises are as relevant to the jumper as to the dressage horse. In dressage tests the movements are not just training exercises but the means by which the performance is judged, whereas in jumping competitions the exercises on the flat are the means of getting the horse to the fence with the best possible chance of jumping it successfully.

At a later stage, the specialist dressage horse performs more demanding movements, such as passage and canter pirouettes, which require a degree of sustained collection. The main purpose of the passage and pirouettes is to 'show off' the beauty of the horse and skill of the trainer and rider, whether in competitions or in displays. To train the event horse or show jumper to perform these movements is probably counter productive in terms of their performance as jumpers and gallopers.

However, the only limit to the basic exercises and combinations of exercises that can be executed is your imagination. Anything that a horse could theoretically do is fair to ask, as long as you keep in mind the physical demands of the exercise related to your horse's ability and physical condition, and its level of understanding and confidence at any point. For example, during counter-canter in a dressage test the horse would be expected to have a lateral flexion slightly in the direction of the leading leg, but in training it is useful to check that the horse is able to offer the lateral flexion away from the leading leg without performing an unintended change of leg. It ought to be possible, so it is worth doing.

The exercises also form a part of the conditioning programme that goes 'hand in glove' with education and gymnastics. In addition to the training exercises performed 'on the flat', the horse's strength and stamina, and therefore indirectly its confidence, will be further developed through the jumping exercises and riding across the country, including hill work. The muscular development and fitness of the horse is often overlooked by riders, particularly in pure dressage.

Conditioning is a process of gradual stress followed by recovery. Without demands being placed on the horse there will be no stress and therefore no conditioning, but on the other side of the coin the horse will not want to cooperate or could be injured if the demands are too great or go on for too long. There has to be a balance, and in finding that balance you will no doubt ask too much on one day and not enough on another, but as long as that aspect of the horse's training is kept in mind then, over time, the balance will be right.

It helps to break the exercises down into separate components. Some horses will try to react too quickly while others will react too slowly. Even when you think that you know what you are doing, you need to make your preparations and then ask for the exercise in a step by step manner, so that it is clear to the horse what is wanted.

The gymnastic exercises should always be done accurately. It is only by attempting to ride circles, turns etc accurately that you will use the leg and rein aids correctly to support your position statement and body language. Riders often appear to wander aimlessly around the arena as they school. In this way they are riding only by feel, rather than a combination of eye and feel. The horse should always be 'on-line' as well as 'in-line' but you can only expect your horse to be 'on-line' if you know where you are going in the first place!

EXERCISE 3

Combine the T-a-F with Circles and Transitions (Walk-Trot-Walk)

The objective

- To achieve lateral and longitudinal submission and acceptance of the contact.

- To improve the quality of the transitions.

- To improve the figure of eight and serpentine.

The exercise

Use the T-a-F as a way of obtaining the lateral and longitudinal submission before the transition into trot, and then ride on to a circle 20 metres in diameter, do a transition to walk, followed by T-a-F outwards and then back into trot on the other rein. This exercise is the basis of the balanced change of rein within the trot in the figure of eight or the serpentine.

Tips for the rider

- *Move across the saddle to what will be the 'inside' before the T-a-F commences.*
  When you start riding the figure of eight or the serpentine, the change of position must come well before the change of direction so that the horse has time to recognize the position statement. The outside rein then allows the lateral flexion to change and then allows the new turn to start, in that order. If the horse does not recognize or respond to the new position statement then the new inside leg has to act. If necessary come back to walk and obtain the lateral submission through the T-a-F and then proceed on into trot again.

- *'Inside leg into outside hand.'*
  The expression means that the new inside leg engages the new inside hind during

the T-a-F, into an outside hand that half-halts and then allows the lateral flexion to come to the inside. The outside rein is therefore the active communicating rein during the turn and subsequently during the circle. It supports the body language by half-halting when the outside fore comes to the ground. The intensity of the half-halt can vary, and sometimes it needs to act as a side rein to support the outside leg in controlling the shoulder when the horse overbends laterally at the base of the neck.

● *The change of lateral flexion in the T-a-F comes about after it has started, not before.*
This is different from the change of lateral flexion in the figure of eight or serpentine which comes about as a result of the horse recognizing the position statement and new inside leg *prior* to the start of the change of direction.

● *Get the timing right from walk into trot.*
The first trot step should be as the outside shoulder is coming forward. This is an easier moment for the rider to recognize than the inside hind coming forward. If the horse draws forward into the contact during the upward transition, then the timing will have been correct. If the horse comes 'above the bit' during the transition, then the likelihood is that the timing of the first trot step has been wrong.

● *Get the timing right from trot to walk.*
The half-halts should be applied down the outside rein as the horse's outside shoulder is coming back, but the first walk step will be in the next stride as the inside hind/outside shoulder are coming forward and the outside hand follows the movement. In this way the horse will come up in the back rather than hollow. At this stage, I recommend that riders come back to walk from rising trot rather than sitting trot, with the objective of coming back to walk on the rise rather than the sit phase of the trot. Assuming that the rider is on the correct rising diagonal (i.e. sitting as the outside shoulder is coming back/inside hind is supporting), it helps with the timing and also encourages the horse to come up in the back during the downward transition. (See the 'Zone' exercise in a later section.)

● *Remember the expressions 'in-line' and 'on-line' and the importance of accuracy.*
At the end of the T-a-F make sure that the outside leg is talking to the forehand to prevent the horse escaping with the shoulder. Soon, the T-a-F outwards on the circle can be changed to the T-a-H during the second half of the turn. After the first two or three steps of the T-a-F, switch the emphasis to the new outside leg to bring the horse's weight back to the hind leg and to control the shoulder.

Common problem

The horse ignores the outside leg and tries to escape through the outside shoulder while being ridden on the 20 metre circle.

● Make the transition to walk and T-a-F outwards again. It will help to teach the horse to respect the outside leg as it is used to tell it to get back 'on-line' and 'in-line'.

EXERCISE 4

Leg-yielding on the Diagonal

The objective

- Lateral submission.

- Acceptance of the contact in the outside rein.

- Teach the horse to engage the hind leg rather than push with it.

The leg-yielding exercise is a gymnastic or loosening exercise that follows logically from the horse's understanding and acceptance of the T-a-F and the half-halting and directional rein aids. The leg-yielding exercise is a relatively simple lateral exercise for the horse to understand, and is a first step before moving on to the shoulder-in, travers, renvers and half-pass.

The exercise

- The horse moves away from the touch of the leg at the girth whilst maintaining the relative straightness of the body.

- There is a slight lateral flexion at the poll away from the direction of movement.

- The horse is said to be on two tracks.

- The inside hind steps forward and across in front of the outside hind (adducts).

Leg yielding on the diagonal.

- The outside foreleg reaches away from the body (abducts) to the same degree.

- The outside hind should step forward rather than away from the body.

- The inside foreleg crosses in front of the outside foreleg.

- The regularity of the steps must be maintained.

Tips for the rider

- Ride through the corner on to the diagonal as if about to make a simple change of rein.

- 'Sit to the inside' – move across the saddle to what will be the new 'inside'.

- 'Shorten the new inside rein' – the new inside rein should be shortened enough so that when the horse switches the lateral flexion over as the leg-yield starts, the elbow on that side does not come behind the hip. It helps to rotate the arm outwards, as this brings the inside elbow closer to the body, so that the rein acts as a positional rein aid once the leg-yield has started (to encourage the lateral flexion to that side) and as a supporting indirect rein.

- The inside rein can also act as a direct rein of opposition to support the action of the inside leg in talking to the hindquarters.

- 'Open the inside hip' – the new inside leg applies its lateral pressure/touch at the girth or just behind but without pulling the heel backwards. Allow the knee to come away from the saddle.

- Start the leg-yield with one or two steps of T-a-F to bring the hindquarters across behind the forehand until the horse is nearly parallel with the long side and the lateral flexion comes across to the other side.

- Control the outside shoulder with the outside leg at the girth while the outside rein limits the bend at the base of the neck but allows the lateral flexion to the 'inside' and can sometimes encourage the outside foreleg to reach further out which will help the inside hind to step further across.

- Allow the rhythm to slow somewhat at the risk of losing some impulsion so as to encourage a greater reach of the outside foreleg and crossing of the inside hind.

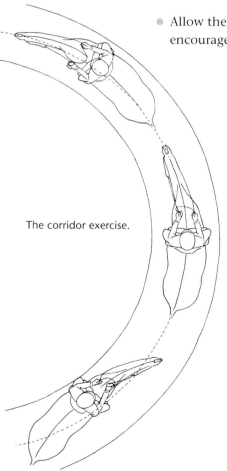

The corridor exercise.

EXERCISE 5

The Corridor Exercise

Leg-yielding inwards and outwards on the circle.

- Imagine a corridor approximately 1½ metres in width on a circle approximately 20 metres in diameter. The horse is travelling on the centre line of the corridor.

- Sit to the outside, shorten the outside rein, then leg yield inwards on the circle just enough to bring the horse's inside shoulder up against the inside wall of the corridor.

- The horse should then offer the lateral submission/flexion to the outside and in so doing bring the outside shoulder back into line. As soon as it does so then sit to the inside of the circle and leg yield back to the outside wall of the corridor.

- The 20 metre circle should remain accurate while performing this exercise.

EXERCISE 6

The Canter and the Transitions: Trot-Canter, Canter-Trot

Once the horse has established a relatively consistent rhythm, balance and posture in the trot this exercise can be introduced.

The objectives

- To achieve the change of pace within the rhythm, in balance and on-line without losing the horse's posture in response to the rider's position statement and body language.

- To maintain the rhythm, balance and posture within the canter in self-carriage.

- To develop the quality of the canter.

- To canter on the desired 'lead' both in true canter and counter canter, before learning how to collect or shorten the stride without losing the quality of the canter.

Trot to canter

When the trot is reasonably correct, the rider puts himself into the appropriate position statement for canter (on the inside lead), then the horse is urged on to lengthen its stride within the rhythm to break into canter, as it would do if loose in the field. The untrained horse will not find canter necessarily at the first stride of asking. As long as the rider is consistent in his body language and position statement, the willing horse will gradually learn to recognize it sooner and pick up the canter without first lengthening the stride in trot. It should remain more or less even in the contact with preferably slightly more contact in the outside rein. It should pick up the appropriate lead relative to the rider's position statement without changing its posture much. If it just rushes off into a faster trot then it should be brought back to the rhythm and asked again while the outside rein half-halts within the rhythm to regulate the trot.

Even the more experienced horse will perform better transitions in response to the position statement and body language rather than primarily from the leg aids. The generally taught system of bringing the outside leg back as the aid for canter nearly always produces a poor canter transition with the horse coming above the bit or against the hand during the transition. This is because the horse will start the canter either by pushing off the front leg or by pushing off the outside hind leg, rather than engaging the inside hind.

The position statement

- Sit to the inside of the saddle with the inside hip slightly forward.

- Shorten slightly the inside rein so that the inside hand is just in front of the outside hand.

- Bring the outside shoulder back.

The body language

- Ask for the canter by 'stepping' into the inside stirrup in much the same way as a child canters around the garden with their hobby horse. Don't expect the horse to respond on the first indication, just repeat until it does.

Common problems

The horse 'hops' into canter or throws its head and neck up.

- The horse is actually holding back during the moment of the transition and using its head and neck as a way of lifting the shoulders into the canter rather than starting the canter from behind. It can be retrained to go forward within the rhythm into canter by concentrating on position statement and only using the leg or whip on the inside to support the body language and energize the horse. This should motivate it to go forward and lengthen its trot stride into canter.

The horse always picks up the outside canter lead.

- The rider should make the position statement more obvious and wait for the moment when the horse gives a feeling of coming in on the circle rather than falling out before 'stepping' into canter. If that does not work because the horse always pushes out through the outside shoulder, try bringing the horse back to walk, make a T-a-F to the outside and then immediately assume the position for canter and ask again, whilst being careful to keep the horse into the contact in the outside rein and performing an 'opening' rein on the inside. Another solution with the very young horse is the figure of eight exercise. In order to obtain a correct canter depart on the right lead, ride a small circle in trot to the left and then change the rein and immediately canter right.

The horse runs faster in trot rather than picking up the canter.

- It may help to tap behind the inside leg with the whip at the moment of stepping into the inside stirrup and using the inside leg. While you do that you can support with half-halts that are repeated down the outside rein to emphasize the desired rhythm.

The horse resists and stops going forward when asked to go into canter.

- This may be because the rider is tightening the leg too much or using the outside leg aid as the signal for canter. It could be because the horse is just lazy, in which case the first priority is forward movement irrespective of whether in trot or in canter. If necessary use the whip to support the body language motivating it to go forward.

Canter to trot

The position statement

⦿ The body comes back to a more central position to be ready for the trot transition, and the outside shoulder comes forward.

The body language

⦿ Asks for the transition by 'thinking' trot rhythm and coming back slightly with the body. This is supported by the half-halt down the outside rein. The horse should trot in the stride following the half-halt as the outside hand allows. In that way the horse will be encouraged to make the transition forward into a good trot rhythm. If the half-halt is held for two strides or more then the transition will be more abrupt (see rules for half-halts).

If the body language asks for trot but the position statement is still in canter, the horse may stay in canter and just shorten its stride in response to the half-halt. This often happens with the more experienced dressage or show jumper schoolmaster who has found that it is easier to stay in canter rather than make the transition back to trot.

If the rider gets into the habit of driving a weak or lazy horse with the seat and leg in every stride, the horse becomes dependant upon it to stay in canter, and then very often the rider's aid for the transition to trot is to cease driving with the seat and leg, which allows the horse to drop into trot. This only perpetuates the horse's habit of relying on the rider's seat and leg rather than remaining in self-carriage. At the most the rider should repeat the leg aid and the driving action of the seat within the canter every other stride with a view to gradually reminding the horse less often. With these horses, the leg supported if necessary by the whip should then be relatively active during the moment of the downward transition to encourage the horse to make a 'change of gear' from canter to trot rather than just dropping out of the canter.

Common problems

During the transition step the horse should draw forward into the contact and in so doing slightly lengthen the outline. If the horse has a tendency to draw forward too much and so fall onto the forehand and run in the trot (usually those with a naturally longer neck), then the rider should be more active with the energizing leg action combined with half-halts to encourage the horse to keep its neck up just before the rein action that asks for trot.

The converse is the horse that draws back with its neck into its shoulders, and then holds back in the trot after the transition (usually those with a naturally short neck). The rider should ride the horse forward actively in canter, with the motivating inside leg action, into the contact in the outside rein. Even if the horse is then inclined to flex to the outside to avoid the contact, it should be maintained until it is felt that the horse volunteers to draw forward into it, which will bring its flexion back to the inside when the outside rein permits. Only when it does so, should it then be allowed to trot. It must be the horse's idea to offer the flexion to the inside and draw forward, and not the rider pulling back on the inside rein. Horses that have this tendency are more difficult to correct than those with the opposite tendency.

EXERCISE 6B

Leg-yielding Combined with Transitions to Canter

The combination of leg-yield on the diagonal, combined with transition to canter at the end of the diagonal, assists greatly with the improvement of the transitions into canter and is a very good loosening exercise for all horses throughout their training.

The leg-yield prepares the horse well by engaging the new inside hind leg prior to the transition and, if ridden well, the horse will be well into the contact in the outside rein at the end of the diagonal. The rider will also be sitting to the inside, and he merely has to bring the outside shoulder back and 'step' into the canter using his body language as described above.

This is one of my favourite exercises. I usually ride one circle in canter at the end of the arena, come back to trot at C or A, then ride on to the next diagonal, set up the leg-yield and then ride from the leg-yield into canter at some stage at or after the centre line. If I ride into canter before we get to the side I must be more careful to keep the outside rein contact and a supporting outside leg to keep the horse straight and 'on-line'.

EXERCISE 7

The Counter Canter

When the horse is able to maintain a rhythm in the canter in reasonable self carriage the counter canter can be introduced.

The objective

- To improve the balance and straightness of the canter.

- To develop the engagement of the 'inside' hind leg.

- To improve the horse's self-carriage prior to teaching it 'flying changes'.

The exercise

The horse is asked to canter with its leading leg on the outside of the circle or line. In the wild the horse may sometimes do this for a while but will tend to change legs when it feels out of balance. Counter canter must be distinguished from 'disunited' canter. By 'disunited' we mean that the horse canters with the leading foreleg to one side and the leading hind leg to the other side. If a horse is at liberty in the arena or field and has to negotiate a tight turn in a corner it will often become disunited for a few strides through and after the corner, even when approaching the corner on the correct lead.

Introduce the counter canter gradually:

- Start with shallow loops away from the side of the arena.

- Half-circles returning to the track in counter canter with balanced transition back to trot before the corner.

- Ride the counter canter on circles starting at 20 metres and then gradually becoming more demanding.

- When the 20 metre circle is possible then start to ride through the corners in counter canter but without asking the horse to go deeper into the corner than it would if asked to perform a 20 metre half-circle.

- Gradually make the corners deeper, but always know in advance the size of the quarter circle that is being ridden, i.e. 15, 10, 8 metres etc so that the exercise can be ridden accurately.

- Do not stay in counter canter for very long before returning to true canter as it will take too much away from the impulsion and lead to the horse looking for too much support from the rider.

- A very good exercise to introduce later when the horse is starting its secondary schooling and working towards collection is the three metre loop either side of the centre line in the 60 metre arena. This exercise must be ridden very accurately to be completed successfully and in order to benefit the horse.

In a correct counter canter in the dressage arena:

- The horse will be straight through its body but with a slight flexion at the poll towards the leading leg. (The horse must be both 'in-line and on-line'.)

- The side of the leading leg continues to be called the 'inside'.

- The horse will be upright with its weight evenly distributed laterally.

- The hind feet follow behind the footsteps of the front feet.

- The canter maintains the same rhythm and regularity as the true canter.

A correct counter canter.

- The contact will be even in the rein.

- The strides will appear the same as in the true canter with the same degree of elasticity and impulsion.

Tips for the rider

Be clear in the position statement by:

- Sitting to the inside of the saddle i.e. on the side towards which the horse is flexed.

- Distributing the weight evenly in the stirrups.

- Keeping the outside shoulder back.

- Shortening the inside rein so that the inside elbow is always at or in front of the hip.

- Having both legs in even contact with the horse's sides with a relaxed inside hip.

Be clear with the body language by:

- Following the movement of the leading leg with the inside hip/elbow.

- Directing the horse through the seat and legs to keep it 'on line' rather than relying on the reins. The direct (opening) rein can help by guiding it around the circle while the rein on the side of the leading leg can be used as an indirect rein but avoid increasing the contact.

- Taking the upper body outwards on the turns i.e leaning towards the wall not away from it, to help the horse with its balance.

Common problems

The horse performs a flying change.

- Be pleased that your horse has a natural ability to do flying changes then:
- Be more clear with your position statement and body language.
- Reduce the demands of the exercise.

The horse becomes disunited.

- As above without being pleased!

The horse over bends laterally in the neck and falls off line with the shoulder.

- Control the bend with the outside rein and, in training, endeavour to gradually obtain the lateral flexion/submission away from the leading leg by ensuring that the inside hand is following the movement sufficiently while the outside rein and outside leg try to keep the shoulder in line.

The horse loses the 'quality' of the canter (rhythm, regularity, posture, impulsion).

- Avoid 'carrying' the horse with a stronger contact. Hand responsibility back to the horse. It is better to take the chance in training that it either breaks to trot or loses its balance in the canter, in which case correct and start again. If necessary the rider can remind the horse every second stride with the supporting aids. The objective over time must be self-carriage.

- Energize with the leg, whip, spur, but without lengthening the stride by using the seat. Only use the seat if the horse shortens its stride in the counter canter.

- Straighten the horse and avoid too much bend at the base of the neck. The loss of the quality of the canter often comes about because the rider tries to prevent the horse from changing canter lead by bending it more over the leading leg. If the horse is inclined to change, then the rider should be more clear with his position statement, including the supporting leg aids, rather than increase the bend at the base of the neck.

EXERCISE 8

The Rein Back

This is introduced when the trot is going forward actively, is regular and has a reasonable rhythm; when the horse understands the restraining aids from the body language supported by the rein actions, and when the horse understands the lateral aids (T-a-F and T-a-H) and is laterally submissive.

The objective

- To reinforce the response to the body language and the restraining aids.

- To increase the engagement of the hind leg and the connection over the back.

- To take the weight back to the hind leg so improving the longitudinal balance, and so is a useful correction for the horse that is on the forehand.

- To use in developing the collected paces.

The exercise

- The horse is asked to step backwards.

- The steps should be diagonal as if in trot but without a moment of suspension.

- The horse should stay straight as it steps backwards.

- The hind leg should remain engaged and flexed, becoming more so with schooling towards collection.

- The rhythm should be the same as for the walk.

- In the early stages the longitudinal balance should remain neutral, but as the horse works more in collection and the transitions become more acute, so the balance should come further back so that the hind leg takes more of the weight.

Tips for the rider

- The first priority is to teach the horse to walk into a halt, which it must then maintain for a while before moving forwards again. With a young horse, the halt does not need to be absolutely square, but the horse should still 'be connected' and 'on the bit'. At this stage it is unlikely to remain absolutely still in its head and neck.

The halt

- Stretch the body up.

- Keep the stirrup as much under the body as possible and transfer some weight from the seat to the stirrup so as to encourage the horse to come up in its back as the walk steps shorten prior to the halt transition.

- Keep the lower leg in light contact with the horse's sides and, if necessary, energize the walk steps without quickening the rhythm to encourage the horse to halt without leaving the hind legs out behind.

- At the point where the halt and rein back are to be executed, use the body language supported by half-halts, in the rhythm of the walk, to bring the horse back to a halt. (See rules for half-halts.)

The rein back

- To ask for the rein back, prepare the body language by stretching up and backwards, and including a slight backward pressure of the lower leg. This conveys the message that the rider wants the horse to step backwards. If the horse tries to move forward, the restraining aid is applied.

- As the horse takes the first step backwards, the rider's body language comes back to neutral and the seat lightens to allow the horse's back to come up. The leg remains in relaxed contact, but still with a slight backward pressure applied alternately. The contact on the rein lightens slightly, especially if a restraining aid has been applied, to allow the horse to stretch the neck forward a little.

- Just before the horse takes the last required step, incline the body forwards slightly and support with the leg to indicate to the horse to move forward again. The rein contact should soften enough to allow the horse to move forward.

Common problems

The horse tries to step to the side.

- Open the rein away from the neck on the side which the horse is trying to step with its hind leg, as well as applying a lateral leg aid on that side.

The horse is very disengaged or becomes so by stepping backwards with the hind leg only.

- If this happens the horse will not be able to rein-back because its back will have dropped and it will have come 'above the bit' or 'behind the bit'. You should walk the horse forward a step or two and then recommence, putting more emphasis on the body language stretching up to lighten the seat and back, while your leg activates the hind leg into a restraining contact. As soon as there is any attempt to step back, no matter how small, the contact should soften and the body language come back to neutral, so that the horse begins to associate the 'pressure' coming off with the acceptance of the backward step.

The horse resists the idea of the rein-back and thinks of rearing.

- The underlying reason is that it is tight or hollow in the back, probably with the hind leg disengaged, as it comes to halt. If you pull on the rein and the horse resists, with the head and neck coming up in your face, the tightening of the jaw and neck muscles will stiffen the back and have a paralyzing effect on the hind leg. The answer is to lighten the seat even so far as standing up and then avoid pulling on the rein to produce the rein back. Pulling on the rein will only work if you are on the ground with the long reins, and even then the pressure must be released as soon as the horse backs off. In that way it gets its reward and learns to back off the pressure. With care, this method does help, particularly with horses that have learnt to use the rear, or the threat of rearing, as a resistance.

The horse runs backwards (usually dropping the neck and going wide behind).

- Try to intervene with the leg to ride it forwards after the first step backwards, and soften the hand. Avoid tipping forwards too much if the horse runs backwards. Inclining the upper body very slightly forwards helps to lighten the seat, but too much and you will not be able to keep your horse 'in front of the leg'.

The diagonal steps become four beat, i.e. the steps are not regular and correct.

- If the horse's steps become four time then, even though the horse is stepping backwards, the rein-back is not correct for a dressage test. The 'broken' rein-back comes about because the horse disengages the hind leg. This is also a coordination problem for the horse and in my experience is difficult to correct.

The horse takes one or two steps backwards and then freezes.

- Try to activate the rein-back with the legs used alternately, but without changing your body language, and be ready to intervene with a restraining rein aid if the horse tries to step forwards when you activate the rein-back with your leg. Often the freezing happens as the horse goes wide behind, which happens when it tightens or hollows its back. If your horse does freeze, then apply a lateral leg action to unstick the hind leg, supported by a direct rein of opposition on the same side and a lighter seat.

EXERCISE 9

The 'Zone' Exercise: Trot-Walk-Trot

Introduce this when the horse is laterally submissive, is 'connected over the back' and has a reasonable, even acceptance of the contact. It should understand and accept leg-yielding and the 'corridor' exercise.

The objective

- To improve the quality of the transitions. This exercise is good for the horse that is inclined to 'drop' or stop in the transitions or lose the rhythm. The transition is not smooth because the speed of the trot and walk are not the same. The downward transition should be thought of as a smooth change of gear in your car from third to second.

- To increase engagement, e.g. when the horse comes onto the forehand and leans on the hand in the transition.

- To improve the horse's posture by improving the connection over the back.

- To improve the acceptance of the contact.

- To develop the elasticity of the steps leading to more cadence or expression in the steps but still in self-carriage.

- To create a 'platform' from which to develop the medium and the collected paces in trot and canter.

The exercise

- This can be performed in canter as well but is most useful in trot.

- Start the exercise on a large (20m) circle. It is a good idea to combine it with the 'corridor' exercise.

- The rhythm of the trot is slowed gradually to the rhythm of the walk, but at the same time the horse is encouraged to maintain its posture (i.e. connection over the back) and the energy of the trot step.

- As soon as the horse starts to recognize the preparation for the transition to walk and slows its rhythm then it is 'in the zone', i.e. in between trot and walk. The rhythm can gradually be slowed more, but the energy must be maintained in the trot step. Then the hind leg will become more engaged, the back will become rounder and the contact will become more 'elastic' as the horse carries itself. The trot will develop slightly more cadence in the steps.

- The horse is kept in the zone for a few steps only at the beginning, and then ridden forwards on a longer stride. Gradually the horse can be held in the zone for longer, and the demands for a slower, yet more cadenced, trot are increased by activating the steps of the hind leg within the rhythm.

- Once the horse has understood and accepted to come into the zone, the rider has the option to:
  a. Bring the horse back to walk and then ride forward to trot again.
  b. Ride forward into a lengthened stride, using the increased cadence in the trot to develop the medium trot steps. As soon as the cadence and rhythm are lost, the horse is brought back to the zone before being asked again.

- The exercise requires an acceptance by the horse of the 'connection over back' and the engagement of the hind leg that comes through the lateral submission. This leads to a better acceptance of the contact and to straightness. Initially, the horse may look for a way to avoid the increased engagement, which may cause problems if the 'basics' are not totally established. It is therefore necessary to complement this exercise with the exercises done previously, and always be prepared to go back a step or two if necessary.

Tips for the rider

- It is a good idea to do this exercise in rising trot until the rider and horse both understand and have perfected it. The 'rise' phase can be used to energize the steps while the 'sit' phase gives the timing for the half-halts.

- The rider's body language supported by half-halts prepares for the downward transition by stretching up and slightly back.

- The half-halts should be executed down the outside rein as the outside diagonal is in the supporting phase of the stride (the 'sit' phase).

- The contact should be constant down the inside rein.

- The whip can be used, if necessary, just behind the inside leg to encourage the inside hind to be picked up and brought forward under the body. To have the desired effect, the whip should be used at the moment of the 'rise'. (see Timing section in chapter 3 – Communication)

- The lateral leg aids are used in conjunction with the rein actions away from the neck if necessary to keep the horse 'in-line' and 'on-line' because its normal evasion will be to become more crooked.

Common problems

The horse pushes out against the hand.

- Use the corridor exercise to achieve lateral submission and thereby longitudinal submission. The horse will tend to push out against the hand when it disengages and attempts to push with the hind leg rather than step under the body. Stretch up and brace the upper body to resist the horse's desire to push out.

- But don't pull backwards on the rein. Even if the horse is quite strong, the horse must be made to realize that it is pulling against itself rather than the rider (it may help to lunge in side reins for a while).

The horse hollows and comes 'above the bit' or 'behind the bit'.

- The horse is not ready for the zone exercise. Use the corridor exercise or, if necessary, a step further back in the training to establish the lateral submission, the 'connection over the back' and reasonable acceptance of the contact.

The horse becomes crooked by swinging the quarters to one side.

- As the horse approaches the zone, it is often a good indication to the rider that they are coming in to the zone when the horse tries to avoid the increased engagement by putting its hind leg slightly to the side rather than under the body.

- Initially, use the lateral leg aids to remind the horse to stay 'in-line' and, if necessary, use the corridor exercise to straighten it. Once the acceptance of this correction has been achieved, the horse will have allowed itself to enter the zone, and should then be ridden forward again or the transition executed into walk.

The horse's step loses its 'spring' or cadence.

- If the rider slows the rhythm but the horse loses energy, its step will become flatter. This is the case even if it is 'laterally submissive', 'connected' and 'up to the bit'. When this happens the horse needs to be motivated to be more energetic.

- Another reason for the flatter step is the hollowing/tightening of the horse's back. When this is the cause, go back a stage to re-establish the 'connection over the back'.

EXERCISE 10

The 'Zone' Exercise: Canter-Trot-Canter

As for exercise 6, introduce this when the horse is laterally submissive, connected over the back and accepting the contact. It must also understand leg-yielding and the corridor exercise. The horse should be able to maintain the canter with reasonable confidence, and be forward thinking in the canter.

The objective

- To improve the engagement of the hind leg in the transitions to produce better balanced and smoother transitions in self-carriage.

- To gradually reduce the oscillations of the head and neck in the canter so that the horse learns to carry its forehand using the 'connection over the back'. This leads to the development of the elastic strength of the back muscles and the muscles at the base of the neck that together support the forehand. (See the section on bio-mechanics.)

- This exercise forms the basis of the work to introduce collection in the canter.

- The trot-canter-trot transitions are a loosening exercise that I regularly use in the early part of a work session with an advanced horse. The canter being a more effective loosening exercise than the trot because of the way it encourages the back muscles to work (see section on bio-mechanics).

The exercise

- The rhythm is slowed slightly, and the length of stride is shortened, so that the speed of the canter is reduced to the speed of the trot as a preparation for the transition to trot.

- The horse is encouraged to maintain its posture and the energy of the stride and so maintain and even enhance the moment of suspension in the canter.

- As soon as the horse starts to recognize the preparation and slows its rhythm then it is 'in the zone'. The energy in the canter stride must be maintained while the horse is in the zone, so that it does not 'break' to trot before it receives the signal to trot from the rider.

- The horse is kept in the zone for a few strides only at the beginning and then is ridden forwards into a longer stride. Gradually the horse can be held in the zone for longer, and the demands for a slower rhythm and yet correct canter with a moment of suspension are increased.

- Once the horse has understood and accepted to come into the zone, the rider has the option to:
   a. Bring the horse back to trot and then ride forward into canter again.
   b. Ride forward into a lengthened stride, using the increased suspension of the canter to develop the medium canter. If the horse quickens the rhythm or loses the suspension, it is brought back to the zone before being asked again.

Tips for the rider

- Start the exercise on a large circle (20 metres).

- Keep the horse as straight as possible, using the outside rein and outside leg to control the shoulder whilst, with a relaxed hip, using the inside leg to keep the inside hind in place behind the inside fore.

- In training it does not matter if the action of the outside rein in controlling the shoulder or in applying the half-halts causes the horse to flex slightly to the outside. In fact it is in itself a good exercise to check on the submission to the outside in canter. As soon as the horse accepts to be straightened and even counterflexed, then the rider must hand responsibility back to the horse to hold itself straight and only 'remind' it when necessary.

- The rider's body language, supported by half-halts, prepares for the downward transition by stretching up and slightly back. Remember that the action of the seat lengthens the stride, while the action of the leg/whip/spur energizes the canter without necessarily increasing the speed. So it is sometimes necessary to transfer virtually all your weight on to the stirrups.

- The half-halts should be executed down the outside rein as the outside fore and inside hind are in the supporting phase of the stride, i.e on the 'downward nod' of the canter. They should be applied, at the most, every other stride and should only last for the duration of the step. It is most important that the rider does not lift the horse with the rein action as the neck and shoulders are coming up in the canter stride. This leads to the horse becoming reliant on the supporting action of the rein, and so makes the contact heavier and the stride flatter.

- The contact should be constant down the inside rein. The inside hip, elbow/hand should always go with the movement, following the leading leg, so as to encourage the maximum expression to the gesture of the leading leg even as the half-halt is applied down the outside rein.

- The horse is reminded to stay in canter and to keep an energetic inside hind by the use of the leg, whip or spur, supported by the other leg to ensure that the horse stays 'in-line' and 'on-line'.

- When the rider wants the horse to make the transition to trot, the position statement changes from canter position to trot position and the seat ceases to follow the canter rhythm. The outside hand applies a stronger half-halt as the outside fore comes to the floor but must then follow into the first trot step.

- Only increase the demands within the zone if the horse is still capable of increasing, or at least maintaining, the 'roundness' of the canter, the moment of suspension and the expression to the leading leg.

Common problems

The horse breaks to trot as soon as the rider prepares for the exercise.

- The horse is backward thinking, due to laziness or anxiety. In the case of the lazy horse, it must be motivated with the leg (whip/spur), even as the rider prepares his body language, and the rider must be clearer in the position statement for canter. But avoid driving with the seat and leg in every stride, at the most use them every other stride.

- In the case of the anxious horse, it is not appropriate to do this exercise until the horse has understood and accepted the earlier work and exercises. It should be first able to maintain a forward going canter without being ridden every stride.

The horse becomes more crooked and comes in with the quarters.

- It is likely that the rider is taking too much contact down the inside rein, and possibly applying the half-halts down the inside rein. The horse should be straightened by using the outside rein and the outside leg at the girth to bring the shoulders back into line. In training, it is a useful exercise to work for the lateral submission to the outside, as in the 'corridor' exercise.

- The rider may have slipped to the outside of the saddle and /or have the outside leg held too far back, which is usually associated with the inside leg being away from the horse. With some horses it is necessary to adjust the position statement frequently. I recommend that, at the least, the position statement should be adjusted every quarter of the circle, but it can be as often as every other stride.

The horse changes behind, becoming disunited.

- The rider may have slipped to the outside of the saddle.

- In straightening the crooked horse, the rider may have brought the inside heel too far back rather than applying the leg at the girth.

● The horse is reluctant to engage the inside hind. Be careful not to demand too much in the zone or for too long before riding forwards.

The canter loses its moment of suspension or becomes irregular (i.e. becomes four time).

● Insufficient engagement of the hind leg, often associated with a loss of the 'connection over the back'. The back becomes tight, if not hollow.

● If the horse is inclined to be lazy or naturally a bit 'flat' in the canter, some riders help the horse to canter by applying lifting actions with the hand or half-halts at the moment that the forehand is coming off the floor. The horse then takes support on the rein to carry its forehand. The half-halts in canter should be applied at the moment that the outside fore/inside hind diagonal come to the floor (i.e. on the 'nod' of the canter).

EXERCISE 11

Progressive Transitions on the Straight line

Introduce this when exercises 1 to 6 can be performed reasonably well, and when the horse is becoming consistent in its understanding and acceptance of the 'basics'.

The objective

● To consolidate and test the work done in the previous exercises, i.e. to establish that the 'basics' have been understood and accepted.

● To develop the means to keep the horse 'in-line' and 'on-line', as well as in a consistent rhythm in its approach to jumps.

The exercise

● Perform progressive transitions between the paces on a straight line instead of in a turn.

● These should be performed at first against the wall/fence, but once the horse understands and accepts the exercises on the wall, they should be done on a straight line away from the support of the wall.

● The transitions should be progressive rather than acute (i.e. trot-walk-trot but *not* trot-halt-trot or canter-walk-canter) at this stage. Although the transitions are progressive, they should be performed with energy but in the rhythm. In the upward transition from walk to trot, the first trot step should be as energetic as the following steps rather than the activity be allowed to build only gradually. I often say to myself or my horse 'Hup, two, three, four…' during that upward transition.

Tips for the rider

- You must prepare your position statement early for the transition.

- You must be clear in your body language and position statement, supported by correctly timed leg and rein aids.

- Imagine you have a 'metronome' ticking inside your head that tells you the rhythm of the pace you are riding. Every action of leg, seat or hand must be performed in that rhythm.

- On the straight line against the wall, the principle of inside leg/outside hand still applies to keep the horse straight through the transitions.

- Away from the wall the straightening starts from the front. The rider must use the positional as well as the directional rein aids to correct the horse when the head, neck and shoulders deviate from the straight line. The lateral leg aids support the rein actions by keeping the horse's shoulders 'in-line' or correcting the quarters if they swing off the line. It may be necessary for one leg to talk to the shoulders in a T-a-H aid while the other talks to the hindquarters in a T-a-F aid.

- At any point on the straight line, there is still an 'inside' and an 'outside' of the horse depending on the lateral flexion at the poll.

- It frequently helps with a young horse to separate the hands during the transitions so that you are better prepared to make the relevant rein actions to correct any deviation.

- The leg should be relaxed at the hip and hanging in an even, light contact with the horse's sides, ready to act to bring the horse back 'in-line' or 'on-line'. If the leg pressure is applied strongly, the horse will tend to ignore or lean against it.

- In training, the inside rein contact should remain the same throughout the transition, even if this leads to an outward flexion or bend as the half-halts are applied in support of the body language. When the horse accepts and responds to the body language and half-halt, the outside rein can allow so that the horse will straighten itself. This principle applies in both upward and downward transitions. (See also the section on control when jumping.)

- In the dressage competition, when riding towards the judges, it may be necessary to hold a positional rein aid on the inside (without pulling backwards), in order to maintain the flexion to the inside when coming towards the judges. When riding away from the judges, it is still possible to do as in training, as long as the acceptance and response is achieved before the point is reached, e.g. the corner, where the judge is able to see the lateral flexion.

- When riding on a straight line away from the wall, it helps if the rider chooses a point (post, tree, jump etc) at which to aim the straight line. The horse must stay 'on-line' during the transition.

- The horse's natural tendency to be crooked (see section on straightness), has to be corrected when necessary without these corrections leading to the horse's reliance on the rider. Self carriage applies to straightness as much as anything else. The rider's role is to remind the horse to keep its body 'in-line'.

Common problems

Horse hollows, overbends or disengages during the transition.

- Improve the quality of the transitions on the circle using the previous exercises.

- Use the leg and hand to work on the lateral submission towards the side to which the horse normally wants to be resistant, even as the straight line is being ridden.

The quarters swing to one side.

- Straighten the horse from the front. Take the rein away from the neck, particularly on the side to which the quarters are swinging, while supporting with the rein on the other side to restrict the bend at the base of the neck. Use the lateral leg aids to support the actions of the reins.

Basic Jumping Training

Introduction

Only when the primary elements of 'flat work', or dressage, are understood by the horse can jumping training commence, although loose jumping can be started even before a young horse has been backed. Without the establishment of the basics of control, it is not possible to expect your horse to respond to your communication with it. The development of the horse's ability to cope with the technical aspects of show jumping and cross-country will mirror its training on the flat, and the most important aspect of that training, as far as jumping is concerned, is the development of the canter work. Basic jumping training will also help the aspiring dressage horse to consolidate its understanding and response to the rider, as well as making it more gymnastic.

The steeplechaser needs only the most rudimentary training on the flat to be able to gallop and jump straightforward fences. The horse is not required to cope with the technical demands of show jumping, e.g. related distances and tight turns, nor is it required to be as 'careful' in its jumping. The parabola of its jump is much flatter than that of a show jumper, because it is jumping at speed. The fences 'give' to a certain extent so the 'chaser can skim them, particularly with the hind legs. Yet quickness of reaction with the foreleg and the ability to measure its own stride are critical factors. As in all facets of equestrianism, some horses are more talented than others, and many steeplechasers would benefit from some elementary dressage work

and jumping training to improve their coordination and their ability to adjust their stride to the fence.

The development of the strength and stamina of the 'topline' muscles of the 'chaser is also important to their ability to jump and 'stay'. So working in a good posture without any requirement for collection must be of benefit to them. Self carriage is as important to the 'chaser as to the dressage horse, show jumper or eventer. The good racehorse that gallops 'on the bridle' (which is not the same as the dressage term 'on the bit', when the horse's head is carried just ahead of the vertical) is sufficiently 'connected over the back' to coordinate its action and to gallop economically.

In a race, the adjustments the horse makes to its balance and stride cannot be dictated by the jockey. The best jockeys are those that interfere the least, just keeping their own balance and thereby helping the horse to maintain its balance.

The parabola of the jump for the steeplechaser is relatively flat compared to the advanced show jumper.

The advanced show jumper has to learn how to jump out of a shorter stride. The parabola it describes over a fence has to be much rounder, with its highest point over the highest point of the jump. The horse has to cope with:

1. The height of the fence and width of the spreads (verticals, oxers, triple bars, water).

2. The related and relatively short distances between fences.

3. The tight turns required in the jump-off against the clock.

4. The different colours, shapes and styles of the fences.

The parabola of the jump for the advanced showjumper is rounder, with its highest point over the highest point of the jump. Baladine Du Mesnil ridden by Olivier Guillon.

The horse's basic dressage training must develop its ability to carry itself in good balance, in a consistent rhythm and in a good posture, 'connected over the back' with an acceptance of the contact. The canter work is the most important part, but the work in trot will help to develop the understanding within the canter work and it also acts as a gymnastic exercise. The same degree of sustained collection is not required of the advanced show jumper as it is of the advanced dressage horse.

The event horse is an all-round athlete and has to be trained to cope with the demands of the show jumping and the cross-country. The show jumping phase is to a much lower height and degree of technical complexity than in advanced show jumping. On the cross-country course the horse must be able to cope with different terrain and with obstacles that vary from being 'big and bold' to very technical. Although its jumping training mirrors that of the show jumper, it must also retain the ability to gallop and to jump some of the fences on the cross-country course at a speed similar to a 'chaser, although not quite as fast.

Responsibilities of the Rider

Understanding the relative responsibilities of the horse and rider within the partnership is essential to success in jumping. The examination of these responsibilities must start with the rider.

Goal setting

In broad terms that means deciding what to jump and when. That decision includes the type of fences, dimensions, order in which jumped etc. The progress from one level to another is also the rider's decision. The horse's confidence is a key element in the training, and the decisions made by the rider on behalf of the horse are key decisions (as are those made by the coach on behalf of the rider).

Rhythm, length of stride, line

The rider knows what test or exercise he is setting for the horse and is therefore responsible for setting the length of stride, rhythm and line required for the approach to the jumps.

Body language, position statement and communication

The rider must communicate through his body language and position statement, supported by the leg and rein actions, as often as is necessary but without interfering with, or taking away from, the horse's responsibility to carry itself. The same responsibilities apply to the rider between the fences as apply in the basic dressage. Between the obstacles and usually some way from the fence, particularly in the turns, the rider is responsible for monitoring the horse's energy, balance, posture and straightness. There are, however, important differences in the way the rider communicates with the horse in the approach to the fence compared to the basic dressage work. These differences are to do with the importance of not distracting the horse from its attention to the obstacle in the approach, whilst still obtaining its acceptance and response to the aids.

Balance, security and control without interference over the jumps

The ability of the rider to allow the horse to use itself to the maximum over the jumps is the key to getting the best out of its jumping. This independent security comes from good balance combined with the ability, at times, to hold your position with your legs. Whereas the neutral position of the upper body for advanced dressage is more or less at the vertical, the neutral position for jumping is ahead of the vertical. The faster the speed at which your horse is expected to jump, the shorter the stirrup should be and the more forward is the inclination of your body. The same principles regarding balance (longitudinal and lateral) and the influence of the upper body position apply in jumping as in dressage work.

The stability of the lower leg, with the weight dropping down into the stirrup, gives you the maximum contact between the leg and the horse's sides. To stay in balance, the stirrup leather should always be perpendicular to the base of support. In the approach to a jump the stirrup should hang vertically down from the stirrup bar. On the landing side, the faster the speed the more forward the stirrup should be relative to the rider's centre of gravity to cope with the deceleration involved in the landing phase.

A pinching of the knee leads to the heel being pulled backwards and, particularly in cross-country riding, increases the chances of the rider being pitched forward.

This provides the most secure position over jumps even when the unexpected happens, so it is particularly important for event riders. It is not as important, and is not always easy to do, in advanced show jumping when the jumps get very big, but the best riders come close to achieving it. A common fault that affects the stability of the lower leg is the inward rotation of the leg causing a pinching of the knee against the saddle. The heel is then pulled backwards and, particularly in cross-country riding, the chances of falling off or pitching on to the horse's forehand are much higher.

Good balance combined with a secure and correctly placed lower leg enables you to keep an independent contact through the reins. Your hand grip of the rein in jumping should be softer than in dressage. This is an important difference. In dressage the half-halts are used either to remind the horse to listen to your body language or to dictate the rhythm in the pace. It does not matter so much if, in training, this correction becomes sharper to get the horse's attention and response. In the approach to the jump, however, the control must not cause your horse to be distracted from the obstacle.

If your horse wants to quicken by lengthening its stride to the fence, hold it with the braced upper body language supported by the firm holding rein but without pressing with the seat deeper into the saddle which will have a pushing effect. The holding rein is applied by tightening the fist around the rein and should be done more down the outside rein. It does not matter if it brings the horse's head to the outside. Once the horse has accepted the control then the softening hand allows the horse to straighten the neck.

Over the jump your hands should be soft, to the point that at times the fingers, with the exception of the thumb and forefinger, are fully opened. The ideal is that the same soft contact is maintained from take-off to landing. With some horses it is necessary to maintain a stronger contact in the approach and on take-off, but you should still be able to soften the contact completely over the top of the fence and into the landing. This applies particularly when jumping horses that lack confidence or cannot be trusted to jump. Conversely, there are some horses and some situations where a loose rein at the point of take-off gives your horse the freedom it requires or appreciates. The important point is that, by having a consistently correct lower leg position and a good balance, your hands are able to act independently. The reins must not be used as the handlebars of a bicycle to hold yourself on to the horse. Riders should be aware that nerves or anxiety, whether caused by fear or by tension of the competition, will also tend to cause the hand grip to tighten.

Over the jump the hands should be soft to the point that at times the fingers are fully opened. By having a consistently correct lower leg position and a good balance, your hands are able to act independently.

Stability of the rider's position over the jump

At the point of take-off your horse has to engage its hind legs and push its forehand off the ground. The higher the jump and the shorter the stride in the approach, the more the hind legs must engage prior to take off and the rounder the shape of the parabola over the jump. Avoid 'throwing' your body forward at the point of take-off. If you approach the jump in neutral position, i.e. with the upper body ahead of the vertical as appropriate to the speed of the canter, then, if you are in good balance and relaxed, your natural reflexes to stay in balance will take care of you following the jump. By attempting to remain still you give the horse the best chance of retaining its own balance and thereby bringing its own forehand up to clear the jump. Let the horse come up to you rather than you go down to the horse.

Developing the reflex to 'follow'
Training for the rider must include exercises that develop the reflex to follow the horse over the fence with the upper body. We all have that reflex within us but it is sometimes stifled by stiffness, pain or anxiety.

The rate of acceleration affects the degree of 'fold' required as the horse takes off. This is influenced in turn by two elements: the speed of approach and the point of take-off.

- If a horse approaches a fence in trot with the rider in an upright position then the 'fold' must be relatively greater because of the sudden acceleration at point of take-off.

- Conversely if approached at speed in a more forward position then the 'fold' will be minimal.

● If the horse's point of take-off is close to the fence then the fold will be minimal whereas if the horse 'stands off' the fence the degree of fold required will be much greater.

Developing the rider's instinctive recognition of these elements is an important part of the training of the rider. This training is best done initially over grids both from trot and canter.

Despite all the training a rider may have, it is not possible to be perfect. Particularly when riding young horses or when riding on a cross-country course even the best riders will occasionally be left behind. It is always better to be left behind than to get ahead of the horse by 'guessing' with the 'fold'. But in being 'left behind' you must try not to use the reins to hold your position, using instead the hold/grip of the correctly placed lower leg. A young or unconfident horse will often hesitate and shorten its stride and then suddenly take off. When this happens it is the security of the correctly placed lower leg that will hold the rider in position. It is a good idea to use a neckstrap when riding an unpredictable, novice horse, or if the rider is a relative novice.

Over the top of the jump

At the highest point of a jump, as your horse is at the top of the parabola, it may have to stretch to reach the back rail. To give the horse the freedom of its neck and back, so that it can bring its hindquarters up high enough to clear the front and back rails, you may have to reach forward with the upper body to follow with the hands and to stay with the movement. Again, if relaxed and in balance with a secure lower

Over the top of the jump. Tlaloc ridden by Santiago Lambre.

leg position, your reflexes will let this happen naturally. As the fences become higher and wider in advanced show jumping, a slightly shorter stirrup helps, but even then it may not be possible to keep the lower leg completely in position.

As the horse lands

The non-leading leg touches the floor a fraction before the leading leg, and as it does so the horse's head and neck comes up and back, which enables you to come more upright with the upper body without pulling on the reins, assuming the fingers are relaxed. This allows the weight to drop down through the shock absorbing ankle into the stirrup. A common fault is for the rider to lose his upper body posture and collapse onto the horse's neck or shoulders, often with the hands pushing down into the neck to support his upper body and so restricting the horse's ability to take the first stride after landing. If the horse expects this restriction it will often tighten its back over the fence and in so doing touch the back rail with its hind leg. The training of the rider should include exercises both on and off the horse that will develop the tone in the upper body so that he is able to maintain posture as the horse lands.

As the horse lands, a common fault is for the rider to lose his upper body posture and collapse onto the horse's neck.

Length of stirrup

The length of stirrup affects:

- the proximity of the seat to the saddle

- the control of the pace

- the 'fold' over the fence.

Shorter stirrups aid in the control of the horse at speed between the fences, particularly in a steeplechase or on the cross-country. However, the shorter the stirrup the more forward tends to be the inclination of the upper body, and if the stirrup is too short relative to the speed of the canter, it is possible that you will be too remote from the saddle and therefore not able to feel and influence the length of stride in the approach to an obstacle. You may also be less secure over the fence and on landing because you have less contact with the horse's sides with the lower leg. The top steeplechase jockeys and event riders are able to ride quite short and yet in the approach to an obstacle still have enough contact with the saddle and remain secure on landing. When the demands increase in cross-country riding and in show jumping for collection prior to the take-off, then the lower leg and spur must also be in a position to act to support the body language in engaging the hind leg.

The length of stirrup also affects the rider's reflex to maintain balance as the horse jumps the fence. The stillness of the upper body over the fence, particularly when

Top steeplechase jockeys are able to ride quite short but still have enough contact with the saddle and remain secure on landing.

If the stirrups are too long it makes it more difficult to control the speed and the balance when galloping.

approaching the jump in a shorter stride and more upright posture, for example when show jumping, is affected by the length of stirrup. If it is too short, it is like trying to get up from a low chair: you have to lean well forward, almost into a crouching position, because the centre of gravity is too far behind the base of support. The ideal length of stirrup for the novice rider in show jumping and basic jump training is one that enables you to comfortably clear the front of the saddle with the weight well down into the heels. Any shorter is not necessary and will make it more difficult to remain still over the jump. As the jumps become higher or the speeds increase between the fences so the stirrups can become shorter.

Another factor determining the correct length of stirrup is the importance of being able to land into the stirrup with the weight dropping down into the heels. If the stirrups are too long, the rider cannot help but land with some if not all of his weight in the saddle. This will cause the horse to tighten its back, to run away from the fence or bounce the rider back out of the saddle, pitching him either over the horse's ears or at least on to its forehand. People who ride too long often use their hands to lean on the horse's neck to prevent themselves being bounced forwards.

There is no exact rule that can be applied to every situation. Each rider is different in terms of conformation and in the length of leg and upper body. The size, type, attitude and level of schooling of the horse are also variables. A rider who is short relative to his horse may have to ride with a longer stirrup to maintain sufficient contact with the horse's sides. A horse that is naturally fairly long and difficult to engage tends to pull downwards and is often easier to ride with a relatively short stirrup.

Long stirrups may also cause the rider to be bounced out of the saddle on landing, and then pitched onto the horse's neck.

The seat contact with the saddle

The rider's objective must always be to keep an even rhythm and length of stride to the jump. The seat in light contact with the saddle not only gives the greatest security but also a feeling for the length of stride and the possibility to do something about it in the last few strides before the jump. When the horse hesitates, it shortens its stride, sometimes at the last moment. When it 'attacks' the fence, it lengthens the stride to the fence. By being close to the saddle at all times the rider can either use the seat to lengthen the stride if the horse is shortening or be still with the seat and come up with the upper body to use the body language to shorten the stride.

On a novice or unpredictable horse the rider can use the 'Remount' seat, in which the rider has approximately 50 per cent of his weight in the saddle and 50 per cent in the stirrup. This defensive position enables the rider to react quickly to any sudden changes in pace. As the horse becomes more experienced and predictable, then you can ride with less weight on its back, in the light seat, coming more in to the saddle for certain jumps where you foresee there may be problems. This applies particularly to cross-country riding.

Length of rein

The length of rein is governed by the length of stirrup and the inclination of the upper body ahead of the vertical. As a guide, the reins should be adjusted at a length that keeps the hands just in front of a line drawn vertically down from the rider's eyes. The shorter the stirrups and the more forward the inclination of the upper body, the shorter the rein needs to be. If the hands are too far in front of this line then the horse will tend to pull the rider forwards and so make it less easy to use the body language for control. It also makes it more difficult for the rider to give the horse the freedom over a fence.

Conversely, if the reins are too long the rider will tend to pull backwards with the rein to keep control and often come behind the movement with the upper body. The length of rein must be adjusted frequently particularly in cross-country riding to cope with the various different styles of fence and their relative approaches, taking account of the terrain before and after the fence. The rider's dexterity in being able to adjust the rein without losing the contact and control is an important aspect of a novice rider's training.

The horse's conformation and natural way of going will also influence the correct length of rein. Those horses that have a tendency to shorten the neck in the canter have to be ridden over fences with a slightly longer rein because when they jump, they need to have the freedom to stretch the neck forward particularly over the spread fences. Horses that tend to carry the head well forward away from the shoulders can be ridden on a shorter rein because they do not take so much rein over the fence.

Temperament is also a determining factor. Horses tend to be more relaxed when ridden on a slightly longer rein. The shortening of the rein combined with the upper body inclining forward will usually have a stimulating or exciting effect on your horse, and of course the converse applies.

Training the Horse – Its Responsibilities

The objective of the jumping training

In an earlier section of the book, I set out the horse's responsibilities in relation to its basic dressage or flat work. Your horse also has responsibilities in jumping work. The basic jumping training for the horse consists of exercises to develop its understanding and acceptance of its responsibilities and thereby its confidence. As with the basic dressage, there is often a fine line between what is the rider's responsibility and what is that of the horse. The balance may change slightly between training the young horse at home and taking part in competitions.

The training is intended to develop:

* The calm attention of the horse to the fence in a consistent *rhythm, stride length,* and *line.*

* The horse's ability to *measure its own stride* to the fence and, where necessary, to adjust it.

* The *balance* and *coordination* of the horse before, over and after the fence.

* The horse's *technique* and *gymnastic* ability.

* The horse's *confidence* in its own jumping ability, in the rider, and the questions asked of it.

* The horse's confidence in the *colours, shapes* and *styles* of fence to which it is presented.

Rhythm, stride length and line

The basic dressage work should provide the means for teaching a horse to approach obstacles in a consistent rhythm and stride length that is correct for the fence to be jumped, and on the correct line that will bring the horse to the chosen point of the fence and at the chosen angle.

Rhythm x Stride Length = Speed

The basic dressage training develops the horse's ability to adjust its stride length in a consistent rhythm on the flat. The difficulty in the early jumping training is that the horse reacts to the sight of the fence. Some horses will hesitate and shorten the stride, while others will get excited or even panic and lengthen the stride. They can go from one extreme to the other: hesitating to the point of stopping or lengthening to the extent of bolting at the fence.

117

The length of stride in the approach affects the ability of the horse to get its stride right for the jump. The shorter the stride, the more strides there will be between the fences and the more likely the horse will come to a take-off point close to the fence. Conversely, the longer the stride, the more likely the horse is to stand off the fence. A longer stride length makes it less easy for the horse to meet the jumps consistently in the correct take-off zone. There can be no exact stride length that is comfortable for every horse. Some are naturally long striding while others have a naturally short stride. What is important is to set a stride length that is in the middle of the horse's range of possibility. From this point the stride can be lengthened or shortened according to the task ahead. (*Tip:* If you always seem to be finding a deep spot to your jumps, then increase the length of stride well in advance of the jump, and maintain that length of stride in a consistent rhythm all the way to the fence. Conversely if you are always seeing a long stride, then collect i.e shorten the canter stride well before the fence but without losing the impulsion.)

Seeing a stride

It is an important part of the training of your horse to teach it to look for its own stride. The horse, particularly the eventer, must not become reliant on you to see a stride for it. If it approaches the fence at a medium length of stride and in balance, it has the ability to shorten slightly or lengthen slightly as it sees its stride to the fence. If you are in good balance and harmony with the horse, you will follow that adjustment, and as you become more experienced you will recognize the slight adjustment the horse is about to make.

'If an even rhythm and length of stride is maintained, a good stride will come.'

Inexperienced jumping riders are often worried that they cannot see a stride when jumping. This is usually the reason why they find it difficult to maintain an even rhythm and length of stride. Because they cannot see the stride they feel a need to do something, which is usually to shorten until they see a stride and then attack the jump. It then becomes a self-fulfiling prophecy. At the higher levels of jumping, whether in eventing or show jumping, the ability to see a stride is largely down to confidence: if an even rhythm and length of stride is maintained, a good stride will come.

I am a firm believer in the value of loose jumping especially with the younger horses. It teaches them to look after themselves both in terms of seeing their stride and in maintaining their own balance. It also gives riders confidence to see that the horse can do so without assistance.

Balance and coordination

The horse must learn to maintain its balance, both longitudinal and lateral, in the approach, take-off and landing.

The *longitudinal* balance that the horse develops through its basic dressage work will help it to learn to maintain that balance while jumping, particularly when having to jump fences in close proximity to each other. The ability to hold its balance will enable it to maintain an even length of stride within related distances (three +

strides between fences), combinations (one or two strides between fences) and bounces (in/out fences). That balance comes from the development of the horse's posture and self-carriage within both the early dressage work and the early jumping exercises. The improved balance while jumping also enables your horse to coordinate its jumping action to produce a more careful jump. Young, brave horses may appear at first to be careless, but as they become better balanced on the flat and over jumps they become more careful, because they find that they *can* keep their balance and avoid hitting the jumps.

Lateral balance is also important and comes about through the basic dressage work to straighten the horse. Not only must the horse learn to approach the jump 'on-line' but also 'in-line', so that it stays straight over the jumps. The novice horse will often have a tendency to drift to the left or right in the take-off or on landing. This is because it pushes off one hind leg more than the other and, because it is not straight, it pushes its shoulder away from the strong hind leg. If you try to correct this tendency to drift off line by using a stronger rein contact over the jumps or between the jumps, you will interfere with the horse's ability to use itself over the jump and you are also likely to cause it to lean more on that rein for support. So the problem only gets worse. The horse must be encouraged to correct itself. The best way to do that is to use guide rails within the jumping exercises. These guide rails include cross rails, sloping poles, etc.

In the landing, and the strides following the landing, the lateral balance must also be maintained. Horses that land and then lose their balance forward and 'run on' will often lose their lateral balance as well and fall out on the turns, especially if the rider uses the inside rein to bring the horse back under control. Hence the importance of 'control' down the outside rein when jumping and also the work on straightening the horse in basic dressage.

The same issues of 'straightness' and 'control' that apply in basic dressage apply equally in jumping training, but they become more obvious in the jumping. Hence the value of jumping training even for the horse that is intended as a pure dressage horse.

Technique and gymnastic ability

The horse's natural ability as a jumper is reflected in its jumping technique and its gymnastic ability. Of course many other attributes, both mental and physical, are involved in making the perfect jumper. The horse with a perfect technique to be a show jumper will not make a very good steeplechaser. The modern event horse has to have more of the attributes of the show jumper than the 'chaser, given the increased technical demands of the modern sport.

The basic jumping training for most horses, except the most naturally talented, must include exercises to improve its jumping technique. Some technique problems are inherent in the horse, while others are produced by mistakes in early jumping training or induced by rider mistakes at the fence. It is important to differentiate between them. Some young horses that are physically immature will have technique problems that will improve with maturity.

It also has to be realized that some horses have technique problems that limit their ability to perform well or safely as the fences get bigger or more demanding gymnastically, no matter how much training they receive. The experienced rider or trainer will recognize this, but the less experienced rider will often need to be told. This applies particularly in the sport of eventing, where unsafe jumping technique can be life threatening to the horse or rider. Every horse has a limit to its capabilities and there comes a point where the horse, despite all the best training, cannot achieve any better.

With the use of grid exercises and different shapes of jumps it is possible to improve your horse's forehand or hind leg technique or the way it uses its back over the fence. These exercises will also gradually improve its gymnastic ability so enabling it to jump higher fences cleanly. The horse's confidence comes from its realization that it can do what is asked of it, which in turn leads to its enjoyment of it. It is easier to lose a horse's confidence than to gain it, so care must always be taken to increase carefully the demands within these exercises.

Despite what some riders or trainers think, horses instinctively know that hitting a fence hurts and will do their best not to do so. Sometimes they appear not to be careful, but in fact it is only that they are unable to avoid hitting the fence because they do not have the ability to get themselves out of trouble.

Of course some horses have a lower pain threshold than others and will try harder to avoid hitting a fence than others. In the case of some top show jumpers, they are so careful that they would rather stop than hit a fence. The angle at which the leg hits the fence and whether it hits the fence with the hoof or the leg will also affect the degree to which the horse feels it. The level of excitement, fear or nerves will also affect its sensitivity.

So it is important when asking your horse to do these exercises that you give them every opportunity to concentrate on what they are being asked to do. The exercise session must not be rushed. A careful analysis of what the horse is doing is important at every stage so that you can address the problems that arise in a logical order.

Shapes, colours, styles and surroundings

An equally important part of basic jumping training is introducing the horse to the varied shapes, colours and styles of fences. Initially at home, but as soon as possible away from home, in unfamiliar surroundings, the horse needs to be introduced to all the different types of fences that it will have to negotiate. The young horse may become quite comfortable jumping plain poles and natural fences at home, and show good technique over reasonably large fences, but then when it goes away from home to jump over different colours, shapes and styles of fence it may go back to being a novice again. It is only by gradually accustoming the horse to all these different possibilities and different situations that it will perform as well away from home as it does at home. At some stage in the training, many horses actually start to perform better away from home than they do at home because they have more respect for the rider and the jumps away from their comfort zone.

Basic Jumping Exercises for Horse and Rider

Horses do not all have to follow exactly the same path in their training. In the early stages some are 'natural' jumpers, while others do not become good jumpers until they mature and become better balanced through the basic dressage training. Each horse should be treated as an individual.

For this reason, not every jumping exercise will work for every horse. There are some horses for which even apparently simple exercises, such as trotting over poles, are counter productive because they are so naturally careful that they want to jump the whole grid in one leap. Logically, one would expect that, by repetition, the horse would eventually learn to trot down a line of poles, but sometimes the horse just becomes more upset. This is particularly so in the case of horses with a 'sharp' or nervous temperament.

The important point is that one should always be prepared to experiment and to keep an open mind. It may be necessary to stick with an exercise for a while until the horse understands it and becomes more accomplished. On the other hand, if the horse is only getting worse rather than better, it is sensible to try another exercise. The ability to jump is a natural one, and a horse is able to jump a large fence even if it has never been trained in its life. We should not think that we always know best.

These exercises should be considered as 'tools' in your 'training bag'. As you progress with a horse's training, you can pull out the most appropriate exercise either to deal with an apparent problem or to further develop the horse's coordination, gymnastic ability and confidence.

Where do we start?

It is possible to start jump training with a single pole on the floor out of trot and then gradually raise the pole until it becomes a jump. The first time they jump the pole, some horses will clear it by a metre! Even when re-presented a few times they may continue to leap over it. Some horses are naturally careful and just instinctively hate to touch a pole, while others jump high initially because they are 'spooky' and see a gremlin there. Of the careful ones, some remain consistently careful, while others soon lose respect for the pole. There are some horses that are so careless, disrespectful or uncoordinated that they trip up over the pole. Whatever they do, it is important that the rider does not interfere with their responsibility to look after themselves either intentionally, or through loss of balance, or because of anxiety.

It is very important that the trainer on the ground is as observant as the rider as to the length of stride that is comfortable for the horse at any particular stage in its training. One objective of training, both in basic dressage and in basic jumping, is to teach the horse to be able to adjust its stride length. The distances suggested in the following exercises are to be taken as average distances and you should be prepared to adjust them, especially in the early stages of the training, so that the horse is comfortable. Then gradually the demands can be increased. In the case of a horse with a naturally long stride, the emphasis will be on teaching it to shorten, whereas with the short striding horse the emphasis will be on lengthening the stride. Care must always be taken not to overface the horse, because confidence is crucial to the development of the jump training.

The exercises included in this book are not the only exercises that can be done with a horse or rider. They are exercises that I have used and find useful. Most of these exercises I have seen used by other riders and trainers. A good rider and trainer will always be looking for new ideas to add to their database of knowledge. The only limit is the depth of your inquiring, analytical mind and your imagination. Normally, one can take one of these exercises and consistently achieve a good result, but there will always be the exception to the rule. What is important is that the rider or trainer must keep in mind both the 'end' goal of the training as well as the 'immediate' goal. The 'end' goal is what the horse is to be asked to do in competition, for example, show jumping, eventing or 'chasing, while the 'immediate' goal refers to the particular detail that is key to the horse's development at that particular stage in its training.

EXERCISE 1

Trotting Poles and Cavalletti

Introduce

- As soon as a reasonable response to the rider's simple aids has been established.

- To re-school a horse that tends not to pay attention to the jumps, or a horse that changes its rhythm and stride length in the approach, or that tends to hollow the back over jumps.

It can be included in the rider's training as soon as reasonable balance in the light seat has been achieved.

The objective

- Improve the rider's balance and ability to maintain an even contact through the rein while in the light seat or light rising trot.

- Encourage the horse to pay attention to what it is doing, to maintain an even rhythm and gradually encourage it either to lengthen or shorten its stride depending on the setting of the poles.

- Encourage the horse to be better coordinated.

- Complement the basic dressage work in developing the horse's posture and topline, and in developing more cadence in the steps, particularly as the poles are raised off the ground.

The exercise

- The exercise is developed from walk, and then trot, initially over single poles until the grid is expanded to include any number of poles, usually five to six. The poles are set at an approximate distance of 1.3m. Be prepared to adjust the distance to suit the natural length of your horse's stride. The distance can then be lengthened or shortened from that point according to the goal.

- When adding extra poles, it is advisable with the novice 'sharp' horse to add alternate poles first (i.e. at 2.6m) in case it tries to jump the whole grid or canter down the line. It is also a good idea to spend some time walking through the grid until the horse is relaxed.

- The poles can gradually be raised as the horse becomes comfortable with the exercise. Raising alternate poles initially or raising just one end alternately are options worth trying. Old fashioned cavalletti help here, but one does not see them used much these days.

- The grid should be approached in a light rising trot or a light seat with the weight mainly in the stirrup, with sufficient tone in the upper body for the hands to remain away from the horse's neck and to maintain an even contact to keep the horse as straight as possible on the line. Make sure you look straight ahead, not down at the poles. It is your horse's job to pay attention to the poles.

- The horse should be encouraged to maintain an even rhythm and stride length, in-line and on-line and with a good posture, i.e. 'connected over the back'.

Trotting poles.

● Through the grid, the horse should be encouraged to draw its neck forward as the contact is softened slightly through a relaxed fist and a 'following' arm. Depending on the setting of the poles, the rider's body language should adjust by going more forward as the stride lengthens or coming more upright to allow the horse to shorten its stride. It is better to cease rising through the grid, so that your body remains as still as possible.

● After the grid the rider must correct any changes that have occurred to the horse's rhythm, length of stride and posture as it went through the grid.

Common problems

The horse rushes, perhaps even trying to jump the grid all in one.

● Start in walk with alternate poles. If the horse still rushes in trot, make the approach shorter. The rider can assist by dictating the rhythm in the approach with his body language supported with a holding rein on an even contact. As the horse starts the grid then the contact is softened slightly.

The horse loses its outline.

● This often happens when the horse's posture is not sufficiently established in the basic dressage work. If the posture is 'held' by the rider then it will be lost as the contact is softened down the grid. It can also happen with the lazy horse, in which case it helps if the rider keeps a more upright posture down the grid and is able to use the leg to maintain the activity and engagement of the horse's hind leg.

Loses straightness and line.

● Widen the hands to channel the horse and use the legs appropriately to bring the horse back into line.

Loses rhythm and regularity over the poles.

● Either shorten the distance between the poles or increase the horse's length of stride by energizing and going forward with the body language into a yielding contact. Use a dressage whip if necessary to support the energizing leg and be careful that the body language is not causing the horse to slow down by coming behind the movement. Raise the poles to encourage the horse to pay more attention, but initially walk through the grid and do not be tempted to look down to help your horse to sort it out. That is its job.

Variations

● Arrange the poles on a large circle. By doing this, it is possible to vary the length of stride without changing the grid, by riding towards the inside or the outside of the poles. Use the legs, a guiding inside rein and supporting outside rein to keep the horse in-line and on-line.

- Approach the grid diagonally to vary the length of stride.

- Increase the height of the poles to develop the horse gymnastically.

- Use as an introduction to a jumping grid.

Simple Grids

Introduce

- When the horse is established over trotting poles. It is not essential that your horse establishes a calm rhythm over the trotting poles before you start to introduce them to small jumping grids. I have known some horses that have never settled well over trotting poles but have accepted the grids of jumps with just one placing pole at the start. These horses were quite 'buzzy' in their jumping and eventually accepted the trotting poles, but only much later in their schooling. If I had waited until they accepted the trotting poles, I would probably never have started their jumping.

- When the rider's balance can be maintained reasonably well over the trotting poles and on the flat. It is important to have a horse as a schoolmaster who is honest and forward going, but that does not rush, so that the rider can concentrate on his style over the jumps.

Objective

- To build up a horse and rider's confidence in jumping bigger fences without having to worry about getting the stride right.

- To develop the horse's rhythm in good self-carriage over jumps.

- To help the horse to understand and accept combinations of fences, i.e. doubles and trebles etc.

- To develop the horse's balance, gymnastic ability and reflexes.

- To encourage the correct use of the horse's back over the jumps and the correct fore/hind leg technique.

- To teach the horse to lengthen and shorten its stride in self-carriage between the jumps.

- To develop the horse's reflex responses.

- To improve the horse's straightness over fences.

- To develop the rider's balance, posture, coordination and relative stillness over jumps.

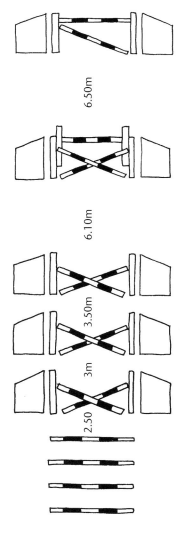

Simple grids.

● To develop the independence of the rider's arm and hand actions and the stability of the lower leg.

The exercise

● Set the distance from the last pole of the trotting grid or from the placing pole at 2.5m from the first element of the jumping grid.

● Start with one small jump, either a cross pole or a straight pole with a ground line.

● Gradually add further elements with one non-jumping stride between the fences. The distance between the first two elements should be set slightly shorter (6m) than between the following elements (6.5m). When approaching from trot or later in the training from a collected canter, the horse's first jump over the cross rail will not have as long a trajectory as over the subsequent jumps.

● The first element is a placing jump, the second element is a sloping spread, e.g. a cross rail in front with a rail behind and then the third and subsequent element can vary between verticals or oxers.

● Start with the grid against the side of the arena to help to encourage the novice horse to remain straight.

● If necessary, assist the horse by placing guide poles so that the rider does not have to use the rein to keep the horse straight, and so that the horse focuses on the line.

● Approach the grid in an active trot, and from not too far away (12 metres from the corner), with the forward position just as you would have in approaching the trotting poles. Later the grid can be approached in canter when the horse's flatwork is sufficiently developed that it can maintain its canter without the constant support of the rider.

● Through the grid, remain in a light seat close to the saddle but with all the weight in the stirrups, and maintain a very light contact with a relaxed fist and the hands slightly away from the neck. Remain as still as possible over the jumps, looking straight ahead and allowing the horse to come up to you. One often sees riders overfolding because they have been left behind at the beginning when the upper body has been too upright in the approach.

● On landing after the last jump maintain the canter until a rhythm is reestablished, perhaps riding on to a circle with a controlling outside rein and a guiding or opening inside rein. Then make a good transition back to trot. If the horse lands on the outside lead continue to ride positively forwards through the turn so that it is encouraged to make a change of lead naturally to keep its balance as it would do if jumping loose. In doing so, maintain the upper body posture, keeping the outside shoulder well back and the weight in the inside stirrup. I often see riders allowing their horses to fall or drop back into trot when they are jumping, even though they are capable of a good transition when schooling basic dressage.

It is important to relate the flat work to the jumping at all times so that it becomes a habit for both the horse and rider.

- Use the grids on both reins. You will find that your horse will have a preference for jumping in one direction more than the other until it becomes straighter in its basic dressage work. Its performance and reactions will also be affected by the position of the gate or stables in relation to the grid. Use this to help you initially, by jumping towards home with a reluctant horse and away from home with an excitable horse.

Common Problems

The horse rushes.

- Make the turn into the grid closer to the start of the grid. Approach from walk, but in doing so make sure the upper body is inclined forwards and the reins are sufficiently long, with the hands wide apart, so that as the horse accelerates it is possible to follow with the contact without having to slip the reins. The main thing to avoid is tightening the contact as the horse jumps down the line. With a horse that rushes, it also helps to change the grid frequently and perhaps include fillers to encourage it to pay attention and slow itself down. Adding poles on the floor in the middle of the non-jumping stride also helps to focus their attention.

The horse is careless.

- It may appear at first that a horse is careless because it hits the fences, but this often happens because the distances between the fences are too short. It is important to keep an eye on the take-off and landing spots to ensure that the distances are set comfortably for the horse. Only gradually, in conjunction with the dressage work, shorten the distances.

The horse hollows the back and does not concentrate.

- This can happen because of rider error in being behind the movement with too much weight on the back and a tight fist over the fences. If it is not due to the rider, then the horse will gradually improve as the demands of the grid are increased along with the dressage schooling. There are some horses that defy all the rules and jump carefully with a good foreleg technique and clean behind but without apparently basculing at all. This is often because they have sufficient ability that it is not until the fences get much higher and wider that they feel a need to use their backs. The tightening of the back also happens with horses that are nervous and worried about what is going on around them. Some horses look backwards as they jump instead of focusing on the jumps. In the racing world such horses would often run in blinkers to encourage them to concentrate.

The horse drifts to one side.

● Use sloping poles as guide rails to encourage it to bring itself back to straightness. This problem can also happen because the distances are too short and the horse is trying to find room.

The horse loses impulsion.

● This happens either because the horse is lazy or because it is nervous, spooky or confused. It is important to differentiate. If in doubt, one must assume that the horse lacks confidence and either reduce the heights or remove elements until it is happier. Even then it may need the support of the whip either from the rider or an assistant on the ground to encourage it to go forward and be positive. If one allows the horse to become too deliberate the problem tends to get worse. I find the use of a dressage whip in early training over the grids is more effective than a short whip or spurs because it can be used without taking the hands off the reins. The time to apply the whip is as the horse comes over the last trotting pole or the placing pole so that it has an energizing effect without distracting it from the jumps. It is better to use it at the first sign of hesitation rather than wait until the impulsion has been lost. The horse that is too cautious or is lazy will tend to find the distances long, so it is important to adjust them immediately if this is the case. In setting the distances for this type of horse, I prefer to have them slightly short rather than too long.

The horse runs away from the fence on landing.

● This could be a sign of well-being, in which case it will soon settle, or it could be a sign of panic or temper. If the rider immediately pulls at the horse's mouth on landing, then the horse learns to expect it and will brace itself for the pull as its lands, and in so doing will put itself more on the forehand, so the problem gets worse. If the horse runs away from the fence, the outside rein should be the dominant one used to support the body language which draws up and back, without sitting heavily into the saddle, but keep the lower leg in place. Do not brace the lower leg forward and pull back on the inside rein. If the horse bends to the outside as the outside hand is used that is not a problem because, as soon as the horse accepts to slow down and responds to the engaging action of the inside leg and the body language, then the softening outside hand will allow the horse to straighten.

Variations

There are numerous variations in gridwork that can be used. The number of possibilities are only limited by the rider's and trainer's imagination. What is important is that particular attention is paid to the distances by looking at the take-off and landing zones to make sure that the highest point of the parabola is over the top of the fences. Only gradually shorten or lengthen these distances to develop your horse gymnastically.

EXERCISE 3

Canter Poles

Introduce

- As the canter work within the basic dressage becomes established and the horse is able to maintain a rhythm in the canter with only occasional reminders from the rider's leg, whip or spur. The horse gradually becomes able to maintain an even length of stride within the rhythm in reasonable self-carriage. At this stage it is possible to include single poles on the ground, on the track and on the circles.

- It is not necessary to wait until the horse's canter is good enough to collect or lengthen, only that the horse knows that it is its responsibility to maintain the canter not the rider's.

The objective

- To work on the quality of the canter, the even stride length, the rhythm and the self-carriage, whilst at the same time the horse has to concentrate on measuring its own stride to the pole. It must learn to 'look', 'adjust' and then 'avoid' touching the poles.

- To develop the rider's ability to look after his own responsibilities, whilst at the same time monitoring the horse but without taking over its responsibilities.

- In particular to work on keeping a soft inside rein contact even if the outside rein sometimes has to support the body language with a holding rein.

- To work on the forward seat in light contact with the saddle without driving or pushing with the seat.

- For the rider to work on monitoring the horse's rhythm, even length of stride, accurate line and straightness whilst negotiating the poles.

The exercise

- Poles can be placed at random around the arena, either on the track or on a circle, but not on a straight line one after the other because that becomes a related distance.

- At a later stage the poles can be laid on a straight line at a distance of just over 3m apart. Again, be prepared to adjust them to the horse's natural stride length and only shorten them as the horse becomes able to collect its stride without being either restricted by the rider or taking support on the reins.

- The canter poles laid out in this way on the straight line in the approach to a fence can be used later in the training to encourage the horse and to teach the rider the feel for the even length of stride within an active 'springy' canter in the approach to the fence.

Common problems

The horse keeps hitting the poles.

- Either the distance needs changing between the poles or the horse takes too much support on the rider's inside hand. Remember to ride with the inside fist relaxed even if the horse then bends to the outside.

The horse over-jumps the poles.

- This may happen at the start due to freshness or spookiness, but the horse will soon settle down. If there is room for another stride, but your horse does not take it and instead launches at the pole, this is likely to be caused by you having a contact that is too strong. The strong contact is often combined with a driving or pushing seat because you do not trust the horse to stay in canter.

The horse does not stay on-line.

- A horse that is inclined to rush will tend to fall in on the turn while the horse that does not go forward will tend to fall out. In addition, the natural tendency of the horse to be crooked will often lead to a loss of lateral balance and cause the horse to over-bend laterally in the neck and fall out through the shoulder. The more this happens the more the rider is inclined to increase the contact in the inside rein. The basic dressage work to keep the horse in-line and on-line must continue even as the horse is asked to canter over the poles, but has to be all the more correct to avoid the increased use of the reins leading to a stronger contact.

Variations

Place three poles on a 20 metre circle, and ride the canter on each rein. This is a useful preparation for riding the same exercise over jumps and is a good exercise for horse and rider to work on maintaining an even rhythm, length of stride and even turns on the circle.

EXERCISE 4

Canter to Small Jumps

Introduce

- When the canter can be maintained reasonably well in self-carriage, so that you are not having to push with the seat at every stride to keep the canter, nor having to keep a strong hold to prevent the canter from getting faster.

- When the horse has mastered trotting to small jumps in a reasonable rhythm.

- When your horse is lazy and so loses the impulsion too much when approaching from trot.

The exercise

- Set up an ascending vertical i.e. a small fence with a groundline set slightly out from the base of the jump so that the horse cannot get too close to the base of the jump.

- Introduce initially by keeping the canter going forwards after jumping a small fence from trot.

- Then introduce jumping from the canter having first done a good transition to canter. Once the rhythm has been established, approach the jump while endeavouring to keep your horse in-line and on-line just as you would in training the dressage.

- It is best to be in a light seat so that you can readily adjust your seat depending on whether your horse lengthens or shortens its stride in the approach. The leg, whip or spur is there if your horse loses energy within its canter.

- Work on trying to maintain the same canter after the jump as before. Some horses will slow down after the jump, others will accelerate.

- Take as much time as you need to re-establish the canter before approaching the next jump from canter.

Common problems

The horse accelerates or even runs away on landing.

- Discipline the horse in the same way as you would execute an acute transition in the dressage arena. Avoid pulling with the reins in the first stride on landing without first using the appropriate body language. Some horses need the discipline because they are exuberant, while others accelerate because they lose their balance after the jump.

The horse does not stay straight in the approach or tries to run out.

- In the approach keep your position more in the 'remount' or even dressage position so that you have more contact with the saddle, and then hold your hands apart with the objective of keeping your horse on-line and in-line. A horse that runs out will always accelerate towards the jump, so try and keep the rhythm the same by using your body language supported by your hand actions. Make sure you have your eye on the jump well in advance. If you take your eye off the jump you will tend to lose your line.

The horse gets its stride wrong and gets too close to the jump.

- Try to ride a more forward canter on a longer stride, but help the balance by staying in a more upright position and avoid getting in front of the movement with your upper body by trying to fold too soon. It is better when jumping these small jumps at this stage to be slightly left behind than ahead of the movement.

The horse consistently takes-off a long way from the jump.

● It is probably because your contact is too strong. Try to ride on a softer contact and keep a more even rhythm to the jump. Don't make the mistake of trying to look for a stride at this stage, because you will then forget to think about keeping an even rhythm.

EXERCISE 5

Small Courses, Including New Shapes, Colours and Styles

Introduce

As soon as your horse is able to maintain the canter to single jumps in a reasonable rhythm and to maintain or recover that rhythm fairly soon after the jump. At this stage your horse may be a bit spooky about any different shapes, colours and styles of jump, but if you concentrate on the basics of the jumping and start small, building up along with its confidence, then it will gradually accept the fillers.

The exercise – Use of different shapes and styles of jump

Cross-rails are used to encourage the horse to focus on the centre of the fence. As the cross is raised so the angle of each rail becomes steeper and the gap between each side becomes narrower. This encourages the horse to be more careful with the foreleg. High crosses should not be used on their own without a ground line or a back rail for novice horses, but are useful with more experienced horses. When used as the front element of a spread fence they encourage the horse to focus on the centre of the fence and to draw the foreleg forwards towards the back rail. This provides an encouraging shape of jump for the novice horse.

Cross-rails.

Ascending verticals have a ground line set in front of the fence as a general rule equivalent to half the height of the jump. Ascending verticals are used in training to help the horse to cope with vertical fences by preventing it from getting so deep to the fence that it is unable to avoid hitting it. The ascending vertical is the appropriate shape for the young horse, the novice rider and, in training, for the more experienced horse that is not so sharp with his foreleg. The ground line prevents the horse getting too close to the fence.

Ascending vertical.

True verticals include planks, gates and walls. The accurate take-off point is approximately the same distance away from the jump as the height of the jump. Most horses and riders find it difficult to jump these fences accurately. Because of this recognized difficulty, the temptation is to over shorten or collect the canter in an attempt to see a stride to the fence. This brings the take-off point closer to the base

True vertical.

of the fence, which makes it difficult for the horse to draw the foreleg up and forwards over the fence. The key to jumping true verticals accurately is for the horse to have a balanced canter and an even length of stride to the fence and for the rider to avoid over 'folding' but rather to allow the horse to come up to you.

Ascending spreads include the triple bar. The take-off point for an ascending spread is approximately one-and-a-half times the height of the fence away from the back rail, but as long as the approach is sufficiently active and forward, the accuracy of the take-off point is not so important. If the horse is a bit 'off' the fence then the increased speed will enable the horse to clear the back rail, while if the horse gets too close, the foreleg will still have room to draw forward over the fence. The difficulty arises when a spread fence is approached off a relatively tight turn. The rider must then actively ride the horse forwards off the turn so that the canter is already sufficiently forward to cope with the width even before the horse is square to the fence. For some riders the wide triple bar causes anxiety because of the width and as a result the negative thinking brings about the very problem the rider is worried about i.e. that the horse will not be able to reach the back rail. Once the rider appreciates that this jump is very forgiving to the rider and horse as long as he rides forward to it then the rider will gain confidence and so will the horse.

Ascending spread.

Oxers, including true and ascending oxers, have a take-off point approximately one-and-a-half times the height of the oxer away from the centre of the spread. The highest point of the horse's jump will be over the centre of the spread and has to be sufficient to allow it to clear the back rail with its hind leg. It must have enough forward momentum to cope with the spread and yet, at the point of take-off, be sufficiently engaged and balanced to be able to clear the front rail. Horses tend to respect oxers more than verticals, and for this reason the first fence of a course is usually an ascending oxer to encourage the horse and rider. A true oxer, where the front rail is the same height as the back rail is more difficult for the horse and rider because the front rail presents the same problem as a true vertical but then the horse must stretch for the back rail. When the jump is relatively high and wide in advanced show jumping, the horse must ventriflex its back to clear the back rail. This flexibility of the horse's back to both bascule over the top of the fence and yet ventriflex the back on the landing side is a key element that differentiates the talented show jumper from the event horse.

Oxer.

Common problems

Refusals

Your horse may refuse for a number of reasons. Novice horses refuse because of a lack of confidence. They may be spooky or not like the appearance of a fence, or they may think the fence is too big. They may also refuse if their stride brings them to an impossible spot, very close to a fence. Even experienced horses may refuse at the last moment if they think they are on an impossible stride. This often happens with experienced horses in combinations if they do not think they can cope with the distances between the fences, i.e. too long or too short. A horse that is resistant or 'nappy' may refuse because of a reluctance to go forward rather than because of the fence. The rider can sometimes be the cause of a refusal if he restricts the horse with the reins or, having held a strong contact in the approach to the fence, 'drops' the horse at the point of take-off.

Each situation is different and must be dealt with differently, so it is important to analyze why a horse refuses and to address the problem correctly. But it is also important that the horse learns from the start of its training that a refusal is not an easy option. The horse has a responsibility to have a go as well as the rider. Furthermore, the rider should not have to be perfect every time. One of your horse's responsibilities is to get you out of trouble. If it stops then it must know that you are not pleased with it. To what extent you scold the horse will depend on its attitude and the cause of the refusal. Equally, the rider has a responsibility to set the questions fairly and be prepared to change the exercise or improve his riding to avoid causing the horse to refuse.

Running out

This may happen for any of the reasons that a horse refuses. The difference is that in the case of a run-out the horse accelerates and runs through the contact to avoid the jump rather stopping. Just as with refusals, the horse must learn that it is not an easy option, but at least a horse that runs out is going forwards if also sideways. Your responsibility as a rider is to correct the crookedness that allows the shoulder to escape in the same way as you would do in the dressage training. The horse will tend to bend in the neck away from the direction of the run-out, so maintaining a stronger contact, if not a flexion, towards the side to which the horse tends to run out will help to keep it in line. It must also learn to maintain an even rhythm and length of stride to the jump. A horse that runs out will tend to lengthen the stride and accelerate towards the jump in the last few strides, often giving the rider the feeling that it is enthusiastically going for the jump and then 'ducking' out at the last second.

If your horse runs out, you should halt immediately, scold it, turn back towards the jump but without turning a circle and then represent it to the jump. If the horse is young and the fences are small, it is usually better to approach the fence again from a relatively short distance and, whether in trot or canter, you should control the speed and the line by coming to the fence in a more upright position, keeping the hands apart to create a corridor with the reins. Keep a firm contact with the lower legs and, if necessary, use spurs depending on the sensitivity of your horse to your leg.

Rushing

A young horse will not rush in its first attempts at jumping. It will tend to have too much respect or fear of the fences. A horse learns to rush because the rider rides it too strongly to the fence. A highly strung, forward going horse will soon learn to rush if over ridden in the last few strides. Sometimes horses rush through exuberance, sometimes through panic apparently shutting their eyes as they race at the fence. A horse may refuse at the start of the training and then, having been scolded with the whip or the spurs, may rush at the fence in fear of the rider.

As with refusals and run-outs, it is important to analyze the underlying reason for your horse rushing. In the case of the horse that is panicking or is frightened of the jumps, the exercise must be made easier and the rider can then concentrate, as with the flat work, on teaching the horse to maintain a rhythm and an even length of stride both before the jump and after the jump. A horse that is frightened of its mouth will often rush the more the rider pulls on the rein. Sitting deeper in the saddle tends to have a driving effect as well as tightening the horse's back and so often makes the problem worse. It is usually better to take more weight on to the stirrups whilst bracing the back to support the restraining rein actions.

The exuberant horse will usually relax and cease rushing after it has done enough work, as long as the rider does not make the problem worse by 'hooking and firing'. A rider who is not confident of seeing a good stride to a fence will often over shorten the canter before the fence while looking for a stride and then, upon seeing the stride, will attack the fence with seat and leg. This teaches your horse to rush at the fences in the last few strides. By focusing on the rhythm and an even length of stride both before and after the fence, rather than on looking for a stride, you can teach your horse to do the same. This is as much an issue of confidence for the rider as it is for the horse.

Laziness

Horses that jump in a lazy manner will often shorten their stride before a fence and then leave themselves too much to do when they get to the fence. The primary correction with such horses is to ride them actively away from the fence with the leg and, if necessary, the whip. In this way they will learn to attack the fence in anticipation of being sent on strongly after it. In addition the horse can be reminded in the flat work between the fences to remain forward thinking and energetic.

Spookiness

Spooky horses are often good jumpers once they have become accustomed to the different shapes, colours and types of fence. They often react by jumping higher and being more careful, but some tighten in the back and do not jump so well. Those that jump well are not a problem, but the ones that tighten need to be ridden in many different situations and over different fences until they become more relaxed and less spooky. Some horses are spooky only at certain types of fences, such as ditches or water trays, and require plenty of practise over small versions of these obstacles until they accept them. Even then, if they have not seen one for a while they are often spooky when they come to see it again.

PART TWO

Secondary Training

'If you teach your horse to go with a light hand on the bit, and yet to hold his head high and to arch his neck, you will be making him do just what the animal himself glories and delights in.'

Xenophon, The Art of Horsemanship
(Xenophon, born approx 430BC)

CHAPTER FIVE

Collection

THE PRIMARY PHASE OF the training is never complete but, at some stage, your horse should move on to secondary training where the emphasis is on collection and the use of that collection in performance. Without the basics, it is not possible to have collection, and throughout the training, even as your horse performs and competes at a higher level, it is necessary to come back again and again to the basics.

The dressage horse is required to show collection in walk, trot and canter. So is the event horse in the dressage arena, though to a lesser degree. The show jumper has no direct need for collection in trot, but has to be able to collect its canter. It needs to be able to shorten its stride length without losing the energy in the step. This gives it the power and the accuracy for its jump. The event horse must also be able to extend and collect on the cross-country course when required.

Defining Collection

Collection involves:

- A change in the horse's longitudinal balance, causing a transfer of weight towards the flexed hindquarters, giving an 'uphill' appearance.

- A raising and arching of the neck, which remains still (i.e. does not oscillate up and down).

- A shortening of the horse's stride within the same rhythm, combined with an increase in energy, or 'spring', in each stride, i.e. impulsion. In German this is called '*schwung*', a word with a ring about it that, for me, combines the notions of swing and power.

In primary training

- The horse is taught to understand and respond to the rider's communication through body language supported by the actions of the leg and the rein.

● This understanding and acceptance is consolidated through the early training exercises that have a gymnastic purpose and lead to the horse learning to carry itself in a posture from which collection can be developed.

● The basic dressage exercises combined with the complementary jumping exercises, the hill work and the general conditioning, prepare the horse for secondary training.

In secondary training

The horse learns to collect in response to the rider's body language and through the exercises that it is taught in this phase of its training. These exercises require varying degrees of collection and can be divided into three groups.

● The *elementary* collecting exercises include shoulder-in, pirouettes in walk, acute transitions and small circles. To be executed, these exercises do not require much collection, but as the demands within the exercises are gradually increased and the rider's body language asks for more collection, they bring about a higher state of collection in the horse.

● The *intermediate* collecting exercises include travers, renvers, half-pass and early piaffe steps. These exercises require a greater degree of collection before they can be ridden and, as the horse learns to perform them well, they bring about even more collection. When in difficulty with these exercises, the solution usually lies in going back to one of the elementary collecting exercises or some element of the basic training, and then trying again. The collection brought about through these exercises is then used to develop expressive flying changes and the extended paces, in particular the extended trot and canter and related transitions.

● The *advanced* exercises are reserved for advanced dressage and are less relevant to jumping training. They include series changes down to tempi-changes (i.e. one time changes), counter changes in half-pass, canter pirouettes, piaffe and passage. These are both collecting exercises and, in the case of the piaffe and passage, exercises that demonstrate the quality of the collection. When in difficulty with any of these exercises the solution lies in improving the quality of the collection, which often means returning to previous exercises and may include going right back to the basic training.

Requirements for Collection

1. *A good 'connection over the back', engaged hind legs, straightness and the horse drawing forward into the contact.*

The basic dressage that formed a part of the primary training prepares the horse for the work in collection, in particular the lateral submission leading to straightness and longitudinal submission. The freeing and lightening of the forehand as the hind leg is engaged and active is dependent on the supporting role of the horse's topline. The muscles of the neck and back, if stretched and supporting, will draw up the base of the neck and lead to its raised and arched appearance. This must be volunteered by the horse rather than carried by the rider's hands.

The stretching of the neck upwards and forwards leads to the freedom of the forehand and a rounder action coming from the shoulder because the muscle (brachiocephalic) that draws the forearm forward is attached at the poll. (See section on bio-mechanics.) The more forward is the fixed point from which the muscle pulls, the more forward will the foreleg be drawn. Conversely, the head and neck drawn back into the shoulders, whether with the horse's face at the vertical or ahead of the vertical, will have a restricting effect on the movement of the forelimb.

As the horse's top line becomes stronger, in particular the neck muscles that support the forehand, and as the hind leg is engaged and flexed, so the horse is able to elevate the forehand without using the oscillations of its head and neck as a way of lifting up the forehand.

A dressage horse is collected and submissive to the extent that its head hangs from the poll more or less at the vertical, but the show jumper or event horse, that must concentrate on the approaching fence, should not be expected to have its face at the vertical because it can focus on the jump better when it has the face ahead of the vertical.

2. *Willingness to flex the hind leg leading to the lowering of the hindquarters associated with the transfer of weight.*

The hind leg, placed well forward under the horse, must be encouraged to act as a shock absorber and a spring, so that the ride becomes more comfortable and so that the energy stored by the muscles in the shock-absorbing phase is re-imparted into the next step or over the jump. This gives rise to the elasticity of the steps in dressage and the power and athleticism in the jump.

This flexion of the hind leg slows down propulsion, and therefore a greater effort is required to push off the hind leg in the next phase. Achieving the willing flexion of the hind leg is partly a question of understanding by the horse, which comes about through the exercises used within secondary training, and partly a question of the conformation and strength of the hind leg, in particular the angles as well as strength and soundness of the stifle and hock joints and physical strength of the groups of hindquarter muscles that are involved. These propulsive muscles of the hind leg are also the supporting or shock absorbing muscles, and their strength is developed gradually through the basic work as well as through hill work and jumping.

The demands for greater collection can only be increased gradually as the horse matures physically. If it is asked too soon for sustained collection it will lose confidence, and then either 'give up' and lose energy, or look for a way to avoid collection by becoming crooked, stiffening the hind leg or even napping and rearing.

3. *A strong but contained desire to go forwards, leading to a compressed energy like a coiled spring.*

A lazy horse that is reluctant to go forward cannot be taught to maintain collection in self-carriage. It will always have to be held together. The inner energy, or desire to go forwards, can easily be stifled in the early training if you do not hand responsibility to the horse to keep going on its own without being driven at every stride. It can also be lost if the rider asks for too much collection too soon.

The training must be sensitive to this aspect above all others. Just as in the primary training the order of priorities placed energy or forward thought at the top of the list, so the same order of priorities applies in the secondary training. We must be prepared to go back to basics frequently to re-establish and also to take the pressure off.

The jumping horse has the advantage of increased motivation. If it enjoys its jumping and if its confidence is nurtured by not being over-faced, then the jumping work will help to maintain its enthusiasm and hence its natural energy.

The Objective of Collection

Lightening of the forehand and increased agility leading to:

- Elasticity of the steps, giving rise to increased cadence and expression in the dressage test.

- Accurate show jumping and increased athleticism on the cross-country.

- Increased power in jumping.

- More expression in the extended paces.

The Use of Collection

Collection is a preparation. It should not be seen as an end in itself but as a means to an end. It prepares the horse for the performance.

In the case of the dressage horse, the accumulated impulsion generated in the collection is either contained within the collected movements, leading to the execution of those movements with grace, expression and apparent ease, or is used in a forward and upward direction. A good extended trot can only come from collection. In High School dressage performed, for example, in the Spanish Riding School, where the 'Airs above the Ground' represent the performance, the preparation is extreme collection either sustained in the levade or leading to its use in an explosive upward and forward direction in the capriole and courbette.

The movements the dressage horse is asked to perform at Grand Prix level are tests of the ability of the horse to hold a sustained collection in self-carriage. Before reaching Grand Prix, the dressage tests at Prix St George and below, whilst being tests of the schooling at that level, also include exercises that form part of the training or preparation for the more demanding movements at Grand Prix level. Exercises such as shoulder-in, travers and renvers are primarily schooling exercises even though they have a place in the dressage tests. In the case of the dressage horse there is a grey area between what is a test and what is a training exercise.

There is no such grey area in show jumping or cross-country riding. The collection is a preparation for jumping. In jumping, the accumulated impulsion is not contained for long and is used in an upwards and forwards movement over the jump. The quality of the jumping is to a large extent a reflection of the quality of the collection that precedes it. Whereas in dressage competitions prior to Grand Prix level it is possible, to some extent, to cover up the problems that arise from insufficient or incorrect collection, in jumping or cross-country it is not so easy. Although the degree of collection required of the advanced eventer or show jumper is less than the advanced dressage horse, the quality of that collection has to be as good or better, because ultimately the horse and rider's safety are at stake.

The Relevance of Collection

In **dressage,** collection is equally important in all three paces. In advanced dressage, it has to be to a high degree and sustained for longer periods, and it has also to be done without losing any regularity of the steps.

The *pirouette* demands the ultimate in terms of collection in both walk and canter. The horse is expected to keep marking time regularly with the hind legs more or less on the spot while the forehand comes around in a circle. The canter pirouette places great strain on the muscles of the hindquarters and the top-line because of the degree to which the longitudinal balance is altered towards the hindquarters and the consequent flexion and lowering of the hindquarters.

The *piaffe* and *passage* require the greatest degree of collection in trot. In piaffe, the sustained flexion of the engaged haunches enables the horse to elevate the forehand without travelling forwards. In the passage, the 'coiling of the spring' produced in the engaged hind leg, together with the muscles that support the top-line and provide the connection to the forehand, lead to the increased cadence of the trot. This produces an elevated gesture of the foreleg at the same time as the active hind leg remains in a semi-flexed state throughout.

In **show jumping** the requirement for collection is focused on the canter. There is no requirement for collection within the trot work and the only requirement for collection in the walk is in order to improve the transition to canter, the simple changes and the flying changes.

The degree of collection required in the canter in advanced show jumping approximates the degree of collection required of the advanced dressage horse but only for short moments. As the demands in terms of size of fence and technicality of the course increase, so the horse must be able to collect and extend on demand, and then use the contained energy within the jump.

The stride must not just be able to shorten but must at the same time retain if not increase the amount of energy in each stride. The canter can be likened to a football that is gradually filled with air and becomes more bouncy. It is worth watching an athlete in his run-up to the high jump rail to see the springiness in his stride.

above left The canter pirouette, the most demanding movement in canter in terms of collection. Christine Traurig on Etienne.

above right The piaffe, shown by Emile Faurie on Virtue, and (*left*) passage, shown by Claus Balkenhol on Goldstern, the movements demanding the most collection in the trot.

In **eventing** the horse is required to perform in the dressage arena as well as in the show jumping arena and on the cross-country, so it must show some collection in all three paces. The degree of collection required in all three paces is less than in advanced dressage, and, in canter, it could be argued that it is less than is needed for advanced show jumping, given that the jumps are much smaller. However, the quickness of reaction and athleticism required on the cross-country course requires the ability to collect instantly when necessary. A horse that is galloping long and flat, on the forehand, is not able to get itself out of trouble quickly.

In the dressage arena, even at four-star level, the movements in trot are prescribed to be ridden in a working trot, although some degree of collection is required in riding the smaller circles, the shoulder-in and the half-pass. Collection is also needed in the preparation for the extended trot, and it generally leads to the development of more expressive paces.

The FEI dressage tests at three and four-star level now prescribe collected canter rather than working canter. This accurately reflects the need for the event horse to be able to collect the canter in order to cope with the technicalities of the modern cross-country courses.

The Rider's Role in Collection

One of the rider's short term goals will be to ask the horse to collect its stride, usually in preparation for something else, for example a pirouette or a jump. You have to teach your horse how to collect and to recognize your body language that means collect.

Stretch up and become more still with the seat in the saddle. Remember: the use of the seat governs the length of stride while the use of the leg creates energy. To indicate to the horse that you want it to shorten its stride you must cease to push with the seat especially in canter. With some horses, the mere act of 'following' the canter with the seat has a slight driving or lengthening effect. Of course, you must be ready to use the seat if your horse tries to shorten its stride too much and stops thinking forwards. A common fault in collection, both in dressage and jumping, is the use of a strong driving seat which then has to be contradicted by a strong restraining rein action and leads to the horse becoming stronger in the hand, either leaning or pulling. Alternatively it can lead to a tightening or even hollowing of the horse's back.

The same principle for achieving collection applies when riding in the forward seat in the jumping arena or on the cross-country. The upper body must draw up and back to indicate to the horse to collect the stride. The more collected you want the canter, the more upright the body must come, but never to the point that it comes behind the vertical because in this case you will start to have a driving effect with your seat. The weight of the body should remain distributed between the seat and the stirrup, and your horse should recognize the slight changes in the weight distribution.

The more the weight comes into the saddle (without a driving effect) then the more the weight is transferred to the hindquarters. The positioning of the seat in the saddle has an effect on the longitudinal balance of the horse. By sitting a bit further back in the saddle (without pushing with the seat) and with an upper body stretching up, you will have the effect of transferring the weight backwards. The effect will only be temporary. It is the act of making that change in position, within one stride, that will have the rebalancing effect. After that you must return to the centre of the saddle and, if necessary, repeat the action.

The body language must be supported by half-halts. These must, as ever, be applied down the outside rein. The frequency of the half-halts depends on the reaction from the horse, but they must never be applied in every stride. The most often that they should be used is every other stride. If you get a rhythm in your mind of applying the half-halt every other stride then you can simply 'adjust the volume', as you would do on a radio. Increase the volume if your horse is not listening, or turn the volume down if your horse has understood and is sufficiently collected in self-carriage, but never switch the radio off. In that way you will be better able to keep the rhythm and get the timing right when you do need to half-halt.

This is crucial. One of the objectives in achieving self-carriage in collection is the reduction in the movement (oscillation) of the head and neck within the paces, particularly in walk and canter but also in trot in the movements of piaffe and passage. The application of the half-halting rein action should be timed to reduce this oscillation. The hands and arms should cease to follow the movement as much and, by becoming more still, you indicate to the horse that you want it to stop using its neck as part of the movement.

The moment to apply the rein action in the canter is at the moment of the 'downward nod' of the head and neck, which is at the same time that the horse's outside front foot comes to the floor. It is often tempting, particularly when the horse is struggling in collection and losing energy, to use the rein action to 'lift' the forehand off the floor rather than use the energizing action of the leg, whip or spur. This can happen when a horse that is lazy intimidates its rider to the extent that the rider is unwilling to use the whip or spur to get a reaction. This can also happen when there is a loss of balance on to the forehand and the horse then uses the oscillation of the neck to lift the forehand off the floor

The half-halt actions down the rein in themselves will not be effective in obtaining a response to the body language of collection without impulsion derived from energy and lateral submission. It may be necessary to use the touch of the leg, whip or spur to achieve that. The leg can have a simple energizing effect or it can have an engaging effect, depending on how it is used. (see 'Communicating by touch' in chapter 3.) It is also used to elicit the lateral submission, which is a pre-condition for collection. Generally, the leg should not be applied at the same moment as the half-halt. (See section on half-halts.)

Elementary Collecting Exercises

The rider obviously has an important direct role in working towards collection through the way he uses his body language supported by seat, legs and half-halts. However, just as important are the various exercises which place the horse in a position to offer collection. You can then build on the collection offered and develop your horse's confidence and ability to maintain collection. The basis of these exercises is the loading of the hindquarters at the same time as handing responsibility for support of the forehand to the horse.

During the primary training, exercises are used to achieve lateral submission and thereby the longitudinal submission leading to the increased engagement of the hind leg, the connection over the back and straightness. Work towards collection can then be developed through gymnastic exercises: shoulder-in – pirouettes – reducing the size of circles – acute transitions – (trot/halt/trot, canter/walk/canter) – travers and renvers – half-pass. The demands are increased through these collecting exercises and then the pressure taken off by returning to the basic exercises.

It is only by increasing and sustaining the demands that the horse will become stronger; but if the demands are unreasonable, the horse will lose confidence and defend itself by resistance. Equally, you can sometimes not be demanding enough. The extent to which the demands are increased will vary from horse to horse depending on temperament and physique.

The Shoulder-in

Introduce

When the horse is prepared to offer the lateral submission to the inside through the leg-yielding exercise as well as remaining straight through the body.

The objective

'The difference between leg-yielding and shoulder-in is the bend around the inside leg.'

To cause the horse to bring the inside hind leg forward and under the body and therefore slightly closer to its centre of gravity at the moment of support. This helps to transfer the weight more towards the hind leg. That is why it is a collecting exercise. The important *difference between leg-yielding and shoulder-in is the bend around the inside leg* required in the shoulder-in compared to the straightness required in leg-yielding.

The exercise

- As the name implies, the shoulder-in involves the positioning of the horse's shoulders on the inside track. The horse's forehand should be at an angle of about 30 degrees from the track.

- The horse should offer the lateral submission to the inside and so be bent uniformly around the inside leg. The lateral flexion at the poll should lead to the horse's head hanging vertically from the poll without any tilting.

● In the classical shoulder-in, the degree of bend should be the same as for a six-metre circle, or volte. Looking at the horse from above, the pelvis/hips of the horse face forwards along the track so that a line drawn through the two points of the hips would be at 90 degrees to the wall. The horse's shoulders are off the track to the extent that the horse's outside foreleg is on the same track as the inside hind leg. This means that the horse is moving on three tracks.

● At the start of the work in collection the degree of bend is no more than for a ten metre circle.

Position Statement (as for all lateral work – see page 77)

In preparation for the movement:

1. Sit to the inside.

2. Shorten the inside rein so that as the horse flexes to the inside in response to an allowing outside rein your elbow will remain just in front of your hip.

3. Open the inside hip to engage the inside hind but keep an even contact with both legs so that the subsequent touch of the outside leg at the girth brings the forehand on to the inside track.

To start the movement:

4. Bring the inside rein slightly away from the horse's neck to keep a straight line to the horse's mouth.

5. Bring the outside hand closer to the withers, but don't allow the horse to find support on the rein by pushing its neck against it.

6. Point the outside foot down the line of the shoulder-in.

Shoulder-in.

Restraining Rein Actions – Half-halts

Tips for the riders

In preparation for the shoulder-in, the *inside rein* must be shortened sufficiently to allow the hand to maintain the lateral flexion without any backward pull on the rein. In general, the inside hand should be kept just in front of the outside hand. The inside rein should never pull across the withers, as it will block the impulsion and engagement of the inside hind and cause the horse to fall outwards. It also tends to lead to over-bending to the inside at the base of the neck. The axiom of 'straight line from elbow through the hand to the horse's mouth' applies equally to the horizontal plane as to the vertical (side to side as much as up and down).

The role of the *outside rein* is to regulate the pace and the bend. The half-halts promote greater collection by extending the moment of support of the inside hind leg. Keep the outside hand near the withers and act with a half-halt every time the outside forefoot comes to the ground (i.e. every other stride) but the intensity of the half-halt varies in relation to the response – remember the radio analogy!

A frequent error is to use the inside leg to push the quarters over with a backward pressure, often combined with the drawing up of the heel instead of *opening the inside hip*. At the same time, the outside leg comes off the horse, and the fence or wall of the arena takes over the role of the outside leg. Since, in most cases, dressage tests ask for the shoulder-in along the track, riders often get away with this until they have to ride the exercise on the centre line. For this reason it is a good exercise to ride the shoulder-in away from the wall, for example along the three-quarter line or on the centre line.

It helps to *point the outside foot down the line* along which the shoulder-in is being ridden so that if the horse drifts outwards with the quarters or shoulders it will come against the outside leg, while if it drifts inwards it will come against the inside leg. The outside leg should be positioned so the stirrup leather is hanging vertically from the stirrup bar at, or just behind the girth, to correct the horse if it steps away from the inside leg rather than coming around it, or if it falls out with the shoulder.

Training the horse

- The shoulder-in is developed out of leg-yielding and small circles.

- A well-ridden corner will set the horse up for the shoulder-in. The horse is asked to come around the leg into the shoulder-in as if it were going to come on to a small circle.

- Both of the rider's legs should be effective by their presence in maintaining the uniform bend and thereby the engagement of the inside hind, rather than by a continuous pressure. Once the horse has understood and accepted your position for the shoulder-in then it should maintain it without the constant pressure of the leg or reins.

- If the horse is genuinely laterally submissive, it will come around the inside leg and take the outside rein whilst accepting the rhythmical and correctly timed half-halts.

Common problems

Too shallow an angle to the track with excessive bend at the base of the neck and the shoulder falling out.

- This is very often caused by the rider slipping to the outside, using too much inside rein and inside leg without controlling the bend with the outside rein and outside leg.

Excessive angle with insufficient bend through the body, combined with hind legs crossing. In effect the horse is performing a leg-yielding.

● These problems are usually caused by the incorrect position statement and application of the supporting aids on the part of the rider, and are, at least in theory, relatively easy to resolve.

The horse comes against the inside leg and refuses to respond to the correction.

● The rider must return to the basic exercises explained previously and even, if necessary, to the T-a-F exercise until there is a better response to the lateral leg aid.

The horse tilts its head or resists lateral flexion at the poll.

● This is a more difficult problem to resolve as it originates from the horse's defensive reactions in the jaw and at the poll. The reaction can be caused by the overuse of the inside rein to obtain the bend, which will often result in the horse tilting the nose outwards and the ears inwards. To resolve this problem it is necessary to go back to the basic work to achieve lateral submission, and then when achieved be careful not to use too strong an inside rein. The real solution lies in persuading the horse to relax at the poll and take the outside rein, accepting an even and light contact in both reins through the exercise.

  The important point to remember with the shoulder-in is that the emphasis is on the horse bringing its body towards and around the inside leg, even though in terms of the direction of the movement the horse is seen to be moving away from the bend. This is why the shoulder-in is more closely related to the pirouette and the half-pass than to the leg-yield.

The Pirouette in Walk

Objective

To increase the mobility of the forehand and transfer the horse's weight more towards the hind leg.

The exercise

This is a development of the turn about the haunches described in primary training. The difference between the pirouette and the T-a-H is one of degree. In the true pirouette the horse is required to mark time with the inside hind as the forehand comes around. The degree of engagement of the hind leg and rounding of the back is therefore greater.

  In preparation for the movement:

1. Assume the same *position statement* as for shoulder-in except that the inside rein must be brought a bit closer to the neck as for an indirect rein. The outside hand is taken very slightly away from the neck to allow the lateral flexion to the inside

Pirouette in walk.

whilst keeping the horse straight on the line being ridden. This, supported by the touch of the inside leg, will encourage the horse to engage the inside hind leg.

2. Collect the walk through the body language by becoming more stretched up. Cease following the walk with the seat, but touch with the leg if necessary to keep the energy in the walk steps whilst maintaining the rhythm in the walk.

To start the movement:

3. Apply a half-halt down the outside rein at the moment the outside fore comes to the floor followed by a touch of the outside leg at the girth, as the foreleg comes forward, to encourage it to reach across the body in front of the inside foreleg, just as with the T-a-H.

4. Monitor the energy of the steps to make sure the inside hind leg remains active. Use the legs alternately in rhythm with the walk, varying the sharpness of the touch depending on the reaction.

Tips for the rider

- *Correct the position statement at least once during the pirouette* because you will tend to slip to the outside. This correction should lighten the seat for one step, which encourages the horse to keep its back up.

- *Keep the inside rein close to the neck as a positional rein* to maintain the lateral flexion to the inside, but encourage the horse to think forwards by using it with an upward action directed towards the opposite ear, as you would with an indirect rein.

- *Use the half-halts down the outside rein to support the body language,* asking the horse to remain on the spot.

- *The outside rein action can be applied as a direct rein of opposition* to support the outside leg in controlling the quarters if the horse has a tendency to swing them out. This often happens towards the second part of the pirouette. Be careful to allow sufficiently with the outside rein between the half-halts in order to allow the forehand to come around.

Common problems

The quarters come in at the start of the pirouette.

- This is usually because the rider's outside leg is too far back and the inside hip is not 'open' enough to apply the touch of inside leg while the lateral flexion is established to the inside. This often leads to the pirouette being too large or off the track.

There is a loss of lateral flexion to the inside, often combined with the horse stepping short or backwards.

● Riders often use the outside rein pressing against the side of the neck as a support, or even a substitute, for the outside leg talking to the forehand. Whilst bringing the outside rein to the neck without an increase in the contact (indirect rein) is correct at the moment the outside foreleg is reaching forward and across the body, increasing the contact by pulling the rein across the neck will always block the movement.

The inside hind leg 'sticks' or becomes inactive.

● This happens because the rein actions block the pirouette, or because the horse is lazy and the rider is not quick enough to react with the inside leg.

The pirouette lacks collection and is more like a small circle with the quarters in.

● This happens when the walk is not collected sufficiently before the start and the hind leg is not sufficiently engaged.

Acute Transitions (trot-halt-trot, canter-walk-canter including simple changes, trot-reinback-trot)

Objective

To achieve collection through the engaging and loading effect of the downward transitions combined with the shorter and yet more elastic and active steps produced from the upward transitions.

The exercise

To be performed correctly, the horse has to learn to control its longitudinal balance on the hind leg. The energy of the forward movement must be controlled and momentarily stored, like a spring, through the flexion of the well-engaged hind leg combined with the muscles of the top line (posture muscles). It is then re-imparted into the next step or stride. The tension in the muscles is an elastic tension rather than a bracing or blocking tension. If the horse braces these muscles and locks the joints, the transitions will appear abrupt and the quality of the pace after the transition will not be enhanced.

As with the shoulder-in and the walk pirouette, these transition exercises initially require a degree of collection, but they also teach the horse to collect. They do so by placing a demand upon the horse to which it will naturally respond by adopting a 'posture for collection', as long as it is both 'laterally submissive' and 'connected over the back'.

1. Trot-halt-trot

Preparation for the transitions When preparing for the transition to halt, the position statement and body language are the same as for the zone exercise. It helps to have a rhythm in your mind that reminds you of the trot rhythm appropriate to your horse. That rhythm or 'music' should have some life or dance quality about it rather than be just the dead tick-tock of a metronome, so that it encourages you to keep the steps active and elastic as well as regular and rhythmical.

Riding and training Start the exercise on a circle because this makes it easier to monitor and maintain the engagement of the hind leg and the 'connection over the back'. Adopt the position statement for riding a circle, i.e. sit to the inside with the inside hip open. At the moment of the transition, make sure the body language clearly says halt, and support with the actions of the hand whilst keeping the legs in contact with the horse's side. Soften the fist just before the transition is finished. (An analogy here is making an emergency stop with your car: to avoid throwing your passengers backwards and forwards, the brake has to be eased just before the car stops.)

A useful exercise to establish the correct feel for your body language is to execute a transition from a run to a halt on your own feet without losing your balance and then directly into an active run again. In the upwards transition, from halt to trot, the body language is expecting the trot and therefore fractionally gets ahead of the first step. The quicker you want to stop and the faster you want to run the more obvious will be your body language, so the more obviously will you feel what is the appropriate body language when you are on your horse. But keep in mind that one of the objectives within dressage training is to minimize the obvious aids.

The touch of the leg, which supports the body language, must be followed by a momentary taking-off of the leg. Remember the requirement for a second's delay between touch and reaction. If the horse is repeatedly lazy in taking the first step directly into trot, then the whip must be used at the same time as the light touch of the leg to support the body language. In this way you will teach your horse a conditioned reflex response to your body language.

In this exercise much depends on the rider's level of expectation and inner feeling for the transition. If the rider has no sense of crispness or urgency then neither will the horse.

If however the horse is tense and over reactive then you will have to use a lighter touch of leg and be careful not to get left behind during the transition, which will cause the horse to tighten the back muscles and push with the hind leg into the first trot step rather than bring the inside hind forwards. As ever, the key is the connection over the back.

Establishing the square, engaged halt When your horse is working correctly 'over the back', is straight, is in good horizontal balance and performing the 'zone' exercise well, then the establishment of the engaged, square halt should happen naturally. At the point of the transition, you must remember to soften the hand just before the horse takes the last step, so that it does not step backwards or leave a hind leg out behind. It also helps to draw your upper body up and take the thigh off the saddle just before the halt is established to give the horse a chance to keep its back up and hind leg engaged. If it is tight in the back it will halt with the hind legs out behind.

The trot steps into the halt must maintain an even activity. If the last step is lazy, then the horse will leave the hind leg out behind. The young horse does not find it natural to be square in halt. Once it has learnt to remain immobile in the halt, then some training to teach it to be in the habit of squaring up will help for the dressage tests. The horse should develop a conscience about it. Such training involves touching with the whip or spur on the side that it leaves its hind leg back. If it is inclined to rest a hind leg in the halt, then touch on the other side. Even the best riders need someone on the ground to shout quickly which hind leg is back, or if the halt is square, because it not always easy to feel, especially if the surface on which you are riding is not absolutely even.

Common faults; trot-halt

Loss of rhythm or halt too abrupt.

- This can happen when your horse is not really going forwards in self-carriage, so it stops on the front leg rather than with the hind leg being engaged and acting as the shock absorber. Try to move the horse laterally during the transition or put it into a slight shoulder-in position towards the side to which it is laterally blocked.

Resistance to the hand so the horse hollows or comes above the bit.

- This usually occurs because the horse does not want to stop or because you pull with your hand rather than use the body language supported by the rhythmical and correctly timed actions of your hand. Your lower leg should stay in contact to keep the hind leg engaged and so maintain the connection over the back. If you sit too 'heavy' and do not stretch up to lighten the seat, the horse is also likely to hollow its back, which will lead to the resistance.

The horse halts with the hind leg out behind.

- This happens when the horse is not sufficiently engaged. Remember to keep the leg in contact during the transition and, if necessary, use each leg alternately, particularly in the last two or three trot steps into the halt.

The horse does not stay straight or goes wide behind into the transition.

- The neck may be coming too short during the transition, or you may be too abrupt and perhaps over demanding in the transition, so the hind legs swing to one side or the other because they cannot find any space under the body.

Common faults; halt-trot

The head and neck come up against the hand.

- The horse comes above the bit because the first step is taken with a front leg, instead of the inside hind leg, and the back drops or tightens. You can help by keeping the horse 'up to the bit' during the halt with a feeling that it stays up in the back, and then ask for the first trot step with the inside leg coinciding with the release of the hand and the body language.

The transition to trot is not directly from halt.

- You must motivate the horse to be more 'switched on' and quicker in its reactions.

The horse does not remain straight on the line you are trying to ride, e.g. the centre line.

- This is probably because it is not straight in the body, i.e. 'in-line', or because you apply a prolonged pressure of one leg as the signal to trot so your horse leg-yields away from it. Within the transition to halt, and then within the halt, it may help to work for the lateral flexion at the poll towards the side that the horse is inclined to fall towards in the upward transition.

2. Canter-walk-canter

Position statement and body language During the *canter*, the horse must clearly feel your position statement for canter even as your body language supported by hand and leg prepares for and then asks for the transition directly to walk.

During the *walk*, the position statement should come central in the saddle so that there is no confusion for the horse between the position for canter and the position for walk. Then, depending on whether you want a canter depart on the same leg or on the other leg, i.e. a simple change, you must prepare your position statement by sitting across the saddle to the relevant side, shorten the inside rein, take the outside shoulder back in order to advance and open the inside hip at the same time as your body language still denotes walk through the rhythm and a relaxed following seat.

Riding and training canter-walk Several factors affect the horse's ability to perform the downward transition smoothly from canter to walk:

- Posture, including straightness, balance and engagement of the hind leg. The hind leg has to be sufficiently engaged to be able to act as the brake. The longitudinal balance has to be sufficient that the horse is at least in horizontal balance without the support of the rider's hands. If the horse tries to make the transition on the forehand, it will lose its balance forwards and then have to trot a few steps before coming to walk. This is of course why the exercise is a collecting exercise. To perform the exercise at all, the weight has to be transferred back to the hind leg, and in improving the quality of the transition the horse's ability and understanding of collection improves.

● The speed of the canter has to be as close as possible to the speed of the walk before the transition is performed. A good analogy is a person stepping off a moving bus. If the bus is moving much faster than a walking pace then it will be impossible to jump off and keep your balance without 'hitting the ground running'. In order to reduce its speed and yet remain in canter the horse has to find a way of shortening its stride. It can do this on the forehand by losing impulsion and thus the moment of suspension in the canter, which leads to a four-time canter. It can do it by rounding its loin, engaging its hind leg and using the hind leg to hold its balance. If the hindquarters are strong enough the horse will be able to keep the impulsion (*schwung*) in the canter and thereby increase the gesture of the leading front leg, which is not needed to prop up the forehand as much.

The rider can help by using his body language, supported by half-halts down the outside rein, to denote a shorter canter stride. The body language talks by becoming stiller with the seat. As explained earlier, the seat governs the length of stride, the leg is for energy. You must try to relax the hips and have a feeling of taking the thigh off the saddle and yet still be able to touch, if necessary, with the lower leg/spur/whip to energize the horse to try a bit harder to stay in canter within this shorter stride. Do all this without losing your position statement for canter.

As the horse tries to come towards a more collected canter, it will often tighten in its neck and back. It shows this by oscillating the head and neck up and down. Work on achieving the relaxation at the poll, or lateral submission, by persuading it to offer a lateral flexion to the outside, and at the same time help it by occasionally lightening the seat. This lightening will happen naturally if you are in the habit of correcting your lateral position in the saddle regularly.

A slight positioning of the horse into shoulder-in without excess neck bend will also help to oblige your horse to engage the inside hind, particularly if it is inclined to become crooked as the canter becomes more collected.

By working on the quality of the collected canter through the connection over the back with impulsion, the rider is making the best preparation for the transition to walk. The mistake I often see is the rider preparing for the downward transition by taking a firmer rein contact, sitting deeper with a driving seat and so causing problems with the balance, self-carriage and engagement of the hind leg. In other words, losing the quality of the canter.

The first few times that you ask the horse to make a transition from canter to walk, it is necessary to ask firmly enough as if you wanted a transition to halt. The horse will not be able to hold its halt even if it momentarily comes to the halt, and so if your hand softens at that moment the horse will walk. When the horse has experienced this acute transition a few times then it will be possible to aim for walk rather than halt and so the transition will be smoother. If your horse is inclined to pull and run through the half-halts, then a prick of the spurs (slightly more inside than outside to produce a slight lateral effect), at the moment that your body and your half-halt ask for the transition, will produce a reflex response for the hind leg to jump under the body. This is a time when there is an exception to the general rule of 'leg without hand/hand without leg'.

Later in the training, when you ask for a transition from canter to halt, the way of asking is exactly the same but the body language must hold the halt rather than ride the walk. Riders will often try to go directly from canter to an immobile halt, but that produces an abrupt transition on the forehand. It is better to ask for a good transition to walk, and then as you hold your body language in the halt position (as described above for the transition from trot to halt), the horse will square up.

Common faults

The transition is not directly to walk.

● This is either because the horse's posture is not good enough and so it does not hold the balance and weight on the shock absorbing engaged hind leg, or because the canter stride is too long before the transition, and the horse is not able to change speed so dramatically within one stride.

The horse resists or has problems in the outline within the transition.

● This usually comes about because the posture was not correct before the transition, or because the rider uses the pulling hand instead of the body language supported by the momentarily fixed hand. It can also happen if the rider forgets to soften the hand through the transition.

Walk-Canter Having set your position statement for canter, learn to feel the moment within the walk when the inside hind is coming forwards so that you can then take the first canter step with your body language and supporting leg actions at the moment that the inside hind leg comes forwards, which will coincide with the downward nod of the horse's head in the walk.

Within the canter-walk-canter exercise, whether ridden as a simple change or keeping the same canter lead, the walk should be regular and in a rhythm before the canter depart. The walk should not change as the position statement for canter is set up. It may therefore be necessary to apply rhythmical half-halts or keep using a light and alternate leg action with a relaxed hip so as to remind the horse to maintain a correct walk. However, it is also important that the horse learns to recognize, through the consistency of the position statement, that the canter depart is coming. Some horses will need a wake up call to switch them on so that you get a feeling that they do recognize that the canter is coming, whereas other horses who are inclined to anticipate may need relaxing and yet reminding to stay in walk until you take the first canter step.

As it takes the first step the horse's shoulders come up through the withers, the head and neck draw forward and the rider should hold his position as the horse takes the first stride. Do not get ahead of the movement. It helps to expect the delayed response, even with an advanced horse. If it goes on the first time of asking then you will be pleasantly surprised. A firmer contact in the outside hand during the transition helps to stabilize the head and neck, but a stronger inside rein contact will block the canter stride and provoke a resistance.

Walk to canter.

Common faults

Your horse comes above the bit in the transition.

- It may be necessary to go back to transitions between trot and canter. Be careful that the outside leg is not 'asking' for the canter. Remember that the transition must come from the position statement and the body language, supported mainly by the inside leg. The outside leg should be kept at the girth in a more supportive rather than active way. Work on the lateral submission to achieve the connection over the back. It helps to check on the lateral flexion to the outside before the transition. When the horse accepts the lateral submission, the canter transition will come through without the horse coming against the hand. When the transitions from trot to canter are without resistance, it is possible to employ the same technique in the transition from walk to canter.

Your horse is crooked in the canter transition.

- It could be because the inside rein is too tight combined with the outside leg being too far back and being used to ask for the canter. Keep your horse 'in-line' and 'on-line' with a relatively soft inside rein contact during the transition.

Intermediate Collecting Exercises

Voltes (small circles) in Trot and Canter

Objective

To set the horse a more difficult gymnastic exercise that will oblige it to collect. The objective within the exercise is to maintain the regularity of the steps and the rhythm whilst increasing the impulsion or *schwung* in the pace. This is achieved by increased lateral submission, leading to increased engagement of the hind legs and the lightening of the forehand, so that the contact on both reins, and in particular on the inside rein, does not increase, if anything it should come lighter. The exercise is complemented by the shoulder-in and the pirouette and prepares the horse for the travers, renvers and half-pass.

Definition

'Volte' comes from the French word meaning circle. In dressage parlance it is defined as a circle of six metres diameter. The actual size of circle that is appropriate in training is relative to the size of the horse and its length of stride. The demands of the exercise must be sufficient to challenge the horse, yet be within its capabilities.

Riding and training

The position statement is the same as for any lateral work, i.e. sit to the inside, shorten the inside rein, open the inside hip. The immediate goal is to keep your horse 'in-line' and 'on-line' and to maintain an even contact so as to encourage it to turn in response to your position statement and body language, supported by the actions of leg, in much the same way as for a turn-about-the-haunches or pirouette. The rhythmical half-halts applied down the outside rein, every second stride, remind the horse to stay 'on line' and yet allows it to turn and to offer the lateral flexion. The half-halts also remind it to maintain the rhythm. The appropriate touches of leg, usually the inside one, energize the pace to keep or enhance the *schwung*, whilst the outside leg is able to talk either towards the forehand or towards the hindquarters to remind the horse to remain 'on-line'.

In the trot, the small circles can also be ridden as a figure of eight to improve your horse's balance, responsiveness and lightness. It will tend to find one easier than the other and so be able to maintain the regularity, rhythm and cadence more easily. In riding from one circle into the other the position statement and then the lateral flexion at the poll should change just before the change of direction. The ultimate goal for the rider in this exercise is to be able to ride the figure of eight with the reins in one hand!

Common faults

Your horse loses the regularity of the steps.

● It is probably because it cannot cope with the size of circle. Its ability to cope and maintain the rhythm and regularity of the steps is dependent on its willingness and ability to maintain the 'connection over the back', leading to the engagement of its hind leg, and to balance and straightness. This is a 'chicken and egg' situation, as with all the collecting exercises. To be performed well the exercises require all these attributes, and yet to develop all these attributes requires the horse to be challenged by these gymnastic exercises. It is up to the rider to set the goal for the horse and then to analyze its response in order to remind, motivate and encourage the horse as appropriate, and also to adjust the size of circle according to how well it copes.

The contact becomes stronger on the inside rein, usually together with the horse overbending in the neck to the inside.

● It is likely that you are relying on the rein too much to turn the horse. It will then be more inclined to fall out through the outside shoulder. Try working for the lateral submission and flexion as in the 'corridor' exercise described in the primary training section to bring the shoulders back on to the line, and then allow the flexion back. Another option is to include more transitions back to walk, followed by pirouette, to remind the horse to listen to the position statement and outside leg, so that after the half-halt it offers to bring the shoulder around in the direction required. It may be necessary also to include some work on a slightly larger circle in shoulder-in position to engage the inside hind leg and obtain the lateral submission to the inside. Keep in mind the overall goal of achieving self-carriage with the horse 'in-line' and 'on-line'.

The lateral flexion to the inside is lost.

● It could be because you are keeping a stronger outside rein contact in an attempt to bring the horse's shoulders around with the rein instead of the leg. Remember the half-halts should only last one step even if you have to repeat them every second stride and even if you have to turn up the volume on your 'radio'.

Travers, Renvers and Half-pass

Objective

To increase the collection and freedom of the forehand by strengthening the load carrying muscles of the hindquarters and to teach the horse to abduct the inside foreleg and bring the outside hind leg under the body. These three exercises are very similar in terms of the position required of the horse. The travers and renvers complement and build on the role of the shoulder-in to develop greater collection and

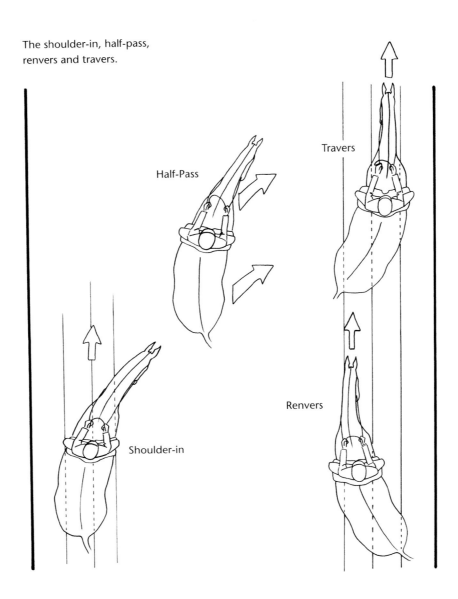

The shoulder-in, half-pass, renvers and travers.

so the lightness of the forehand. They are more demanding for the horse than the shoulder-in and they prepare it for the half-pass. The relevance of the half-pass is more as a test of the quality of the 'collection' than as a training exercise. Gradually the demands in the half-pass are increased within the dressage tests in terms of the degree of lateral movement required, which in turn requires the horse to offer more lateral submission and so bend around the inside leg.

Definition

During the travers, renvers and half-pass, the horse is uniformly bent from poll to tail in the direction of the movement. As with the shoulder-in, the degree of bend towards which the horse should gradually be trained is the same as for a six metre circle or volte. If the horse is genuinely laterally submissive, it will offer the lateral flexion at the poll without any tilting of the head. In the travers, renvers and half-pass it may help to imagine that your horse is a unicorn with the spike on its head pointing at the marker.

In *travers*, its shoulders and forelegs remain on the track, more or less facing in the direction you are riding, while its quarters are on the inside track with the outside hind leg immediately behind the inside foreleg, so that, as in 'shoulder-in', your horse is moving on three tracks. In a dressage test it is necessary to show slightly more angle because from the judge's perspective it never quite looks enough.

In *renvers*, the horse's position is much the same but its shoulders and forelegs are positioned on the inside track, more or less facing in the direction of the movement, while its hindquarters are on the track or line. Traditionally the travers and renvers are ridden along the wall, so it is easy to remember that in travers you face the wall whilst in renvers you face away from the wall. The renvers is not required in any dressage tests but can be incorporated in freestyle tests quite effectively. It is particularly useful as an exercise to improve the half-pass.

The *half-pass* is in effect the same as a travers, but it is ridden on a diagonal line across the arena rather than along the length of the arena. The horse should be flexed at the poll, looking at the point towards which it is being ridden. The

The travers.

forehand should at all times be marginally ahead of the hindquarters to the extent that, when looked at from in front, the horse's head should be in front of the inside hip. The demands of the half-pass increase relative to the angle at which it is ridden across the arena. In Medium dressage tests, this is along the full diagonal in a 20 x 60 metre arena (i.e 20 metres to the side and 48 metres forwards), whereas in the Grand Prix tests, the half-pass is ridden from quarter marker to half marker, (i.e. 20 metres lateral with 24 metres forwards).

As the demands within these lateral movements increase, in particular in the half-pass, the horse must be able to offer more bend through its body to be able to look in the direction of the movement and yet not be trailing the hindquarters. It must be able to abduct the inside foreleg in the direction of the movement and take the outside foreleg across the body in front of the inside foreleg. At the same time it must reach sufficiently forward with the outside foreleg so that it does not hit the back of its outside knee with the front of the inside knee as it brings that leg forwards. The inside hind leg must step well forward as well as abducting in the direction of the movement, while the outside hind leg steps forward, across and under the body.

The quality of the half-pass is judged in terms not just of the positioning of the hindquarters behind the shoulders and the degree of lateral movement, but also in

The half-pass. Gestlon Krack ridden by Anky van Grunsven.

terms of the quality of the 'collection', reflected in the rhythm and regularity of the steps and the impulsion (*schwung*) that enables the cadence of the trot or canter to be maintained within the movement.

For travers, renvers and half-pass the hands should be positioned towards the outside hip.

Position statement for travers, renvers and half-pass

- As for all lateral work; sit to the inside, shorten the inside rein, open the inside hip. (The 'inside' refers always to the side to which the horse is bent.)

- In shortening the inside rein, rotate the arm slightly so that the fingers point slightly upwards, and take the inside rein towards the neck as an indirect rein.

- Open the inside hip without applying pressure so that the inside knee and toe point in the direction of the movement.

- The difference between the position statement for travers, renvers and half-pass and the position statement for leg-yielding and shoulder-in, is in the positioning of the hands. For leg-yielding and shoulder-in, the hands should be carried more towards your inside hip, whilst for travers, renvers and half-pass the hands should be positioned towards the outside hip.

However, the rein length must always be adjusted so that the hands/reins, whilst coming to the neck or withers, never cross.

Riding and training the travers and renvers

- Use shoulder-in and small circles to establish the lateral submission and the uniform bend.

- Initially in training, the travers is set up from the circle or out of a corner. The position statement must be made early so that when you get to the point where you want to start the exercise, your body language, combined with a half-halt on the outside rein away from the neck (as in a direct rein of opposition) and a touch of the outside leg at the girth, start the lateral movement. Later in the training, it is possible to set up the travers from a straight line or from the 'shoulder-in'.

- When riding the renvers along the wall, the outside of the arena becomes the 'inside' of the renvers.

- Both the travers and the renvers can be performed on a circle as well as on a straight line, both of which are useful training exercises for the half-pass (see below). It is also useful to ride these exercises away from the wall or fence of an arena but then you must imagine one. Use a post or tree in the distance as a marker towards which you ride.

- The timing of the half-halts coincides with the outside front foot coming to the floor. In trot, of course, this is the same moment as the inside hind is in the support phase.

- The touch of the outside leg or spur at the girth or just behind should be timed to coincide with the outside front leg starting to come forwards. A common fault is the rider's tendency to pull the heel up and backwards and apply too much pressure with the outside leg.

- The body language encourages the horse to move laterally and forwards by moving towards the direction of movement so as to keep the weight into the inside stirrup. While the travers is being ridden, you can adjust the angle. To increase it, bring the outside shoulder back to support a half-halt away from the neck and the touch of the outside leg. To reduce the angle, bring the outside shoulder forwards, allowing with the outside rein and touch with the inside leg. This also encourages the horse to move forwards and bend a bit more.

- At the beginning of the work in collection, just as with the shoulder-in, the degree of bend for the travers and renvers is relatively slight. The important element is the lateral submission at the poll, rather than the angle to the wall/line. As the horse's understanding and ability to engage and collect improve so does the horse's ability to bend 'around the inside leg'.

Riding and training the half-pass

- The half-pass is ridden in much the same way as the travers. It is ridden out of a corner or small circle but along the diagonal line instead of down the long side. When riding out of a corner, try and ride deep into the corner so as to reinforce the lateral submission. The position statement must be made early before the corner or half way round the circle, and is the same as for the travers. The half-pass is then started with a half-halt down the outside rein while the body language, supported by the touch of the outside leg, which should not be held too far back, takes the horse along the line.

- By concentrating on sitting to the inside of the saddle, with the weight in the inside stirrup supporting your inside hip, and the inside knee and hip open so that the inside foot is pointing at the marker towards which the half-pass is aimed, you can focus on riding forwards along the line keeping the uniform bend and in particular the lateral submission and flexion at the poll. The combination of the touch of the outside leg directed at the quarters and the supporting half-halts directed towards the outside hip will encourage the quarters to catch up to the forehand. If your horse tries to cross the line, then half-halt more strongly down the outside rein. If it tries to move sideways too quickly, by leading with the hindquarters, then it must be ridden up to the line with more inside leg. The goal is to be able to maintain an even contact with the legs as well as with the reins.

- Riders often make the mistake of applying too much outside leg pressure to push the quarters over, to which the horse responds either by leading with the quarters or by losing the bend to the inside. The stronger the constant pressure of the outside leg, the more the horse interprets the demand as being for leg-yielding and so tries to flex to that side. The rider will also tend to pull himself to the outside of the saddle and block the movement with the inside rein.

- In the early attempts, the diagonal line along which the half-pass is ridden should not be too acute. For example, the line from quarter marker to centre line or vice versa (e.g. F-G, G-F) is demanding enough. The priority must always be on maintaining the lateral submission and the quality of the pace, rather than on how far you can take your horse across. As the horse understands, and the degree of collection improves through the work in shoulder-in and travers, so the demands can be increased.

- The renvers is a particularly useful exercise to perform after riding the half-pass from the centre line to the side, as it reinforces the role of the inside leg in maintaining the lateral submission and bend at the end of the half-pass. This helps you and your horse to get into the habit of maintaining the quality of the half-pass right through to the end.

Common faults in travers, renvers and half-pass

Most of the faults or problems that arise originate from the 'basics'. As the demands for collection are increased within these exercises, so you will find it difficult to maintain the lateral submission, the connection over the back and engagement and activity of the hind legs. It is always best to use a 'softly softly' approach to the training of these movements or exercises. As soon as you 'try' too hard, you will apply too much pressure with the leg or hand and the horse will brace against them or misunderstand.

When riding travers or half-pass, the horse starts with the correct lateral flexion and bend and then loses it or tilts the head.

- Your position statement may be incorrect, especially if you are pressing too much with the outside leg. When you lose the lateral flexion, ride forwards either straight or in slight shoulder-in position, whilst working on it. If you are riding the half-pass, you can even ride back in the opposite direction in leg-yielding. This helps to reinforce the bend around the inside leg and the lateral flexion at the poll.

  A useful preparatory or training exercise for the shoulder-in, travers, renvers or half-pass is to ride your horse straight along the wall or line encouraging it to offer as much lateral flexion as possible without tilting its head and without bending at the base of the neck. Initially it will try to offer shoulder-in or travers, but with appropriate use of the legs it should be corrected so that its body remains as straight as possible on the line.

The steps become irregular to the point that some horses look lame.

- The horse may be abducting the inside hind too much rather than stepping forwards, and probably leading with the quarters. This is usually associated with the loss of the lateral submission to the inside. It can also happen when the horse is inactive with the outside hind leg, leaving it on the floor for too long as a result of losing its posture or 'connection over the back'. In this case, ask for less angle in the movement but work on maintaining the lateral submission and the horse's posture as a priority.

The steps become shorter and the rhythm changes.

- You are probably trying too hard, causing your leg pressure to be too tight, if not the pressure of your lower leg then the pressure of your thigh grip. The rhythm tends to quicken with a tense horse, as its back tightens, and slows with a lazy horse. Try to remain relaxed in the hips and, if necessary, touch with the whip to support the leg action rather than apply more pressure with the leg.

Introduction to Piaffe

Objective

Piaffe is considered by most riders as an exercise reserved for the Advanced dressage horse. So it is, as a movement in competition dressage, but as an exercise to develop collection, the training towards piaffe is a useful gymnastic tool. The work teaches the horse to adopt the posture required for a higher degree of collection. It is a natural movement for a horse that has a good posture and is in a high state of excitement or energy but is restrained from releasing that energy in forward movement. Instead, the energy is released by trotting on the spot.

The objective in introducing this gymnastic exercise at this stage in the training is to teach your horse to recognize the position statement and body language for the piaffe, so that out of that understanding comes the possibility of teaching it to adopt a posture that will lighten the forehand by taking more weight on the flexed hind legs even as it is ridden more forwards. This understanding is useful not just for the dressage horse but also for the show jumper or event horse, because it becomes easier to prepare them for a jump or to bring them back into balance after a jump. The work towards the piaffe, which is equally valuable for the training of the rider as for the horse, may not always lead to the achievement of a dressage test piaffe in terms of the rhythm, height and number of the steps, as this requires a particularly gifted horse both in temperament and physical attributes.

Definition

In performing a classical piaffe, the horse trots on the spot with a well engaged hind leg that is flexed through all the joints from the croup to the fetlock. The energy is contained within these flexed muscles of the hindquarters and through the strong connection over the back, leading to the elevation of the forehand when the neck is raised yet with a submission at the poll. The classical piaffe looks natural, with an even rhythm and regular steps. Each diagonal pair of legs alternately supports and then elevates equally, with a slight moment of suspension so that the horse really looks like it is springing from one diagonal to the other rather than just stepping. The engaged and flexed hind legs support most of the horse's weight, which allows the front foot to be lifted well.

As explained previously in the section on bio-mechanics, the back muscles in an elastic state of tension support the horse's spine and the rider, and provide the 'connection over the back'. This allows the raising of the neck to have an engaging effect on the hind leg. The combination of the raised neck with the submission at the poll, both lateral and longitudinal, leads to the flexed and engaged hindquarters supporting more of the weight of the forehand. This is a natural reflex, but it can be blocked by the horse, in particular when it loses the lateral submission by bracing the muscles at the top of the neck.

Position statement

For the piaffe this is in some ways contradictory. It is subtle, and yet it must be very clear and consistent, so that your horse learns to recognize it.

● Your seat must be central in the saddle, your upper body stretching up with your neck drawn up and back to your collar, so that it has the effect of bracing your back but with a non-driving or pushing seat. You must sit on your horse's back in such a way as to encourage it to keep its back up, so that it can round its loin and engage the hind legs.

The training towards piaffe is introduced at this stage of the horse's training as a gymnastic exercise to develop collection. Richard Davison riding Askari.

- The reins must be shortened so that the elbows are always just in front of the hip and the hands in front of the withers.

- The legs should be very relaxed at the hip, hanging down with the heel as close as possible to the vertical line drawn down from the shoulder through the hip to the heel. The toe is lifted upwards to brace the knee. The more relaxed or light the contact between your thigh and the saddle the better. This is only possible if the contact through the rein to your horse's mouth is light.

Body language

This must convey energy for the piaffe and yet at the same time a desire to stay more or less on the spot. This energy is conveyed through your posture supported by the touch of leg, whip or spur, rather than through anything that you do with your seat. Your horse should by now have learnt to react positively to the touch of leg, whip or spur by thinking 'energy' and 'forwards'.

The stiller your body and seat the better. As soon as you try to push or drive with the seat, the horse will either start to push with the hind leg, rather than sit and wait, or will tighten and hollow the back. The energy that is 'created' through the body language, supported by the leg, whip or spur, is then contained by half-halts that say to the horse 'wait' or 'stay here'.

Riding and training

The training and development of the piaffe is a natural extension of the secondary training. The piaffe should not be introduced until a good 'connection over the back' has been established and, through the lateral work, the horse has become relatively straight and is 'laterally submissive'. The key to the piaffe is the 'lateral submission' at the poll. The pirouette, shoulder-in, travers and renvers introduce the idea of collection and form the basis for the work towards increased collection in the piaffe. The best indicator of 'lateral submission at the poll' is the willingness of the horse to offer the lateral flexion at the poll in these exercises without tilting the head.

When introducing piaffe, the preparatory exercises are the T-a-F and the pirouette, both to energize the hindquarters and engage the hind leg as well as to transfer the weight to the hind leg. Very often a good place or time to introduce the idea to the horse is when it is excited or keen, such as when returning to the stables from work or when excited by some outside stimulation. Using a slight downhill slope is particularly helpful in encouraging the engagement of the hind leg. As long as there is a good 'connection over the back', then you can help by raising the horse's neck whilst working on the relaxation at the poll through slight lateral flexions, at the same time working as always to keep it 'in-line' and 'on-line'.

The rider's responsibility is to adjust the demands in terms of energizing and restraint. You should learn to recognize the rounding of the back and lowering of the croup, which is associated with the engagement of the hind leg. The most important advice to give to a rider who is just starting to work with the piaffe is that it does not feel like trot and do not expect to feel much under your seat. The engagement and flexion of the hind leg leads to a dropping feeling alternately under each seat bone, rather than an upward lift. You must avoid driving with the seat to try and create a trot feeling. The stiller you sit with the seat and the more relaxed the hip, and therefore the lighter the contact of the thigh and lower leg, the better. You must correct the horse's tendency to avoid engaging the hind leg by becoming crooked. The horse's responsibility is to respond to the energizing or stimulating actions and yet accept the corrections of leg and hand.

It is important that your horse recognizes that, when it offers a piaffe position and a couple of diagonal steps, the pressure comes off. Immediately halt, relax and reward. Then ask again. Do not keep up the pressure for long. If it does not react at all to the energizing aids, then it may be necessary to 'stir it up' by the sudden use of the leg, whip or spur to cause it to jump forwards. I often refer to this as a 'double barrel' because both legs and spurs or whip are used simultaneously, as a surprise, to cause the horse to jump forwards. If it overreacts and panics, then the pressure must come off sooner, either by halting and relaxing or by allowing it to go forwards into trot. There is a fine line between asking or expecting too much and not energizing enough. The most important point to keep in mind is that the end product must be a natural, active and elastic step from one diagonal to the other with a slight moment of suspension, rather than a mere earthbound stepping action.

The work towards the piaffe steps should not be too intense or prolonged. I prefer to use the word 'play' rather than 'work'. It is important that your horse does not associate this training with pain or discomfort, because that will lead to it blocking its reflexes or more serious resistances. A few minutes within a training session at most, or just a few steps when your horse feels excited, will lead to a more natural piaffe. Even when the horse becomes relatively established in the diagonal steps, the work to increase the elevation and lowering of the croup must be in short sessions and always related to its natural talent and energy. It must always see 'light at the end of the tunnel'.

Few horses have the talent for a piaffe that would score well in Grand Prix dressage competitions. Most horses can however adopt the posture for piaffe and offer one or two diagonal steps. At this stage in the training that is sufficient as the work towards the piaffe steps is primarily aimed at improving their posture and ability to collect, rather than achieving the ten to twelve regular and rythmical steps required in the dressage tests. The feeling that both the rider and the horse get from this work can then be carried into the other collected work, in particular the downward transitions from trot to halt and within the collected canter work towards canter pirouettes.

Common faults

The horse becomes crooked as soon as you put yourself into piaffe position.

- It helps to work initially along the wall to assist in keeping the horse straight. A slight shoulder-in position can also help if your horse has a tendency to push the quarters against the inside leg, but avoid bending the horse in the neck too much.

The horse is very tight at the poll and wants to push with the hind leg instead of engaging and lowering the croup.

- Use the basic exercises of T-a-F to engage the hind leg and the pirouette to take the weight back to the hind legs.

The horse comes against the hand or braces the muscles at the top of the neck.

- This causes a stiffening of the back and prevents the engagement and flexion of the hind leg. Work tactfully with the hand and appropriate touches of the leg to obtain the lateral submission as in the 'corridor' exercise described within the primary training section. In loosening the horse at the poll, encourage it to flex first to the side it prefers to flex and then to the other.

The horse comes croup high to avoid engaging and flexing the hind legs.

- The straightening and disengagement of the hind leg is associated with the lowering of the neck. The correction is to raise the neck whilst still working on the lateral submission at the poll.

Useful Exercise Combinations

Combining exercises helps both to improve the responses to the rider's body language, position and aids as well as to improve the lateral submission, posture, balance and impulsion in the collected paces. Combining also helps in preparing horses for subsequent movements. Many of these combinations are to be found already within the movements set out in the dressage tests, such as the volte combined with the lateral movements. However, it is worth experimenting with other combinations to resolve problems as they arise.

Exercises to include in walk and trot

Shoulder-in to walk to half-pirouette as a way of encouraging your horse to keep the weight back to the inside hind in the collected trot and to improve the response to the controlling role of the outside leg and half-halts down the outside rein.

Shoulder-in to travers on the straight line and vice versa to improve the horse's response to your body language, leg and rein actions, and to improve the freedom of the forehand and expression of the steps in the collected trot.

Shoulder-in and travers on a circle to develop lateral submission and collection by working initially on the engagement of the inside hind leg and the transfer of weight to the hindquarters, and then on the freedom and expression to the forehand. It leads to the increased willingness of the horse to offer the bend around the inside leg and is a useful preparation for the half-pass. But be careful with the travers as many crooked horses already have a tendency to disengage the inside hind by bringing the quarters in.

Half-pass right to leg-yielding to the left or vice versa to improve the horse's balance, its response to the inside leg and its lateral submission in the half-pass. When your horse comes against the inside leg in the half-pass and does not accept its controlling influence then you are forced to 'hold' the horse with a stronger contact down the inside rein.The objective is to feel that you can control the lateral movement with your leg rather than with your reins. The objective with the inside rein is to act as a 'positional' rein and to maintain a relatively passive even contact.

Shoulder-in left to renvers right or vice versa to improve the lateral submission and suppleness leading to the horse's willingness and ability to change its lateral flexion and bend from one side to the other within the lateral movements and without loss of rhythm or regularity. A similar exercise within the half-pass is to change the lateral flexion during the riding of the half-pass.

Exercises to include in canter

Canter to walk to half-pirouette to canter to improve the quality of the collected canter in self-carriage. You should take time to make sure that you go through the correct step-by-step process before each transition and before the pirouette to set up your position statement correctly, and then to ride the pirouette actively but in the rhythm with your body language supported by the rein and leg. Focus as well on the timing of your aids in the transitions to canter and from canter back to walk. (see section on Acute Transitions: canter-walk-canter.) Gradually, as your horse learns the exercise, it will start to anticipate and you must be ready to correct with the half-halts and leg.

Canter in shoulder-in position to strengthen the supporting inside leg in the canter. In performing this exercise it is very important to limit the bend in the neck and keep the shoulder 'in-line' with the outside rein and outside leg. Because the horse's natural tendency to be crooked is at its greatest in canter, I use this exercise with care, making sure that the ultimate objective of straightening the horse and persuading it to use its inside hind correctly is achieved, rather than just leading it to becoming more crooked. One often sees horses in dressage tests being ridden down the long side, or on the centre line, with excessive neck bend in a shoulder-in position in an attempt to convince the judge that the horse is straight.

Canter on small circles or voltes in travers position to improve the horse's balance and strength in the collected canter, but this must be ridden with care. I do not recommend the travers and renvers exercises in the canter work because your horse already has a natural tendency to do it, usually more so to the right than to the left. However, when working on the collected canter on very small circles, say less than eight metres, the travers can play a role in developing the quality of the collected canter and preparing the horse for the canter pirouettes at the next level of training as long as the inside leg is ready to control and engage the inside hind leg.

Canter half-pass into a slight shoulder-in position on the centre line to reinforce the controlling influence of the inside leg and the position statement, sitting to the inside of the saddle above the inside hind with the inside hip open and the inside leg at the girth. One often sees riders slip to the outside in the half-pass, which makes it difficult to keep the inside leg in contact, and so the horse's balance is lost as is the impulsion or *schwung* in the canter.

Counter canter on small circles and tighter serpentines requires increased engagement of the inside hind leg (inside in this context always means the side of the leading leg) as long as the rider corrects the horse's tendency to overbend laterally. Make sure you do not slip to the outside of the saddle and keep an even contact both with the reins and the legs. Use the body language supported by the legs to turn the horse rather than pulling on the reins.

Using Collection in the Training

The elementary and intermediate collecting exercises enable the development of the extended paces and related transitions, in particular in trot and canter. The collection and straightening of the canter produced through this work also prepares the horse for the work on the flying changes, which are required not just of the dressage horse but also of the advanced event horse and show jumper.

Medium and Extended Trot

Objective and definition

In the extended trot, the horse should cover as much ground as possible. Maintaining the same cadence, it should lengthen its steps to the utmost as a result of the impulsion from the hindquarters. The rider should allow the horse, remaining on the bit without leaning on it, to lengthen its frame and gain ground. The fore feet should touch the ground on the spot towards where they are pointing. The movement of the fore and hind legs should be similar (parallel) in the forward moment of the extension. The whole movement should be well balanced and the transition to collected trot should be smoothly executed, without loss of rhythm, by taking more weight on the hindquarters.

Riding and training

The development of the extended trot comes initially from the 'zone' exercise described in the section on primary training which leads to the medium trot. The intermediate collecting exercises lead to the increased impulsion and engagement of the collected trot and the loading of the hindquarters. This in turn together with

Medium trot. Farbenfroh ridden by Nadine Capplemann.

the lateral work leads to the freedom of the forehand that enables the horse to 'open' the shoulder and reach further in the extended trot to cover more ground in each stride.

Common faults

The horse goes wide behind or croup high.

- This problem arises when the horse is not willing to remain engaged with the hind leg. This may be because its conformation makes it hard for it: horses that have a straight hind leg or hocks that rotate outwards excessively (this is a common Thoroughbred problem), are more inclined to disengage. The appropriate exercise to improve the engagement within the medium and extended paces is the 'zone' exercise combined with the shoulder-in on a large circle, which is then combined with the development of the medium trot on the circle. When the medium trot is better on the large circle then the extended trot can be ridden on the straight line and, by encouraging the horse to maintain an elevated neck and forehand without coming above the bit, the horse will be encouraged to draw the foreleg up and forward more. (See the role of the brachicephalic muscle in the section on bio-mechanics.) This will give space to the hind leg to come forward and under the body. A useful picture to keep in mind here is the 'wheel' illustration (see page 76)

The foreleg makes a bigger and more elevated gesture than the hind leg.

- In this case the horse is not really going forwards to the contact. The horse is not genuinely 'connected over the back'. The hind leg may be well engaged but without sufficient impulsion and the neck may be too elevated. The correction is to ride the medium trot more actively forwards, to start with in rising trot on a circle until the horse takes the contact and draws 'over the back and through the neck' forward into it.

The extended trot starts well but loses balance, and therefore the cadence and rhythm, after a few strides.

- This problem can be caused by tension or over exuberance causing the horse to push itself with the hind leg over the point of balance. The correction is to remind the horse through the combination of body language and half-halts down the outside rein to maintain its balance and the rhythm. It also helps to encourage the horse to maintain a more elevated forehand by appropriate actions of the rein and an alternate leg aid to dictate the rhythm within the extended trot.

The horse drops the bit or comes above the bit at the start of the extended trot.

- This problem is similar to the previous one but may also happen in the case of a horse that is not lazy and may in fact be tense. The back drops and the energy in the hind leg is not transmitted through and over the back to the forehand. The correction is to go back to basics to establish a better connection over the back through the exercises described in the primary training.

The horse comes against the hand and loses the rhythm and cadence during the transition from extended trot to collected trot.

● This problem happens when the horse loses its balance or through exuberance does not want to come back to collected trot without leaning on the rein. The horse must learn to listen to the rider's body language and when it ignores the half-halts then a transition should immediately be made to walk or halt. While the restraining rein actions are applied as sharply as is required to get a response, the touches of the leg or spur must act sharply enough to activate and engage the hind leg so that it acts as a brake rather than to push against the rider. When practising the extended trot on the diagonal or down the long side, such a horse should be in the habit of knowing that, more often than not, it will be asked to perform a transition to walk or halt. Further work on the 'zone' exercise, to develop increased engagement and impulsion, will also help to maintain the rhythm and produce more cadence in the downward transition steps.

Flying Changes

Objective and definition

The objective of the 'movement' is to make a change of lead in canter without losing the canter. A horse at liberty will naturally change leads when cantering or galloping around a field in order to keep its balance. Every young horse at liberty is different in respect of whether it has a natural balance and good moment of suspension in its canter and so makes a 'correct' flying change during the moment of suspension or chooses to change first in front and then behind or even through trot.

The show jumper or event horse finds it easier to maintain a good canter on a turn to a fence if it has the ability to make a flying change. One often sees horses coming off the turn in a disunited canter or in counter canter. The term 'disunited' refers to a canter in which the front legs are on one lead, usually inside, while the hind legs are on the other lead. Some trainers refer to it as a 'cross-gaited' canter. A 'disunited' canter implies a 'disconnected' canter. The hind legs are, in effect, not sufficiently engaged. A counter canter will limit the tightness of the turn that can be ridden, and usually reduces the power of the canter, so the horse may come to the jump without enough impulsion.

Dressage horses and advanced event horses are required to show one or more flying changes as 'movements' in the dressage test. There is, or should be, an order of priorities in judging the flying changes. Unfortunately, it does appear at times within eventing dressage, if not within pure dressage, that each judge has a different set of priorities.

The flying change is judged in terms of a number of qualities. If the change of lead is made through trot or walk, no matter how quickly, then it cannot be called a flying change. Some horses are so quick at cheating that an inexperienced spectator or judge will find it hard to detect. They would just notice a brief flat step within the canter. Such changes should not be rewarded with more than a four (insufficient) no matter how smooth, calm or straight they may be. Where the rider deliberately avoids the flying change by riding a simple change or a quick change through trot, then he should really be awarded no marks, as the movement has not been performed. It can be compared with a rider missing out an awkward jump on the course because it might upset his horse.

In a correct flying change, the forelegs and hind legs change leads during the moment of suspension. There may be many problems still to be ironed out in the training, but such a change should be rewarded with at least a five (sufficient). If the horse makes the change over two strides, by changing usually the forelegs in one moment of suspension and hind legs in the next, then the change is said to be 'late behind'. If it changes first behind and then in front, which is not as common, then it is said to be 'late in front'. As will be discussed later, such expressions are not always totally accurate because sometimes the horse is in fact 'early in front' rather then 'late behind'. No matter how smooth such changes may be, they should not be rewarded with more than a four (insufficient). Some horses can be so smooth in performing their changes in this 'incorrect' manner that the inexperienced spectator may find it difficult to spot. Even an experienced judge may find it difficult to detect this fault if the flying change is performed straight towards him, rather than across the arena.

As well as being performed both front and back within the same stride, the flying change must be judged in terms of the rhythm and regularity of the canter both before and after, and in terms of the correctness of the horse's posture i.e. the connection over the back, the acceptance of the contact, the straightness and engagement of the hindquarters before, during and after the change.

Where the rhythm and regularity of the canter is maintained and the horse accepts the rider's aids without resistance, whilst maintaining the 'connection over the back' during the change, then the mark should be at least six. If, in addition, the change is straight, both before and after the change as well as during the change, then, by definition, the hind leg must be reasonably engaged and therefore a seven or an eight would be appropriate.

As the quality of the canter is improved, leading to increased engagement and impulsion giving rise to a cleaner and bigger moment of suspension in the canter, then it is possible to have more expressive changes. The flying change stride appears to be as big or even bigger and more ground covering. As long as the balance is on the hindquarters with the hind leg engaged through the change, so that the horse does not appear to be croup high, such changes would deserve an eight or nine. Increased collection, leading to the lightness of the forehand and an expressive 'uphill' appearance to the change, with a very clear moment of suspension, would lead to the possibility of a nine or ten (excellent).

The degree of collection required of the event horse in its dressage test is less than

Robert Dover showing an example of an expressive and straight flying change with a good moment of suspension.

that required of the advanced dressage horse. So the excellent (ten) flying change shown by the event horse would probably only be an eight or nine for the dressage horse because it would not have enough expression and 'uphill' appearance. The advanced dressage horse also has to be able to maintain its balance and collection with such correct and expressive changes to accurately perform series changes every fourth, third, second and then every stride, whilst remaining straight both 'in-line' and 'on-line'.

Riding and training

The time taken to teach an average horse is six months to a year. During this time, it will be a process of two steps forward and one step back. As with all the training, we use the horse's natural reflexes to help to bring about the response that we want.

These reflexes include the natural desire to stay in balance and remain co-ordinated in the canter. The horse at liberty will not remain in counter canter for more than a few strides, and will only remain disunited for any length of time if it is naturally very uncoordinated or lazy.

The quality of the canter

A good flying change can only come from a canter that is correct. It is not possible from a canter that is in two halves, with no connection over the back, that is not regular (i.e. four time) and has no moment of suspension, or that is not maintained by the horse in moderate self-carriage without constant driving or support from the rider. These are the minimum conditions. The crooked horse can cope, but usually at the expense of crooked changes. A good working canter is sufficient for many horses, as long as it has a good moment of suspension and is in reasonable horizontal balance. A good collected canter adds more expression to the changes and enables more precision. A poor collected canter, with a shorter stride and no *schwung* will produce short changes, frequently with the inside hind leg barely coming through in the change. In short, the ability to perform and the quality of the flying change is a reflection of the quality of the canter.

The talented young horse may be able to perform correct flying changes under saddle from a very young age. Such horses however are rare. In most cases, the young horse will show a predisposition to changing from right to left but no such talent from left to right. Even with a horse that shows such talent, the work to establish the quality of the canter, explained in an earlier section, must come first. Such work includes establishing the 'connection over the back' both on the turn and on the straight line, and also in the counter canter.

One of the goals in this basic work will be to develop the impulsion (*schwung*) in the collected canter that leads to a generous moment of suspension within a regular three beat rhythm. As soon as your horse is confident and able to maintain the impulsion within the counter canter, then it is ready to start the flying changes. Even if it is not totally ready for them, you may wish to start the training, because if you wait for perfection in the canter as I have described, you may never start to teach your horse to perform flying changes on demand.

Three phases in teaching flying changes

The training period can be divided into three phases.

The *first phase* involves training the horse to react to the rider's aid, i.e. body language and position statement supported by the action of the legs. During this phase, exercises are used that are likely to produce a flying change reaction from the horse in response to our signals. When it responds, exactly how well or correctly it responds is not important, as long as it has a go. Gradually, it will learn to recognize and even to anticipate the change. In this respect it is very similar to jumping where the horse may initially be hesitant but may then start to rush when it knows the jump.

Phase 1 – Reacting to the aid

Phase 2 – Improving the quality of the canter and flying change

During the *second phase* the rider/trainer uses the horse's understanding if not anticipation of the exercises and of the change of position statement and body language. The rider works more on the quality and correctness of the canter, yet with the horse knowing that a change is coming a lighter aid has to be applied especially with the leg to bring about the change. Out of the improved collected canter will come the quality of the change. At this stage, quality is more important than being able to ask for the change precisely at a point or marker.

Phase 3 – Precision and quality

In *phase three*, the rider works on precision as well as quality. The horse must learn to recognize the rider's position statement and body language, accept to wait for the signal whilst improving the quality of canter, then precisely at the required point, respond to the rider's signal for the change.

The aids for the change – body language and position statement

The rider asks for a flying change through his body language and a change of the position statement from one canter lead to the next. This is supported by the slight change of leg position, in particular by the new outside leg. One of the best ways to teach a rider the correct feeling for riding a flying change is to ask him to canter along on his own feet and then to skip for the change just as a young child would do when playing in the garden pretending to be a horse. The important points to recognize are the advancing of the new inside hip and the bringing back of the new outside shoulder.

Having the opportunity to experience flying changes on a good schoolmaster can be helpful. However, it has to be borne in mind that such a schoolmaster will not necessarily have the same canter as your horse and so the feeling of the flying change will be different between the experienced horse and the new recruit. Whilst learning flying changes as a rider, or even for the experienced rider teaching a horse, it is essential to have someone on the ground watching. The assistant must be able to recognize a correct flying change, i.e. one that comes through with forelegs and hind legs together in the same stride. In the early stages with most horses, it is difficult to feel whether the change has been correct due to the tension produced. Once you can associate the 'feel' for the correct change, as opposed to the incorrect change, then you will not need the assistant.

As with all training, *the goal must be to minimize the aids*. One often sees riders ask for the flying change with a swinging outside leg aid or by throwing the body from one side to the other, sometimes combined with a 'jerk' on the rein to lift the horse into a change. Those who aspire to compete at the highest level in dressage must keep in mind that, when they reach the stage of performing series changes every second stride or even every stride, they will find it very difficult if they are used to using a 'big' aid to get the change. Remember the maxim: 'there is no limit to how little you can do, there is only a limit to how much'.

To *minimize the amount of excessive body language* and to create the best opportunity to 'feel' the correct change, it helps to get into the habit from the start of looking well ahead of your horse, if not slightly away from the direction of the change. This helps you to keep the correct posture and position with the outside shoulder back and therefore the balance during the change.

The timing of the aid is an important responsibility of the rider. Ask for the change at the moment when the outside front leg comes to the floor. The next phase of the canter is the moment when the original leading leg comes to the floor followed a split second later by the moment of suspension during which the new inside hind leg comes forward and under together with the change of leading leg in front. At first it helps to use your eye to help you but then try and feel without looking.

It is also important to stress *the importance of the rider's supporting leg in the change.* The leg which, before the change, was the outside leg and which, after the change, is the inside leg must be kept against the horse throughout the change so as to encourage the new inside hind leg to come clearly forward in the change. You may notice that when you get to the stage in the training when the horse anticipates the changes, you will often get the best change when you do not want it, for example when riding a serpentine in canter just because you are keeping the outside leg against the horse in the counter canter.

Useful exercises

There is a fine line to be drawn in teaching changes. Repeating the same exercise each time in preparation for the change in the same part of the arena can help your horse to expect to be asked for the change, but if the horse builds up tension and loses the quality of the canter every time that exercise is ridden, or every time you approach that part of the arena, you then have to try another exercise. Some exercises work better with one horse than another depending on their temperament, their natural talent for changes and the natural qualities of their canter. There is no substitute for trial and error in this regard. Every horse I have trained has taught me something new.

Exercise 1 Use the half-pass in canter as a preparation, then ride straight and then change. As you complete the half-pass, the outside leg that has been asking the horse to come over in the half-pass should be kept on the horse as you ask with the new outside leg for the change.

Exercise 2 Ride a small circle (volte) in the corner of the arena. The demands of this circle when ridden with the position statement and actions of leg and hand as for a pirouette will help to engage the hind leg. Then ride out of this very small circle returning towards the track asking for the flying change immediately out of the circle on the straight line back to the track.

Exercise 3 Ride very deep into a corner then from the corner into a shallow loop away from the side, asking for the change to the outside lead to counter canter at the moment of turning into the shallow loop. One would expect this exercise to be too demanding at this early stage of teaching the changes but I find it works well with horses that initially show no inclination to change. You will understand this exercise when you ride a young or green horse in its early canter work. You will often find that they either go disunited or change to the outside canter lead as they come out of a corner because of the difficulty they have in engaging the inside hind during the tighter turns.

Exercise 4 Riding a serpentine with changes over the centre line works well with horses that have a natural inclination to change correctly. In riding the serpentine, the loops of the serpentine must be ridden in such a way that the outside shoulder is well under control. The neck must be kept as straight as possible and then it also helps to make the loops turn back on themselves.

Exercise 5 Horses that have no inclination to change can be started over a pole on the ground. However in my experience, starting the changes in this way nearly always produces the fault of the horse changing in front and then behind and so croup high. In a correct flying change the new inside hind leg comes forward and under the body, whereas over a pole the hind leg pushes as it would do over a small jump.

Tips for improving the quality of the changes in phases 2 and 3

The lateral flexion at the poll should be independent of the flying change. One of the objectives in the training of the canter is straightness. To achieve this the horse must accept the lateral flexion to the outside away from the leading leg as explained in the 'corridor' exercise in primary schooling. In preparing the horse for the flying change, the change of the lateral flexion must be established before the signal for the change is applied. In this way the horse does not learn to change as soon as the lateral flexion is changed, which can often cause problems in straightening the horse in the canter and in achieving straight changes.

The priority within the changes is the rhythm, length of stride and the impulsion. Just as in jumping training, the rider must monitor the canter both before and after the change. By focusing as much as possible on the quality of the canter after the change, the rider will tend to react correctly during the preparation and during the change. If necessary be prepared to come back to simple changes if the horse starts to 'take charge' and either quickens the rhythm or lengthens the stride. The half-halts that are used in support of the body language during the canter should be applied down the outside rein. This means that once the lateral flexion has been changed and you start to ask for the flying change, you should apply the half-halts with the rein that will become the outside rein after the change.

Ask for the flying changes in an every-second-stride rhythm. By repeating the aid every second stride rather than keeping the aid on, you have the opportunity to apply the half-halts and through your position and body language continue to work on the quality of the canter between each aid. It is important that the horse learns to change on the aid and not one stride after the aid. As you move on within advanced dressage to include series changes every fourth, third and second stride, it is impossible to ride the series accurately and to be able to count if the horse has a tendency to change in the stride after the aid.

The flying changes must be 'in-line' and 'on-line'. In the first phase of teaching the flying changes, one can accept that the horse turns onto a circle during or immediately after the change. For the horse this is logical and is the point of doing the change. However, in the second phase the horse should be corrected by the outside rein supporting the rider's body language so that it learns to remain straight 'on the line' after the change. This will help to increase the engagement of the new inside hind and will help in the case of the horse that is inclined to change late behind. When asking for the flying change along the long side of the arena, do so towards the beginning of the long side rather than as you approach the corner. As you ask every second stride and the horse has still not changed before you get to the corner, do not let it change in the corner. Instead ride the corner in a correct counter canter and then ask again either on the long side or if necessary coming on to a 20 metre circle.

More advanced exercises at this stage include:

- Flying changes on a circle and down the long side from true canter to counter canter.

- Flying changes on the diagonal over the centre line.

- Serpentine with flying changes over the centre line.

Once your horse is at this stage in its work on the changes, the training is mainly concentrated on improving the quality of the changes in terms of the engagement of the hind leg, the 'up-hill' appearance, the gesture of the leading leg and the straightness of the changes. The horse is then ready to work on the exercises in advanced dressage such as series changes, counter changes in half-pass, the transitions from medium and extended canter back to collected canter followed by the flying change as well as the flying change within the medium canter required at Grand Prix level. This latter exercise is a real test of the quality of the changes. One sees many riders who can only illicit a correct flying change while their horse is in collected canter because the horse loses the engagement and 'connection over the back' within the medium canter.

Advanced Collecting Exercises

The advanced collecting exercises are reserved for the horse that is specializing in dressage. These exercises are beyond the ability of most horses to perform well. They require a substantial degree of sustained collection that depends on a combination of factors that are rarely seen in most horses. Sustained collection requires strength of frame and musculature, combined with natural energy, to enable the horse to carry the weight substantially on the hind leg in the piaffe and the canter pirouettes. The horse's natural paces will affect its ability to impart the cadence and expression to the step in a well engaged passage and to perform expressive, balanced and straight tempi flying changes. The Thoroughbred whose conformation, physical strength and natural paces are those of a long distance runner will find it difficult to perform these strength exercises with its straighter action than the horses that are bred for dressage which have a rounder action. The exercises require a great degree of contained energy, which, for the purpose of providing a graceful performance, has to be volunteered. A horse with good conformation that is naturally lazy cannot be motivated for long to sustain the effort required at this level. For this reason the number of horses that perform well at Grand Prix level are few and far between. In much the same way, there are not so many horses that are naturally gifted enough to be successful Grand Prix show jumpers or have the speed and stamina as well as courage to be world class three-day event horses.

CHAPTER SIX

Jumping – Secondary School

THE PRIMARY TRAINING introduces your horse to jumping, starting with poles, going through simple grid exercises and then introducing jumping from canter and jumping small courses. This work includes getting the horse used to different colours and shapes. The secondary jumping training builds on this, in parallel with the dressage training. The ability to jump bigger fences, to adjust the stride within related distances and to adjust the balance between jumping vertical fences and spreads is governed by the horse's flatwork i.e. dressage training. Although the dressage work in trot is not obviously relevant to the jumper, what is important is the quality of the canter and the horse's ability to maintain its independent balance in the canter.

Once your horse is confident to jump small fences, up to one metre in height and spread, whether from trot or canter, then it can be introduced to bigger courses and to more technical difficulties. How it performs around these courses will then determine what training exercises are relevant for it. In most cases, the problems that arise at this stage are related either to the horse's dressage training or to rider error. Of course, sometimes they are related to a technique fault on the part of the horse, for example poor foreleg or hind leg technique, which in turn is a reflection of its natural aptitude for jumping. Such technical jumping faults can often be improved through gymnastic jumping exercises.

The most talented jumpers do not have such technical flaws and require only the establishment of their acceptance of the dressage work and correct riding to the fences. Up to a certain height or degree of technical difficulty, even a technically untalented horse can cope if ridden correctly, but at some point every horse will find its limit. The ability of the horse to jump bigger fences and more technically demanding lines is partly governed by natural aptitude, both mental and physical, but also by the horse's dressage training (education, gymnastic, and physical development).

The training exercises introduced at this stage include those that are related to aspects of course riding as well as gymnastic exercises used to improve the horse's technique over the jumps or develop its confidence and experience in jumping

'The sky is not the limit'

combinations. These exercises are equally relevant to training the rider as they are to training the horse. It is always important to keep both parties in mind, i.e. the rider and the horse, when setting the goals for the training session. When the priority is the training of the rider, the exercise must be comfortably within the capability of the horse and, of course, vice versa.

The objective with the course riding exercises is to combine the dressage training with the jumping so that the rider is able to join the exercises together within the jumping round in a competition. This will include jumping different types of fences on the straight line and off a turn, jumping on related distances, whether on straight lines or on curved or 'dog leg' lines, adding or taking away strides, jumping from spread to vertical or from vertical to spread. The rider's responsibility within these exercises remains as in the dressage training, his own position, balance and clear communication with the horse as well as setting and then monitoring the energy level, rhythm, length of stride, line, balance etc. You must remind your horse when necessary of its responsibilities, and sometimes support your horse to a degree, but not take over those responsibilities.

The gymnastic exercises used to improve a horse's technique will differ from horse to horse depending on the problems encountered and its mental attitude and confidence. They include exercises to improve the horse's bascule over a fence, its fore and hind leg technique and its straightness. Gymnastic exercises are also used to develop the horse's confidence and ability to jump more difficult combinations or related distances. There is no doubt that some horses are very careful and will do everything in their power to avoid touching a fence, and there are others who are not so sensitive. Every horse can have the odd rail down in competition, but in almost all cases where a horse is consistently having rails down there is a reason other than that the horse is just plain careless. The cause of the problem is often the rider, as in my experience a horse will rarely have a fence down when jumping loose. However, there may be a postural problem because the flat work is not sufficiently established, or a technique problem, which may be resolved with a combination of gymnastic exercises and a different system when riding to the fences to cope with the particular difficulty.

Confidence is a major factor limiting performance, as much for the horse as for the rider. Confidence relates not just to the horse's trust of the shapes, colours and general appearance of the jumps, but also to the height and width of the fences and combinations of jumps. Horses do not like hurting themselves, and will only willingly jump higher jumps when they are confident. It is easy to overface a horse in training or in competition. Equally, it is possible to make a horse bored or disrespectful of the fences by not making them sufficiently challenging. In this respect, raising the fences is not the only way to keep their attention and interest. Changing the shape or position of the

'Improving technique'

Horses do not like hurting themselves. It is easy to overface a horse in training or competition.

jumps, or setting gymnastic exercises or combinations of fences will also help, as will competing or training away from home or familiar surroundings. This is where the rider's judgement or 'feel' is so important, and is an aspect of the rider's training that cannot be taught in a book.

Mental attitude as well as confidence will also affect a horse's technique over a fence. The bold horse, the nervous horse, the lazy horse or the frightened horse will have different characteristics when jumping and it is important to assess this aspect when dealing with a problem. Many times a young horse who appears careless is in fact panicking, and any attempts to make it more careful by setting more demanding exercises to 'teach it a lesson' will be counter productive. It is always better to assume that a horse basically wants to jump clear if it possibly can, and so find a solution through the flat work or through jumping exercises that do not deliberately try to catch it out. Such jumping exercises are best left to very experienced riders and coaches. Some horses that are spooky react by jumping higher, while some react in exactly the opposite way by tightening in the back and getting less height over the fence.

'All in the mind'

Exercises

In the section on Basic Jumping Training (primary school), the use of canter poles was introduced to teach your horse (and yourself) to maintain an even stride length to the fence and between fences. Once this exercise has been mastered, and the horse is able to maintain an even rhythm, in self-carriage, over a line or circle of poles, it is ready to move on to some more advanced exercises.

Jumping on a Circle

The objective

To maintain an even rhythm and length of stride before and after the fences, with the same number of strides between each fence.

Set up the exercise by imagining that the 20 metre circle is the face of a clock, and put three small fences at 12 o'clock, 3 o'clock and 9 o'clock on the circle. It helps in maintaining accuracy to position two jump stands at 6 o'clock but without rails. The rider's responsibility is to monitor the quality of the canter and control the speed

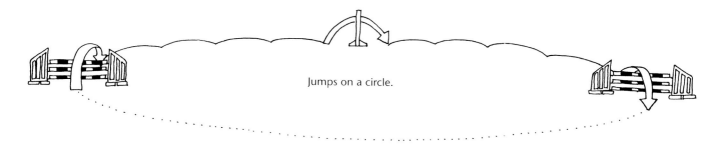

Jumps on a circle.

and the line down the outside rein. It helps to keep the neck straight or even with a flexion to the outside, i.e. away from the leading leg with the primary objective to keep a light inside rein contact.

The exercise

This is started in canter over the poles just to establish the rhythm and line in the rider's mind. The focus must be on controlling the direction and rhythm through position statement, leg and outside rein. Once the rhythm and line has been established in canter, gradually the fences are introduced and raised, keeping the ground line out from each fence. The rider must maintain a very light seat and avoid driving the canter with the seat. The weight must be kept more in the inside stirrup, keeping the outside shoulder back. The rider must not over 'fold' over the fence. The contact must always remain light in the inside rein. If the rhythm and line are lost, or the horse breaks to trot, then come back to walk and start again. Always depart into canter directly from walk and, after completing the circle twice on one rein, make a good transition from canter directly to walk.

Adjusting the Number of Strides in Combinations and Related Distances

A combination has one or two strides between elements while anything over two strides is called a related distance. Anymore than six strides, even if in a direct line, cannot really be called a related distance. I often tell my pupils that there is no such thing as a related distance. One horse may be more comfortable on three strides while another, more short striding horse, will be comfortable on four strides. Even within combinations and 'bounces' I have seen horses, particularly small ones, successfully negotiate the combination comfortably adding extra strides.

When the canter work is sufficiently established within the dressage training and your horse can maintain an even rhythm in the canter, in balance and self-carriage and is able to collect and extend to a degree, then it is possible to train it to adjust the number of strides within related distances.

The objective

To be able to adjust the length of the canter stride whilst still keeping it even and in a consistent rhythm with impulsion, so that you are able to add strides or take away strides between the fences to suit the type of fence or terrain over which you are jumping.

The exercise

In the schooling arena check whether you are able to adjust the canter within an even rhythm and without losing the impulsion within the canter. Count the number of strides between two points, for example between the letters of the dressage arena. See if you can add a stride and then two and then see if you can lengthen the canter, within the rhythm, and take out one or two strides between the points.

When you can do that easily with your horse still in self carriage, i.e. keeping its canter on its own without you having to carry it, then you can try the same exercise over jumps. Set up two ascending verticals at a distance of approximately 26 metres, initially on a straight line and then later on a bending line. Set the canter stride within the middle of the horse's range and maintain the rhythm and length of stride before and after each jump. Count the number of strides between the jumps. When this has been achieved, calmly shorten the length of stride in the canter well before the first jump, but without losing the energy in the step, with a view to adding a stride between the two fences. This will mean being ready with your position and if necessary supporting rein and leg to bring the horse back to the rhythm and length of stride immediately after landing over the jumps.

Then increase the length of stride in the canter well before the first fence, but without allowing it to get flat, so as to ride between the fences on one less stride. It is necessary to work both to lengthen and shorten the stride, but with any horse there will be an emphasis on what is opposite to their natural inclination i.e whether to 'run on' after the fence or be lazy after the fence.

It is important to keep in mind that the shorter the horse's canter stride in the approach to the fence, the closer will be its take-off point to the fence. Conversely, the longer its stride, the more it will tend to 'stand off' the fence. If you always find your horse getting too close to the fences, ride it in to a consistently more forward canter within the rhythm so as to lengthen the canter stride. This will cause it to stand off the fences rather than get too close. This problem often arises when you are too cautious and try to help the horse too much by looking for a stride and so ride 'backwards,' rather than concentrating on developing an active, forward canter between the fences.

Setting the distances in training – when to shorten or lengthen

In competitions, the distances between fences in bounces, one or two stride combinations and within three or four stride related distances are set by the course builder more or less to exact specifications set out in the rule book. However the shape, type and appearance of the fences, as well as the state of the going and the terrain, will have an effect on whether the distance rides long or short. So too will the natural stride length of your horse. A small horse can sometimes have a naturally long, powerful stride, while a relatively large horse can have a naturally short stride.

It is an important part of the training to teach a horse to shorten and lengthen within combinations and related distances. With most horses the emphasis in training is on teaching the horse to shorten or collect its stride within the non-jumping strides. The dressage work helps to teach the horse to shorten its stride without losing impulsion by rounding its loin and engaging the hind leg and so taking the weight more on the hind leg and lightening the forehand. The jumping exercises complement that work as long as the rider avoids using the hand alone to shorten the stride between the fences, which will cause the horse to tighten its back.

Responsibility must also be handed back to the horse in training to collect itself between the fences in combinations. If the horse lacks respect for the fence and so does not try to collect, then gymnastic exercises can be used involving different shapes or styles of fence to teach the horse to have more respect for the fence and so try to collect its stride. Loose jumping work can also help to teach the horse to look after itself.

It is very easy to lose a horse's confidence by setting distances that it finds too difficult, either too short or too long. The rider and the trainer on the ground must recognize whether the horse is finding the distance between the fences short or long. The length of stride and the impulsion of the canter in the approach will of course affect the horse's ability to cope with the distances but, having set the stride length within the mid-range i.e. an energetic working canter rather than a collected or medium canter, then the distances in training should be adjusted so that the horse is comfortable. From this point one can then shorten or lengthen the distances according to any difficulties that the horse may have. A horse will also change within a jumping session and may, at the beginning, require longer distances because it is exuberant or shorter distances because it is spooky. Subsequently, as the session progresses, the distances may then have to be adjusted as the horse relaxes.

Recognizing whether the horse finds the distance long or short, when riding or when assisting on the ground, takes experience. When assisting from the ground, you should focus on whether the highest point of the parabola of the jump is over the highest part of the obstacle. The parabola will be beyond the fence if the distance is too short and the horse may hit the front rail of the fence either in front or behind. Conversely, if the distance is too long, the parabola will be in front of the fence with the feeling that the horse is coming down on the back rail too early. It may then hit the back rail either with the front leg or with the hind leg. If in doubt with a new horse, I always recommend that the distances are set on the short side at the start of the training session, while the fences are small, and then lengthen if required. It is always safer for horse and rider to have the horse hitting the fence on the way up, rather than having the possibility of the horse coming down on the back rail of the fence.

Ground lines

The positioning of the ground line at the base of a jump will have a significant effect on the horse's jump. In show jumping competitions the ground line for most verticals or true oxers is sited immediately under the front of the fence. By adjusting the position of the ground line in training further forward from the fence the profile of the jump is made easier for the horse. The shape of the jump is made rounder and the take-off point is able to come closer to the base of the jump but yet without the danger that the horse may come too close to the jump to be able to clear the front rail.

Positioning the ground rail more forward is particularly appropriate when the emphasis is on training the rider rather than the horse. The horse or rider can then be less accurate in the striding before the fence and still be able to cope. However there are times in the training of the horse when it is appropriate to place the ground line immediately under the front of the fence in order to teach the horse to be more careful.

Your horse should also become used to focusing on the top rail of the fence when jumping rather than always on the base of the fence. In order to encourage it to do so, it is helpful with some horses to take the ground line away altogether, both to single fences and within grids or combinations, even jumping single poles.

Transitions to Walk or Halt Between Fences

The objective

To teach the horse to pay attention to your position statement and body language between the fences so that you are able to regulate the rhythm and length of stride before, and particularly after the fence, without resorting to pulling on the reins, which will produce a resistance in the mouth and a tightening of the back.

Set up a five- or six-stride related distance on a straight line initially, and then ride a good transition to halt, as you would do in the dressage test if asked to ride extended canter back to collected canter and then halt. The important point here is that you are reinforcing the understanding and acceptance of the body language and the engagement of the hind leg. If your horse tends to run on after the fence be sure to use the body language with a light seat rather than a deep driving seat, supported by a touch of the leg or spur to engage the hind leg and by appropriate restraining actions of the hand. Avoid a constant pull on the reins that your horse will just be tempted to lean on or brace against.

This exercise requires the rider to be very clear in goal setting before commencing and then very strict without being rough during the exercise. If you plan to halt between the fences and then change your mind at the last minute, the horse will just become confused and the exercise will be detrimental. As soon as the horse halts he must be rewarded and relax before walking forwards. How often to use this exercise depends on how much your horse has a tendency to run on between the fences.

Figure of Eight Exercise Over a Single Fence

The objective

This exercise teaches your horse to 'turn back' to a fence and to bring the weight back to the hind leg through the turn, but without losing the forwardness of the canter and thereby shortening the stride. It also teaches the horse and rider to maintain an accurate line.

A single fence is set up in the centre of the arena. Initially, the fence should be an ascending vertical jumpable from both directions. Later the fence can be changed to an oxer that can be jumped from both ways. To help the rider focus on maintaining an accurate line, as well as to develop the exercise further, it helps to set up a pair of

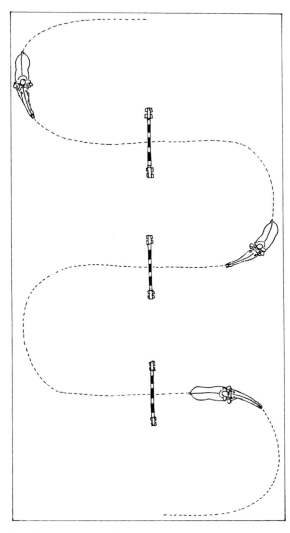

Jumping on a serpentine.

jump stands at a distance of two strides from the jump on both sides, so that later the exercise can be changed to jumping a two stride treble combination.

The active canter is established with the rider focusing on the rhythm and line, and the jump is approached on an angle but as close to the outside of the jump stands as possible so as to keep the angle to the fence being jumped as small as possible. After jumping the central jump, you turn back on yourself around the jump wings to come on an angle to the fence from the other side. The exercise involves controlling the bend at the base of the neck so as not to lose the shoulder to the outside. Turn the horse through your position statement and outside leg talking to the horse's forehand as in a pirouette, trying to keep the contact in the inside rein even and light.

The horse may initially land on the outside lead, but if you work on keeping your seat to the inside and keeping the inside rein contact light then the horse will learn to land on the correct lead more of the time. It is the horse's responsibility to look after its own balance and therefore to learn to land into the correct lead or if not to change immediately. This they soon learn to do. It is a mistake to help them by returning to trot or walk and then cantering off on the correct lead again.

This exercise can be developed further by setting fences on the centre line and then riding a *serpentine over fences* across the centre line. The system is basically the same as for the 'figure of eight' exercise.

Another variation is to place the jump about six to eight metres away from the side of the arena and then after jumping the fence each time turn towards the wall rather than away from the wall.

Technique Problems –
Useful Secondary Gymnastic Exercises

Every horse has its own style of jumping. The style of jump suitable for a pure show jumper is different from the style that is appropriate to the horse jumping at speed, such as the event horse, which must be careful enough in its show jumping and yet not waste energy or lose speed by jumping too high on the cross-country course. The gymnastic exercises that are appropriate for one horse are not necessarily appropriate for another. In training you have to keep in mind at all times the ultimate goal for your horse and to learn to recognize the horse's strengths and weaknesses in relation to that goal. You should also try to recognize the limit to your horse's inherent ability. Not every horse is going to be a superstar just as not every rider will be a champion, and it is easy to lose a horse's confidence by setting exercises and increasing the demands of the exercises beyond its capability.

Keep in mind the expression 'if it aint broke, don't fix it'. Some horses have their own particular style, which may not be classical yet they always jump cleanly. The only reason for changing a horse's technique is when it is causing problems in its jumping relative to the goal.

Also keep in mind that horses react differently to the same exercise depending on their mental and physical attributes. So it is important to keep an open mind and to recognize whether the exercise is producing the desired result or not. Here again, experience is only gained over time and no exact formula or system that will apply to all horses can be explained in a book.

'Bounces'

'Bounces' are two or more jumps set at a distance of approximately three-and-a-half to four metres. They are useful to incorporate in gymnastic exercises that are used to encourage the horse to be more attentive and less inclined to rush the fences, or to be quicker in its reactions and better balanced before and after the jump. They are also useful in teaching a horse to use its neck and improve its bascule.

In riding through a bounce or series of bounces, the rider must remain as still as possible with the upper body so as not to disturb the horse's balance. The lower leg should be kept in close contact with the horse with the weight dropping down into the heel. Approach the first fence in a light seat, with the upper body just in front of the vertical and the majority of your weight in your stirrups, but keep some contact between the seat and the saddle so that you can feel the horse's stride and react if it hesitates and shortens its stride. Once the first element has been jumped, keeping the leg in close contact, take the weight more on to the stirrup and off the seat and hold the upper body in a more upright position. Keep the arm and fist relaxed, and maintain an even but light contact. It is the horse that comes up to you and then away from you as it jumps. Don't over 'fold' over the jumps, as this will upset your horse's balance.

Variations can include jumping a series of bounces comprising cross-rails in a straight line. The height of the cross-rails can be raised gradually to encourage the horse that rushes to pay more attention and slow down; the horse that is inclined to hollow will be encouraged to bascule and use its back more over the jumps. Be careful with the horse that is already hesitant through lack of confidence or is naturally careful, because it is easy to overface it with this exercise. The horse that is lazy and does not go forward willingly should be ridden with a dressage whip so that it can be motivated, if necessary, through the exercise. If it is very lazy or reluctant to go forward then this exercise is not appropriate.

Bounces on a Circle to Improve Foreleg Technique

A series of six bounces comprising single poles or cavalletti set up on gradual turn equivalent to a circle of 20 metres or more in diameter is useful to teach a more experienced horse to be quicker in its foreleg reaction and to pay more attention. The exercise should start with placing poles and then, having progressed to a series of low rails, the demands of the exercise can be increased by raising every alternate pole. This variation in height avoids over-facing the horse and yet keeps its attention. The rider should guide with the inside rein but without pulling, and keep the weight in the inside stirrup with the outside shoulder held back. Initially aim for the centre of each fence and then, depending on how your horse finds the distance in the bounce, you can vary the exercise by riding towards the inside to shorten the distance and encourage it to be quicker, or towards the outside to give it more room if it finds the distances between the jumps uncomfortably short.

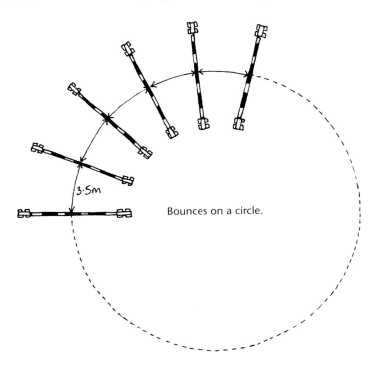

3.5m

Bounces on a circle.

Basculing Exercise

Some horses are inclined to rush their fences and jump with a hollow back. These horses sometimes benefit from jumping out of walk. This exercise is appropriate for fairly experienced riders and helps them to develop a more independent seat and balance, as well as the reflex to follow the movement over a jump. The exercise is not appropriate for horses that are lazy or reluctant to go forwards or for nervous or inexperienced riders.

A placing pole is set up three metres from the jump, which comprises just a single rail with no ground line, initially set at a comfortably low height. A plank is placed on the ground after the jump, approximately the same distance away from the jump as the height of the fence. This plank is intended to encourage the horse to lower its head and neck over the jump as it looks at the plank to avoid landing on it. A pole can be used instead but there is always the risk that the horse may land on

Basculing exercise.

it. As the fence is gradually raised, so the plank is taken further out from the fence. So, marginally, is the placing pole. If necessary, guide rails can be set against each side of the fence to help the horse to focus on the line.

The rider approaches the fence in walk and asks the horse to halt approximately three to four metres before the placing pole. When the halt is established and relaxed, the rider allows the horse a long, loose rein and then applies a touch of leg supported, if necessary, by an energizing 'click of the tongue'. The horse is given complete freedom and responsibility to jump the fence. The rider endeavours to remain with the movement with a secure lower leg position. Only after the jump, as the horse canters away from the fence, should the rider gather up the reins and then bring the horse back to a balanced canter and then back to walk.

As the jump is raised, you should resist the urge to incline forwards too much over the placing pole and then over the jump, but rather allow the horse's jump to come up to you. The feeling when the horse really tries is of the withers coming up to hit your chest. When using this exercise, the trainer on the ground must keep an eye on the horse's foreleg technique. The foreleg should continue to be drawn forwards and the knee flexed. Occasionally, horses will drop the knee and foreleg in bringing their withers up, rather than flex and bascule. In this case the distance from the placing pole to the jump must be increased because the horse's take off point is too close and the highest point of the parabola (shape) of the horse's jump is beyond the fence rather than over the fence.

It is important also to get the balance right in raising the fence. With some horses, the exercise only works when the jump gets sufficiently high that the horse really has to try and work hard to clear it. However, you must also recognize when the horse shows signs of worry by looking backwards or sideways rather than forwards. If the horse hits the rail then immediately lower the fence before coming again, and try next time to stay more upright in your position over the placing pole and the jump. If it tightens its back over the fence it could be because you are not giving it enough rein or you are grabbing the rein over the top of the jump if you get left behind. You have to resist the urge to interfere with the jump.

Use of Guide Poles within Grids to Develop Straightness

For whatever reason, some horses have a tendency when jumping, especially within gymnastic exercises, to drift off the line, normally to one particular side. Guide rails can be used to encourage them to remain straight, so that the rider does not have to interfere with the hands and so increase the contact on one side of the horse's mouth before and over the jump. Such an increase in contact will tend to have the effect of causing the horse to tighten in the back over the fence, which often results in the horse catching a pole with the hind legs.

The guide poles must be placed against the front rail of the fence on not too much of an angle so that there is no possibility of them rolling off the fence as the horse approaches. In most cases, the guide rail is required on only one side of the fence, but occasionally they are needed on both sides, in which case care must be taken initially not to place them too close to the centre of the jump, as they may cause the horse to hesitate. At a certain point, the effect of these guide poles becomes as for the 'V poles'.

The use of 'V poles' to improve foreleg technique.

'V Poles' to Improve Foreleg Technique

When the guide poles are placed on both sides against the front rail, relatively close together, the inverted V shape created has the effect of causing the horse to focus on the front of the fence, 'back off' slightly and draw the knees up and forwards.

This exercise is appropriate for horses that have a tendency to rush down the grid or combination and that project the highest point of their parabola beyond the fence. It can also be appropriate for horses that drop their knees over the fence rather than draw their arm forward and flex the knee. However, in using this exercise, care must be taken not to close the point too quickly with a horse that is not so confident in its jumping.

Improving Hind Leg Technique

If a horse regularly has jumping faults with the hind leg, the fault is probably due to it tightening in the back over the jump, which is caused by the rider failing to soften the hands and rein contact over the fence. Once a horse has learned to brace itself against the rider's hands, it takes time and careful retraining to encourage it to use its neck and back correctly. The rider's ability to soften the hand is dependant upon having an independent balance over the fence and developing the coordination to offer the rein without losing the control of the upper body position.

An exercise to encourage the horse to use its neck and back without tension involves jumping a grid that includes low but wide oxers with the distance between elements gradually reduced. It also helps the horse to learn to use its neck and engage the hind leg in the non jumping strides between the fences if a pole is placed on the floor between each element to encourage the horse to look and lower the neck over the top of the fence.

Some horses that tighten the back have become used to rushing their jumps and may benefit from loose jumping, so that they get used to jumping without the rider tightening the contact as they rush down the grid. The horse must learn to balance itself and stay in a rhythm without the rider having to jump with a tight contact.

I have known some horses with a confirmed problem with the hind leg that have benefited from jumping small fences in draw reins. This is the rare occasion when I believe that draw reins can help in jump training, but they must be used by an experienced rider and on a horse that has a good foreleg technique. Once the horse has accepted the draw rein and stops trying to run through the bridle down the grid, the parabola of its jump will become rounder and it will then come up more with the hindquarters.

Some horses have the habit of snatching the hind leg up underneath the body rather than opening out behind with the hind leg. This happens with tense or nervous horses that are inherently careful. The correction is to work on relaxing them by jumping over small grids with distances that are initially a bit longer than usual, and then only gradually shorten the distances between the elements whilst gradually increasing the width of the spreads. Only increase the height when the horse starts to use the hind leg correctly.

Course Riding Tips

Upright for Uprights and Forward for Spreads

The shape of a horse's jump is a 'parabola'. To jump a fence accurately, the highest point of the parabola should be immediately above the highest point of the fence. The position of this point will differ between a vertical and a spread fence. In the case of a vertical fence e.g. wall, planks, gate etc, the highest point is of course immediately above the vertical, whereas for an ascending spread fence e.g. triple bar or ascending oxer, it is towards the back of the fence. The square oxer will have the highest point over the midpoint between the front and back rails.

This difference has relevance to the rider's position at point of take-off. The rider's upper body should not get ahead of the parabola. When jumping a vertical or a square oxer, the rider should maintain a more upright posture at the point of take-off, thereby allowing the horse's shoulders and withers to come up to the rider rather than the rider going down to the fence. This allows the parabola to clear the front rail. When the parabola is flatter, as when jumping an ascending spread fence or a water jump, the rider's position should be more forwards at the point of take-off to project the jump, or parabola, towards the back rail. Riders are generally taught to 'fold' over a fence to avoid being left behind, but very often this leads to the rider going down to the horse rather than allowing the horse to come up to the rider. If a horse has a fence down by touching the front rail with its front legs, it is often because the rider has overloaded the shoulders by folding down to the horse.

In the case of a spread fence, the horse has to be coming to the fence on a sufficiently forward stride so that the parabola reaches the back rail. For a wide oxer or triple bar, the canter must be ridden forward well before the fence, especially if such a jump is sited off a tight turn. Remember to sit to the inside of the saddle with more weight in the inside stirrup. The turn must be ridden forward from the leg and seat into a controlling outside rein rather than backwards from the pulling inside rein, which will cause the horse to hold back and fall out through the shoulder. The 'rule of thumb' guide for the rider is: 'upright for uprights and forward for spreads'.

Jump to the Inside of the Midline of the Fence

When riding to fences off a turn it is important to maintain an accurate line on the turn all the way to the fence. The horse that gets excited when jumping will tend to fall in on the turns, whilst the horse that does not go forward, because of laziness or reluctance, will fall out. Even a calm but positive horse can lose its balance laterally and should be corrected. The rider's responsibility is to maintain the accurate line to the fence, and it helps the less experienced rider to have as another 'rule of thumb' guide the aim of always jumping towards the inside of the midline of the fence. No matter how tight the turn is, if a line is drawn in your mind at 90 degrees from the centre of the fence, then you should aim to stay to the inside of that line both before and over the fence. As you ride a course of jumps, you will be jumping some fences on the left, off a left turn and some on the right, off a right turn. In this way you avoid the tendency to allow your horse to drift through the outside shoulder either in the approach or at the point of take-off. If your turn overshoots the midline, then you will nearly always meet a bad stride to the fence.

Walking and Riding the Show Jumping Course

When walking a show jumping course, it is important to walk the exact line that you intend to ride. Look for guide points around the outside of the ring that will help to bring you accurately on to the correct line for each jump. Whilst walking, think of all the preparations you will need to make with your position statement; when to move across the saddle, when to think of bringing the outside shoulder back; when

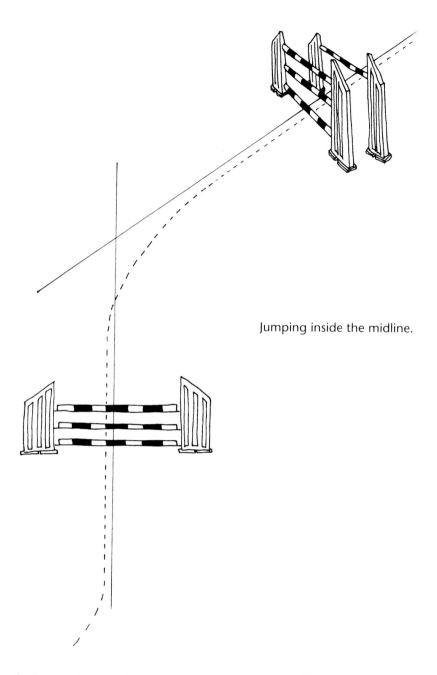

Jumping inside the midline.

to keep the horse's head to the outside so as to control it off the outside rein and only guide with the inside rein; when to re-balance your horse, particularly during or at the end of a line, and when to ride the horse forward with the outside leg on the turn. Think of using the turns, particularly where there is a long gap between the fences, to develop the quality of the canter in terms of the balance, the impulsion and the straightness.

Look for the best approach to the first fence, keeping in mind factors that are likely to affect your horse, such as where the entrance or exit is, the positioning of the fence and whether it will be better to approach it off the left rein or the right rein. As a 'rule of thumb', less experienced riders should always ride to the first fence with a bit more seat and leg, especially with novice horses. Make sure that you have the canter well established, with impulsion and in an even, forward rhythm. It helps to think of riding to the first fence as if it was half way around the course.

Take note of the colour, shape and general appearance of the fences, keeping in mind whether your horse is likely to spook at them, in which case it is better to be prepared in advance to ride more aggressively. This applies to some horses when approaching a combination, particularly a treble. The size and the number of jumps in the combination, together with their appearance, may cause your horse to 'spook' or 'back off'. When riding into a treble combination, it is usually better to come on a forward stride to the first part and then stay up in your position, with soft hands for the second and third parts. If you know your horse is confident, or even perhaps somewhat excited, then it may be better to be very quiet with the seat and leg at the first part in order not to make up too much ground jumping into the combination.

Cross-Country Training

The Responsibilities of the Rider and Horse

In cross-country riding the ultimate goals are to have a clear round in the time and to finish with a sound horse. To achieve this, both the horse and rider must take care of their responsibilities. The rider must have good posture, balance and security in the saddle, as well as positive mental reactions and attitude. The horse must be forward thinking and maintain its own balance. It may need some encouragement from the rider to do this, but it is the horse's job to jump the fence, not the rider's. The horse must look at and work out the problem for itself, and not always rely on the rider.

The rider's responsibility is to make sure that he has a secure position, so that when something goes wrong, which it invariably does, such as the horse stumbling or hitting the fence or decelerating because it spooks, the rider can react quickly enough and remain safe. On the approach to a fence, the rider must make the appropriate preparations in his body and leg position, as well as in the length of rein, to maintain this secure position and yet still be able to react and communicate with the horse at all times

'Safety First'

When approaching a cross-country fence, it is safer to be a fraction behind the point of balance, with the centre of gravity just behind the stirrup. This places you in a 'safety first' position. The stability of the lower leg over the jumps is very important. Your weight should go down into the stirrup, never with the knee clinging, as this causes your heel to swing back as your horse goes over the jump and makes it more likely that you will lose your balance on landing especially if the horse makes a mistake. Your stirrup leathers should be short enough to allow you to be totally clear of the saddle between the fences, thereby helping your horse to gallop more freely, yet when approaching the fence, and over the fence itself, your seat should come close to the saddle and at times deeply into the saddle, for example when your horse tries to stop.

It is safer to be a fraction behind the point of balance, with the centre of gravity just behind the stirrup as demonstrated by Andrew Nicholson.

Position over the fence

When jumping, the seat and lower leg should stay in the same place, but the position of your upper body will change for each type of cross-country obstacle. It can fluctuate between being very forward over a steeplechase fence to leaning well back when you jump into water with a drop on the landing side – such as the lake at Badminton.

The seat and lower leg should stay in same place, but the position of your upper body will change for each type of cross-country obstacle as shown by Jean Teulere.

'In-line' and 'on-line'

The rider's responsibility is to keep the horse 'in-line' and 'on-line'. The body language supported by the seat and leg steer the horse, and the hands guide him. The rider's hand has to be able to maintain a contact with the horse's mouth without interfering with its jump. That contact is the challenge for a cross-country rider. He must keep the connection between the hand and the horse's mouth at all times, ready to correct the horse if necessary, but still allowing it to jump. For example, at times the rider must adjust his reins to be fairly long to give the horse the necessary freedom, over a drop fence, perhaps, but at the same time he must still be able to guide the horse on the line.

At times the rider must adjust his reins to be fairly long but at the same time be able to guide the horse on the line as shown by Blyth Tait on Ready Teddy.

Set the right speed

It is the rider's job to set a speed that is correct for the fence and the terrain. Speed is a combination of rhythm and length of stride. In the approach, the rider, who knows what fence is coming next as well as the terrain before and after, should set the appropriate stride length whilst endeavouring to maintain the rhythm. It may be a short stride for something like a ditch and rail combination or a jump into water, or a longer stride if it's a steeplechase fence or wider spread fence. Whatever rhythm you set, try to keep it as even as possible as you collect or extend the stride. That's where nerves and self-control come into it!

The best riders are able to get close to the optimum time without appearing to be going very fast. They are able to maintain an even rhythm and to ride the tighter lines on the cross-country because they and their horse are in harmony and in good balance at all times. When the unexpected happens, for example when the horse loses its footing or makes a mistake, they are able to react with their position to remain secure yet give the horse the freedom to recover.

Control without a fight

As a horse becomes more confident, it may decide it knows better than you and wants to run faster. It may start pulling between the fences or start attacking the fences in the last few strides and so putting itself into trouble.

The horse that wants to gallop between the fences but then backs off as it approaches a fence can be a joy to ride, as long as you know that it will back off when you do get to the fence. Other horses may be very bold and not back off, and it is the rider's job to set the correct speed in the approach. It is important with such horses

Mark Todd demonstrating control without a fight.

not to end up fighting them between the fences, because that just makes them more excited and teaches them to ignore you when you really do mean slow down.

As has been said all through this book, the hand and leg actions support the body language and position statement. Very often the rider who hangs on or fights his horse between the fences does not really have a sufficiently clear position statement and body language. So the fight is just between the rider's hand and the horse's mouth. To teach such horses to relax, there has to be sufficient lightness of contact between the fences, so that when you really do mean slow down, there is a difference in the contact. The increase in the contact supports the body language and position statement, but must be supported by the actions of the leg and, if necessary, the spur, to cause the horse to engage the hind leg and slow down on the hind leg rather than just pull down on to the forehand.

The steady hold, which may be on quite a strong contact, can be correct with some horses. Even though the contact is strong, the steadiness of the hold means that no signal is being sent that the horse ignores. There is no fight involved in the steady hold that one sees a jockey take in a steeplechase when he wants his horse to stay at the back in the early part of the race. His objective is to get the horse to settle and accept the rhythm. Gradually the horse will do so if there is no fight, and gradually the contact becomes lighter. I always recommend that riders have their reins bridged when riding on the cross-country. This makes it easier to maintain a steady hold by letting the horse pull against itself. A single bridge is better than a double bridge because it allows you to adjust the reins more easily in the approach and after the fences. With a single bridge, in principle both pairs of reins should be held in the outside hand and the inside hand only holds the inside rein. The bridge between the two hands is then pushed into the neck, helping as well to support the upper body as you gallop between the fences.

Andrew Nicholson setting off cross country with bridged reins.

Bits for Cross-country

The first solution that riders usually think of to control their keen horse is a stronger bit. You should be careful to analyze the problem first. Sometimes a stronger bit, such as a pelham or a gag, will produce the desired effect, so that more of the time you can ride your horse on a lighter contact, knowing that you have the stronger bit to get its attention when required. However, stronger is not always the answer. Some horses will fight a stronger bit and will 'run through' it, or they may throw their head up against the pressure and become unsteady in the contact, making it difficult to maintain an even rhythm into the fence.

In these cases a softer bit may in fact work better. With such horses, when jumping, the combination bit can be more effective. As they get excited and want to rush, the combined pressure on the nose as well as on the corners of the mouth is often better accepted. However, it is all the more important with a combination bit or a bitless bridle that the rider does not 'hang on'. The horse must notice and react to the change in contact as the signal supporting the body language and the engaging action of the leg. Whilst it is always a good idea to try a new bit at home first, you will not really know whether it is the answer until you try it in the heat of the competition.

When a horse is pulling hard and leaning down on the bit, the sharp touch of the spur to support the action of the upper body and the hand will produce a quicker response, as long as the rider does not sit heavily and drive with the seat at the same time. Hence the importance of the rider's upper body remaining at or in front of the vertical at all times, even if the horse is pulling hard. If you lean back and pull, you will invariably end up sitting deep into the saddle and driving with the seat.

It is important at all times in training and in the training competitions to keep in mind that your objective is just as in the dressage work: to teach your horse to recognize and accept your communication and in so doing learn to relax and maintain an even rhythm and length of stride. Gradually your horse should become more relaxed and easier to control, even though it may become more confident with the fences.

Cross-Country Schooling

Many of us have a dressage and/or jumping arena to school in, but few have the luxury of a cross-country course connected to their stable yard. Most top riders have to take their horses away to train over cross-country fences. This is what broadens their experience and is an essential part of the cross-country training. Young horses must become confident in jumping fences that are not familiar to them, just as they will have to do in competition.

The particularly difficult thing about cross-country riding is the surprise element, and that is hard to duplicate at home. The horse has to develop confidence in the rider, in its own ability and in its surroundings, so that when it goes to a strange place and gallops over the hill and comes to a fence, it can trust the rider and its own judgment that there is going to be a safe landing on the other side. Often on a cross-country course the horse cannot see where it is going to land.

Although the development in a horse's cross-country education requires that you take it cross-country schooling and to small competitions to build up its confidence, you can also do some useful schooling at home. Exercises that can be taught at home with your own jump poles and standards include simulating things like the rail-ditch-rail combinations, the arrowheads, and the corner fences.

Cross-country schooling is largely about building up a horse's trust and confidence, rather than just blind obedience. The different shapes and types of fence all present potential problems for the horse, as does the terrain over which it must learn to gallop and jump. One of the great advantages for many British riders is that they have had the opportunity to hunt on horseback. This helps to give both horses and riders experience over varied terrain and going, in a very natural environment, and teaches them to concentrate on what is in front of them at any particular moment as well as cope with the surprise element.

Such opportunities are becoming less available, and these days more use has to be made of structured cross-country training. This has also become more important as the technical demands of modern cross-country courses have increased. The horse must learn to look and work things out for itself. It will trust the rider and grow in confidence if this is done over small fences, which allow room for error. The schooling should not generally test the horse. The demands should always be set well within its capabilities. Use should be made of experienced horses to give young horses a lead at times, to help to give them confidence. Of course, the horse must also learn that a refusal or run-out is not an easy option. It must learn that jumping the fences is easy and much more fun than stopping!

The Water Jump

Some horses do not have any fear of water. They have been born in a wet field in Ireland and they have stood in water most of their early lives. Others have never seen a puddle and won't step into one. With these horses you have to introduce them gradually to water. You can get them to follow another horse, or you can lead them into a very shallow puddle. Once you are there, get them to splash around a bit. We have a water jump in our field which can be approached many different ways: the horse can walk straight into it and it gradually gets deeper, or it can drop off an edge into the water, or it can jump a fence into the water. This way the demands are increased – from puddle to jump. You can also teach your horse to follow another through streams, or into bigger lakes or even out to sea! Most importantly, the horse must know that the water is not too deep and that the ground underneath the water is safe. The most important aspect of training in water is not to lose a horse's confidence in the footing or the depth. You must try not to have good ground one day and bad the next.

Introducing young horses to water. You can get your horse to follow another into the water, or you can lead it in. Once in, splash around a bit.

As the jump or drop into the water jump gets bigger, you have to allow the horse more freedom with its neck, so ride on a longer rein. If necessary, be prepared to slip the reins through your hands over the jump but I usually recommend to riders that they lengthen their rein before they get to the fence. As they jump into the water, they can give the horse the freedom it needs without letting go of the reins and losing control of the direction and balance in the water itself. Be careful when adjusting the martingale that it is not too short, as this will cause a downward pull on the horse's mouth as it drops into the water.

Be prepared to slip the reins through your hand over the jump to give the horse the freedom to use its neck.

Stay back with your upper body as your horse jumps into the water so that it jumps slightly away from you. Stay upright in your posture at least through the first stride in the water and then gradually take a more forward position if, for example, there is a long, galloping stretch through the water. There may be only one or two strides followed by another jump out of the water. In this case, you must stay in a more upright position all the way through the water.

Falling off can happen, and the first stride after the landing is often when it happens. Deep water stops the horse's momentum, and very often the horse will stumble in the water in the first stride after landing. Modern water jumps are not normally very deep, so more often the problem is associated with the horse losing its balance as it drops into the water. It may come too forward with its neck, or the rider may lean too far forward on to its shoulders causing it to lose balance as it lands. That is why the rider has to remain in the defensive position, with the stability of the lower leg and the control of the upper body being crucial, whilst giving the

Stay upright in you posture at least for the first stride.

horse the freedom to look and use its neck. The horse's neck is its 'fifth' leg and, if it has the free use of it, the horse will often save itself as it stumbles.

If a rider has a weak upper body position and cannot control it sufficiently with his abdominal and back muscles, he will be pitched forward when the horse lands in the water. You must have the strength to hold your posture as you jump into the water.

Ditches

What scares a rider often has more to do with what scares his horse. If you have a relationship with your horse, you will know what it dislikes. Some horses are frightened of banks, some of water and some just by the shape or colour of a fence. Ditches are very often frightening to riders and horses but, when you walk a cross-country course and you look at that chasm in front of you, keep in mind that the length of a horse's stride when galloping is quite long, and most ditches are less than half that length. Even the biggest ditches I have seen in a competition, for example at Burghley, where there is one wide enough to drive a tractor along it, become a bit of an anticlimax when jumping them on a horse that does not have a fear of ditches.

When a young horse starts jumping ditches, it is important that it recognizes what it is jumping, and that the task is well within its capabilities, even from a halt. If we can jump a ditch a metre wide from a standstill on our own two feet, the horse certainly should be able to, with four feet and a bigger stride. Once it has the confidence to jump from a standstill, while having a good look at what it is doing, then it can be jumped over gradually wider and deeper ditches from a faster pace. At a

Ditches are often very frightening to riders and horses, but when you walk the cross-country course bear in mind that the length of a horse's stride when galloping is quite long, and most ditches are less than half that length.

faster pace, the horse will have jumped the ditch before it even knows how wide or deep it is, but it should not start its training in this way. For many riders, a ditch is as much a psychological challenge as it is for the horse. It is important, therefore, to convey the same degree of confidence and forwardness in your riding as you would like of the horse. The best way to do that is to look well ahead and beyond the ditch, not down into it. This will also help you to maintain the correct position over it.

You should start the training by approaching a very small ditch, preferably from a walk or slow trot, with your body in an upright position and with your reins long, but maintaining enough contact to be able to correct the horse if it tries to turn away from the ditch. You must urge the horse on and over the ditch, giving it as much rein as it needs to lower its neck and look. It will probably jump the ditch from a standstill, so lean forward to allow its neck and shoulders almost over the ditch before it takes off. If the horse tries to turn away or run backwards it must be corrected. As long as it confronts the ditch and does not run sideways or backwards, then it is preferable at first to allow it to make up its own mind when to take off. Be careful to have the lower leg in the correct position and ready to grip if the horse suddenly performs a huge leap. If you get left behind try not to catch your horse in the mouth.

The horse must realize the consequences of not having a go, which will include the use of the whip and perhaps even an assistant from the ground, if it is particularly stubborn. Gradually it can be expected to approach the ditch on a more forward stride until it just skips over without losing its forward rhythm. Some horses always remain spooky with ditches, and they require regular schooling over small ditches to keep them confident. When they go out to a competition, the increased speed with which they approach a ditch will not give them the chance to look down and see how wide the ditch is or see that there is water in it, until they are well over it.

Ditch and Fence

Since the size of a ditch is usually about half a galloping stride, it can actually help you at times. For example, a ditch in front of a fence stops a horse from getting too close to the fence. You should come faster to a fence of this kind because you only have two possibilities: one is that your horse will take off a little bit early, in which case the extra speed is going to help, and the second is that your horse will get close to the fence but the ditch stops you getting too close. Up the tempo, increase the length of stride, keep coming to it, don't look for a stride, let the horse judge when to take off, and don't look down into the ditch!

Start training by approaching a very small ditch preferably from a walk or slow trot.

As you approach a fence with a ditch in front, adjust the reins slightly longer, come into the saddle and ride your horse into the contact a little bit to encourage it to look at the top of the fence. You mustn't give the horse a loose rein and allow it to drop its neck and look down into the ditch, but equally, you must not ride with the reins short and with the horse's neck short. If the horse doesn't feel that it can use its neck, then it's going to say 'I can't jump this fence' and refuse. Remember to keep a contact, but let the horse have a long neck. This advice applies to an open ditch as well as a ditch in front of a fence.

Ditch/Rail Combination

With a rail ditch rail combination – what we used to call a 'coffin' – you should maintain an upright posture in the approach and collect the canter stride i.e. a shorter stride but with increased engagement and impulsion. Increase slightly the length of rein before you get to the fence, so that you can give the horse the freedom to use its neck going in and through. In that way you are always just behind the horse, ready to react if it spooks at the ditch or catches a leg over the fence going in. It is a mistake to look for a stride in the approach, focus only on preparing your position and the canter early enough, and then be ready to ride stronger to the fence in the last two strides to overcome the horse's likely reaction in seeing the ditch on the landing side and hesitating. Each horse is different in its reactions, but it is always better to assume that the horse is going to look at the ditch. This particularly applies when the ditch is hidden until the last moment, such as when jumping into a hollow in the ground.

Banks and Steps Up and Down

When you come up to a bank or steps that you have to jump up on to, it is a bit like jumping an upright fence, so you should approach with impulsion but not a very long stride, so the horse has the energy to get up onto the bank. If you come too fast, then the trajectory of the jump will flatten and your horse may skid across the top of the step because it has not landed high enough. If you come too slowly, then the horse will lose its momentum as it jumps up onto the first step, and if there is another step or obstacle following soon after, it may well not have enough power to jump it.

In jumping off a bank or down steps you should prepare your position and length of rein by coming more upright with the heel down and well forward. Let the reins get longer so that the horse can jump off the bank using its neck. The inclination of your upper body will depend on the height of the drop and whether you are landing onto ground that is level or sloping away from the drop. The higher the drop and

In jumping off a bank or down steps you should come more upright and lengthen your rein.

the more level the ground on which the horse will be landing, the more you have to be ready with your position for the horse to stumble on landing, so it is better to lean further back and, on landing, use the abdominal and back muscles to maintain your core stability as you land. This is just the same as a gymnast jumping off the apparatus and maintaining his balance and posture as he lands. If the drop is not very great and the land slopes away from the jump then you can be more forward in your position. The principle, as always in cross-country riding, is to keep your centre of gravity just behind the base of support, namely the foot in the stirrups.

There are some banks or drops where you want your horse to pop off very slowly. For example, if there is a jump on the landing stride. In this case you want the horse to 'drop' off the bank rather than jump off. So lengthen your rein and reduce the speed to the minimum; sometimes it is best to trot off. Make sure that you have enough leg against the horse so that you are ready to react if it hesitates. An example of this type of jump is the Leaf Pit at Burghley. Riders have sometimes been caught out here by having a hesitation or a stop at the top. They have tried to reduce the speed so much that the horse decides not to go. On the other hand, if they have come in too fast into a tight contact and a short neck, the horse will either launch off the top, or refuse at the last minute because it cannot look at what it is doing. If it does launch from the top, then you are going to land right at the bottom of the Leaf Pit instead of halfway down, and then the horse may crumple on landing.

Bounces

Bounces are incorporated within the gymnastic jumping training at an early stage. There is therefore no reason why they should be a major problem for the horses on the cross-country course. Yet they do often worry riders because they require a degree of trust in the horse's natural instincts and reflexes. There is no time in a bounce for the rider to drive with the seat or overcome the horse's desire to stop in the middle, if it so wishes.

The most important points for the rider to remember are to re-balance the horse and adjust the speed in the approach through the combined use of position statement, body language and engaging leg, as well as the actions of hand, so that the horse comes forward to the first element focusing on the fence without shortening the neck, which will restrict the free forward reaction of the foreleg over the fence. The rider must then avoid over-folding over the fences, which will upset the horse's balance. Imagine what it would be like jumping a series of hurdles with a loose knapsack on your back or a child on your shoulders who pitches backwards and forwards. You would tighten the knapsack or tell the child to stay still. I always recommend that riders think of standing upright in the stirrups rather than folding as their horse jumps the fences. This is the safest position and keeps your weight off the horse's shoulders.

Bounces into water jumps must be ridden more strongly forward than other bounces because the horse will be inclined to back off or hesitate when it sees the water. The shape and height of the bounce going into the water jump will dictate just how forward to ride to the bounce. If there is a good ground line and a rounded profile to the element then you can afford to ride more strongly into it because it is not likely that your horse will get too close to the fence. The only risk is that it hesitates and lands short into the bounce, giving it too much to do at the second element. Approach the fence in a relatively upright position so that you can stay behind your horse all the way into the water.

Corners and Narrow Fences

Accuracy fences are an important part of modern cross-country courses. They include corners, arrowheads, elbows and narrow uprights or 'pimples'. The training over these fences is largely an extension of the work on the flat to teach your horse to stay 'in-line' and 'on-line'. To a degree it is about testing your horse's obedience, but it is also about teaching your horse to enjoy jumping what is in front of it. It must learn that running out is not as pleasant as jumping the fence.

It is important to consider the training from the horse's point of view. It is a natural reaction on the part of a horse to avoid an obstacle in its path. We would be upset if our horse kept running into trees, chairs and other things that are around the place. So we have to teach it carefully, by only gradually increasing the demands. Using guide poles to channel the horse over a narrow fence or to keep it in at a corner will help it to understand the job. I am a great believer in the intelligence of the horse, and so I always set up the flags on either side of the fence when training over narrow fences and corners. It is my belief that horses can learn that part of the game is to go between the flags!

The rider's primary responsibility in the approach to such fences is to set the correct line, then adjust the speed within an even rhythm and adjust the horse's balance if necessary. The rider must focus on maintaining the line with the eye, and must have sufficient contact with the reins to be able to react if necessary. It is a wise precaution to widen the hands in the approach to provide a corridor without pulling backwards. The common mistake in riding to a corner is for the rider to look for a stride. You then either attack the fence on a long stride, loosening the contact and so leaving the door open for the horse to run out, or you over-shorten the horse's stride and neck so that it feels unable to cope with the width of the corner and so refuses or catches a leg on the front rail.

In setting the line for a narrow fence or a corner it helps, when walking the course, to line up a point on the front of the fence with some landmark in the distance, such as a tree, so that as you make your approach some way from the fence you know how to find the correct line. The line you ride to a corner should intersect at 90 degrees the line that divides the angle of the corner in half.

In training over corners, start with fairly narrow corners so that there is a margin for error, and then gradually widen the angle of the corner. Always keep the height comfortably low in training so that you don't get worried about seeing a good stride to the fence. It also helps to get your horse used to jumping fences on an angle, which can gradually become more extreme as it understands. Set up a small vertical fence and begin to jump it from different angles rather than straight on. This will

I always set up flags on either side of narrow fences when training.

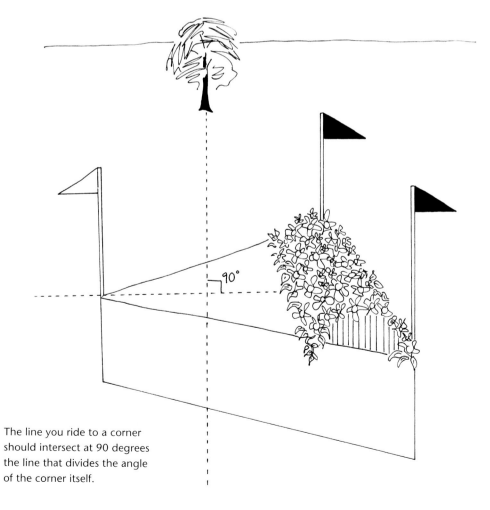

90°

The line you ride to a corner should intersect at 90 degrees the line that divides the angle of the corner itself.

teach the horse to hold its line and not to run out. Your horse must be very balanced to jump an angle, lifting both knees equally. Once your horse is comfortable and keeps its line very accurately with this exercise, then add another set of stands to create the corner. Remember that the accuracy of the line is the most important point, and accuracy should be to within 10 to 20cm of the spot you have chosen on the fence.

Walking the Course

Effective course walking is a vital part of cross-country riding. When riding a cross-country course, the preparations in terms of the speed, balance and line must be made sufficiently early and yet without losing time by slowing the horse down too soon.

The purpose of the course walk is to know what fences have to be jumped, the correct line to be ridden, based on the type and shape of fence, the terrain before and after the fence, and what fences follow, so as to present the horse in the best possible manner. Depending on the importance of the competition and the experience of your horse, you may be looking to ride as tight a line as is possible in order to get as close as possible to the optimum time, or you may be using the competition as a training outing and so time is less critical than a good confidence-giving round.

Always walk the course through your horse's eyes. First impressions of a fence or combination of fences as you approach will be those that your horse sees. You may spend some time working it out and, after walking the line a few times, it may be very clear in your mind what you will do, but don't forget that your horse has not got the benefit of walking the line a few times. It must work it out at speed the first time.

So in walking the line you plan to ride, keep in mind that your horse needs to have time to assess the fence. The greatest danger in the modern sport with the complexities of some of the combinations, involving frequent turns off the direct line, is that the riders can be tempted to ride lines that do not give the horse, particularly when it is tired, a chance to work out the problem.

It helps as you walk your course to identify landmarks such as trees or other easily visible and permanent features that are not likely to be hidden from you by spectators. These landmarks remind you what fence is coming next, where to change gear and collect your horse before a fence, where to find the correct line, where to prepare your position, to lengthen your rein or from where to ride strongly forward.

Remember that the shortest route is the straightest line, so when walking a course at a three-day event, where there is a definite track to follow, always notice where you have to move from one side of the track to the other and how you can negotiate the turns both keeping your horse balanced and yet taking the shortest route that will bring you on to the correct line for the fence. Keep an eye out for the going and avoid following directly in the footprints of the other horses if the going is wet or sticky, unless you are forced to because the fence is narrow or a corner.

At most one-day events you only have time to walk the course once, but at a three-day event you can walk the course three or four times. On the first occasion, I walk it looking for the first impressions that my horse is going to get as it goes around. On my second walk, I look at all the alternative options, always bearing in mind my knowledge of my own horse and its strengths and weaknesses. I also use this course walk to imagine all the possible things that can go wrong so that I have prepared myself with a plan for each eventuality. This includes preparing my position, including leg and upper body as well as my length of rein, for any problems, such as my horse stumbling, hesitating, catching a leg on the fence when it may be distracted. On the third course walk, I focus only on my plan and try to imagine it all going well, yet also being prepared to react. If I have the chance to walk the course a fourth time, say on the morning of the cross-country, then I will use it as a way of pumping myself up and making myself feel really positive and aggressive.

Many of the situations that I have talked about call for good judgement: getting the right balance between speed, control and forward thought, yet allowing the horse the freedom to jump well by guiding it without restriction. Effective course walking will help you to achieve that.

Index

GREYSCALE

BIN TRAVELER FORM

Cut By _Paola Fraemont_ Qty _21_ Date _10-28_

Scanned By_____ Qty_____ Date_____

Scanned Batch IDs

_____ _____ _____

Notes / Exception

_____

_____

_____

_____

_____